NOT FOR EXPORT

NOT FOR EXPORT:

Toward a Political Economy of Canada's Arrested Industrialization

Glen Williams

Canada in Transition Series
McCLELLAND AND STEWART

To the unemployed and the underemployed.

Reprinted 1987

McClelland and Stewart
The Canadian Publishers
481 University Avenue
Toronto, Ontario
M5G 2E9

Canadian Cataloguing in Publication Data
Williams, Glen, 1947-
Not for export

(Canada in transition series)
Includes index.
ISBN 0-7710-8967-8 (pbk.)

1. Canada – Commercial policy. 2. Canada – Commercial policy – History. I. Title. II. Series.

HF1479.W54 382′.3′0971 C82-095265-6

Printed and bound in Canada by John Deyell Company

Contents

Editors' Foreword

The volumes in the Series *Canada in Transition: Crisis in Political Development* draw on concepts and theories from the field of political development in an attempt to place our current national dilemma in historical perspective. As a country embedded from the outset in the political and economic fortunes of powerful neighbours, Canada has encountered unique social, economic, and political obstacles to unity and cohesion. Indeed, the term "crisis" denotes for us the central features of the Canadian experience: a fascinating mix of dangers and opportunities in a rapidly changing international environment.

From this perspective the present volume by Professor Glen Williams, *Not for Export: Toward a Political Economy of Canada's Arrested Industrialization,* could not appear at a more important time. With all its internal problems and threats to national unity, economically Canada's post-war experience was grounded in a growing prosperity. In every region, although in different degrees, economic growth and the extension of the full range of welfare state services transformed the lives and expectations of Canadians. Internationally, while not a member of the predictable "Inner Five" Western industrial states, Canada was nevertheless (with Italy) in the nearly as exclusive "Club of Seven." We might not have believed, with Sir Wilfrid Laurier, that Canada could inherit the twentieth century, but we were at least destined to be among the best and the brightest.

There were, of course, the doubters–those who questioned Canada's branch-plant structure, or its record in productivity, innovation, and industrial export performance–but they were dismissed as gloomy detractors from the mood of general prosperity.

The present economic crisis, which has shaken this complacency, confronts Canada with its most serious challenge since the Depression. Given the current international economic environment, Professor Williams contends that Canada cannot maintain its standard of living on resource exports alone. It is not yet "an underdeveloped country," but structural problems in the Canadian economy, long ignored, must now be addressed to create a viable, competitive, and less vulnerable industrial sector. Dramatic changes in the international system are forcing a new industrial strategy on our timorous and reluctant elites.

Professor Williams' book is essential reading for understanding the roots of the present crisis and the options facing Canada as it heads into the bleak realities of the 1980's and beyond. Both the general reader and the specialist will welcome this important contribution.

David V.J. Bell
Edgar J. Dosman

Preface

Not For Export was born in the traumatic bout of culture shock which afflicts many Canadians who return to their native land after working for some years in an underdeveloped country. In my case, I returned to graduate school in Toronto from a very rural area in Zambia in late 1973 to find my intellectual environment buzzing with the heady left nationalist rhetoric of Canada's colonial "underdevelopment" and the need to liberate it from the tentacles of U.S. imperialism. At the same time, a minority view took the more orthodox Leninist position that Canada was itself an imperialist country.

I had previously reflected on these questions many times when I was in Africa. So, while this debate crystallized an already awakened interest, I often found its expression by Canadians unsatisfactory. Both sides reflected important truths, yet they were so crudely formulated that they could not be reconciled by simply staking out a middle position. Rather, it was from the beginning necessary to transcend both arguments in order to come to terms with the central questions of Canadian politics, economic development, class, nation, and our position in the international hierarchy of wealth and power that each sought to address. This book, then, traces my intellectual search during the last decade for a more satisfactory approach to these pivotal Canadian issues.

Many have stimulated, informed, and encouraged me along the way. In pursuing my doctoral studies at York University and preparing the dissertation which forms the basis of over half of this book, I gratefully acknowledge the assistance of Tom Hockin, David Bell, Fred Fletcher, Mel Watkins, H.V. Nelles, Jim Laxer, Daniel Drache, John Saul, Rob Albritton, and Sten Kjellberg. In refining my ideas at Carleton University, I have greatly benefited from the advice and helpful criticism of my colleagues, including Jane Jenson, Wallace Clement, Lynne Mytelka, Maureen Molot, Dan Butler, and Leo Panitch.

In gathering material for my study, the libraries of the University of Toronto, York University, and Carleton University and the National Library in Ottawa have proved invaluable. The Public Archives provided every possible assistance and I especially thank Sandra Bell and Gilles Malette. The Department of Industry, Trade and Commerce gave me special permission to view certain of its files from the 1950's and 1960's without which the core of the later chapters would have remained speculative.

Finally, I acknowledge my debt to the patience and perseverance of my publisher and series editors, Ed Dosman and David Bell, through all the years and stages of its preparation. All shortcomings in the book are, of course, my own responsibility.

For those who will wonder if our title, *Not For Export*, was conjured up out of nothing by a clever copywriter of catchy phrases, I must report, unhappily for the national interest, that instead we have here a case of art imitating life. Some years ago, when Maureen Molot and I were collaborating on an article for another book, she directed my attention to her typewriter, the product of a well-known branch plant manufacturing in Canada. Just out of view and inside the frame, a label was affixed to her machine, which read as follows:

> Patented 1936 1937 1939 1941
> Made in Canada
> Protected by American and
> foreign patents
> /NOT FOR EXPORT/

Glen Williams
October, 1982

CHAPTER 1

Introduction

Since Margaret Atwood, we have come to appreciate the centrality of the survival symbol to the way Canadians see their environment. "The main idea," she says, "is . . . hanging on, staying alive. Canadians are forever taking the national pulse like doctors at a sickbed: the aim is not to see whether the patient will live well but simply whether he will live at all." [1]

So it was that in the economic crisis of the early 1980's, certainly the worst since the Great Depression, we heard a discordant choir of unqualified failure. Our bankers warned that the country faced economic ruin at home and defeat in world markets. Our politicians cautioned us to "live within our means" and accept "short-term pain" while promoting strategies to restructure Canadian industry and trade. With the relentless erosion of their sector's performance during the last decade, our manufacturers were the gloomiest of all as the boom years of the 1950's and 1960's seemed lost forever. The recession chopped 10 per cent of the nation's already scarce industrial jobs and the Canadian Manufacturers' Association estimated that as many as 400,000 jobs (20 per cent) could be lost before we "hit bottom."[2] Union executives watched with impotent frustration as more than three decades of their memberships' hard-won victories in compensation and job security slipped through their fingers.

A sense of despair and resignation to a dimmer economic future accompanied the increasingly familiar news of factory and even entire community shutdowns. Anxieties were only fleetingly allayed by government promises of industrial strategies based on massive megaproject developments. Sunk before they were properly launched, these schemes fell victim to the indifference or open hostility of the major economic actors they sought to revive. In this context, the introduction of new concepts like "deindustrialization" into our national economic discourse, accompanied by suggestions that Canada was in danger of "regression toward economies like that of Chile or Brazil" and even that this decline may bring Canadians "inevitably to a condition of pastoral servitude by the middle years of the twenty-first century," vividly demonstrates the appropriateness of the survival metaphor.[3]

Canada's Place in the International Economic Order

By its very subject, this book is bound to add fuel to the survivalist dialogue. Indeed, it would take a very determined optimist to find much to celebrate in the historical or contemporary record of Canada's industrial exports which will be presented here. Yet, this is an unintended consequence. I am outlining the case for frustrated potential, not potential catastrophe. Speculation that Canada has been drifting toward semi-industrialized underdevelopment is ill-considered at this juncture. In order to explain why, it will be necessary to clarify our understanding of Canada's unique position in the world economy.

One of the most prominent features of the last two centuries of world history has been a steadily sharpening division in material abundance between the globe's regions and nations. This division has developed along all those dimensions on which a standard of living can be measured – for example, health, education, housing, disposable income, industrialization – to the point that we have come to speak of an international hierarchy of wealth. Social scientists who first examined this stratification believed that economic and social development were evolutionary processes. A society could, therefore, presumably progress along a linear path from a traditional stage to a modern stage. Accordingly, those at the bottom of the international hierarchy were simply caught at an earlier stage of their development, while those at the top provided the model of what could be achieved through modernization.[4]

By the mid-1960's, the unquestioned complacency of social scientists that Canada had made a successful transition between tradition and modernity was shaken. Some authorities started to speak of Canada as a "rich industrialized underdeveloped country."[5] This dramatically different image of Canada in the world order can be traced to growing controversies among social scientists about the stage theory of economic and social modernization. Challenging the former orthodoxy, a new generation of scholars was arguing that development and underdevelopment are not simply stages of a single linear process but have been caused by each other.

According to this new approach, development and underdevelopment in the modern world are the consequences of the economic and political expansion of Europe since the fifteenth century and of the United States since the nineteenth century. Through trade, investment, and even military instruments, these "metropolitan" areas succeeded in draining their "satellites" in Latin America and elsewhere of their reinvestment capital or economic surplus. Because their own economic surplus was unavailable for the expansion of production within the satellites, they failed to develop and, indeed, regressed as local economic activity was distorted to meet external requirements. At the same time, this surplus served to fuel further economic growth in the metropolitan countries. Thus, the operation of a hierarchical chain of exploitation/appropriation linking nation to nation and even city to countryside was held to be the fundamental feature of the world order.[6]

As we shall observe in later chapters, a social science tradition stressing the negative features of our links with more advanced economic centres was already well established in Canada prior to the appearance of the underdevelopment thesis. To some extent, this earlier tradition accounts for the persistent and often uncritical application of these ideas to the Canadian case. A view of Canada teetering on the edge of full-blown economic underdevelopment has been reinforced by a number of characteristics Canada shares with more obvious satellites in the world economy. Such similarities include extremely high levels of foreign direct investment, a weak and fragmented industrial sector, a formidable dependence on resource exports, and a state and economic elite which has nurtured and protected foreign interests in Canada. These parallels have sparked portrayals of post-World War II Canada as a client state in the American Empire that enjoyed a temporary "special status" in the wake of the expanding U.S. economy of the 1950's and 1960's but that, in the long run, is doomed to a steady erosion in its standard of living as American exploitation intensifies. [7]

Ultimately, those who argue that Canada's position in the world economy is that of a dependency or colony or resource hinterland headed more or less directly to underdevelopment have more to explain than their model allows. Although it is true that the Canadian political economy shares some important structural similarities with underdeveloped countries, these are by no means recent nor, it would appear, determining. Rather, Canada has maintained throughout her history a position near the top of the international heirarchy of wealth in spite of her seemingly perpetual "colonial" status.

What, then, was different about Canada to distinguish its evolution from more classical underdevelopment? The answer to this crucial question requires an understanding of development and underdevelopment that goes beyond such one-dimensional concepts as the exploitation/appropriation chain. Advances in the study of international political economy during the last decade have made this possible. For instance, Samir Amin distinguishes between two different socio-economic formations – a developed capitalism of the centre and an underdeveloped capitalism of the periphery – which, he submits, together compose a world system of capital accumulation.[8]

In spite of the apparent similarities noted above between Canada and the peripheral nations, Amin's work leads us to conclude that at a more fundamental level our political economy does not share the essential characteristics of underdevelopment. There is, for example, no large gap in productivity and wages between economic sectors in Canada as there is in the periphery where the modern capitalist mode of production is often surrounded by more traditional pre-capitalist elements. Nor can the Canadian economy readily be cut up into a number of poorly integrated fragments that have fewer connections with each other than with the centre economy which dominates them. In this, the peripheral case, the economy is disarticulated or extroverted in the sense that foreign exchanges of goods and services are of relatively greater significance than domestic exchanges. Canada, like other central nations, has a basically autocentric economy in which progress in one economic sector spills over into other sectors of an interconnected internal market.[9] Finally, foreign investment, although dominant in both Canada and the periphery, plays a different role in our central economy. Here, because of our relatively large and integrated internal market, foreign investment has historically produced more positive than negative effects on economic growth as opportunities have existed for the reinvestment of profit in new sectors of the economy. By contrast, in the periphery, where few such opportunities for reinvestment exist, growth has been blocked by the resulting repatriation of profits.

Canada's location within the centre of the world economy can best be understood when it is remembered that Canada was developed as a colony of settlement, an offshoot, of the European social formation and, from the beginning, shared many of its most important characteristics. Economically, Canada always enjoyed relatively high wages in comparison to the rest of the world. Politically, it possessed the elements necessary for the evolution of liberal-democratic political institutions. Both of these factors were key to the unfolding of Canada as a new country of the centre. Let us take each in turn.

Put briefly, Canada was not integrated into the world economy along the peripheral route of the European colonies of military occupation and economic impoverishment such as India and Africa. On the contrary, most Europeans who immigrated to Canada, particularly skilled labourers, did so freely, induced by the opportunity to improve their material condition. Definite lower limits were placed on Canadians' incomes by their ability either to move into independent farming or to emigrate to the more prosperous U.S. So it was that by Confederation, even before the formative years of our modern industrialism, Canada already possessed one of the highest standards of living in the world.[10]

Canada's high wage economy was to influence greatly the course of our industrialization. For instance, high wages made for relatively rich consumers and, accordingly, stimulated investment in our productive capacity. By contrast, manufacturing in the limited markets of the poverty-stricken periphery was starved of capital. Equally important, high wages forced the employment in Canada of the capital-intensive labour-saving industrial technology which became typical of the central economies, rather than the craft, cottage, and labour-intensive techniques of the periphery.

The course of our industrialization was also to be influenced by the development of Canadian liberal democracy. At variance with the direct administration of its colonies of military occupation by London, the U.S. War of Independence had eventually opened the door to the propertied elites of the white Dominions for local autonomy in most matters. In the British North American colonies, the progression from representative to responsible, and, finally, federal government gave our political and economic elites considerable scope to make decisions about the course of their own economic future. Such opportunities were firmly denied to comparable elites in much of the periphery until the post-World War II period.

This is not to suggest that, shorn of imperial control, the Canadian state simply became a mere instrument of a domestic ruling elite or class. In fact, just the opposite occurred. In the selection of our national economic strategy during the late nineteenth and early twentieth centuries the state required considerable autonomy in order to mediate and adjudicate the many substantive policy disagreements that arose among various groups within the capitalist class. Further, both the emerging industrial proletariat and the farmers were schooled, in some degree, in the British constitutional practices of free association and speech. Armed with an ever-widening franchise, these groups met with a measure of success in applying their weight to various sides in these debates.[11] To be certain, as in other centre political economies where it framed both social and economic reality, the logic of the capitalist accumulation process guided such major policy debates and decisions. This limitation, however, should not obscure the significance of the liberal democratic form in this matter. Canada's economic development strategy during its most formative early years was not externally imposed in any crude or direct fashion. Rather, as in other centre countries, it was shaped through the complicated interplay of social and economic forces mediated by the state.

All of this should not be taken to mean that as a centre nation, Canada historically pursued the kind of industrial strategy typical of such countries as Great Britain, Federal Germany, or even the United States. Indeed, the burden of the argument of this book is that Canadian development has been strikingly different insofar as it has overemphasized resource extraction and underemphasized industrial expansion. Yet, if we are to draw the proper lessons from these differences, it is essential that we place them in their correct context from the beginning of our discussion. Catastrophism and survivalism, while romantic and dramatic, are extremely misleading in the Canadian case because they leave us with too few tools to understand what has happened in the past and what is likely to happen in the future. The disastrous effects of resource export dependency, which are so painfully obvious in Latin America, in Canada are largely contained and modified by a developed economy with a high standard of living and an imposing industrial capacity. In turn, this developed economy is managed by a correspondingly developed state and class structure which has always demonstrated the ability to act in defence or promotion of what it perceives to be the national interest – capitalist accumulation with social harmony.

With this context firmly established, we can proceed with our inquiry into Canada's failure to develop a substantial trade in finished manufactures. Our focus is admittedly far more specific than our discussion to this point. Nevertheless, it will soon become apparent that we have chosen a pivotal location from which to examine Canadian economic and industrial development generally.

Canadian Industry in World Markets: The Ledger

Scarcely any symptom of Canada's industrial weakness has received as much comment in the last decade as its failure to export its products at a level appropriate to our developed modern status in the world economy. This failure has taken place in a century in which manufactured goods have established themselves as the most dynamic sector of world trade. Moreover, among manufactures, the most technologically advanced and highly finished categories, such as machinery and transport goods, have led the way. By comparison, trade in textiles has stagnated.[12]

The international success of manufactured exports has been so pronounced that it has led a number of observers to link it to economic development.[13] Industrialization is said to be associated with economic development because it leads to increases in both labour productivity and real incomes. In turn, relative levels of industrialization and worldwide industrial competitive power can be measured through manufactured exports because industrial growth enhances trade potential. This accounts for the "remarkably close relationship over the past 60 years in the relative growth rates of the main industrial countries and their shares of the world export market in manufactures."[14]

Not only is a high level of manufactured exports usually a feature of economic development, but underdevelopment is often associated with an export structure dominated by primary products and/or intermediate or semi-manufactures.[15] In correspondence with these trends, international trade in manufactures has polarized with a few developed centre nations on one side and the many nations of the periphery of the world economy on the other. Indeed, during the first half of the twentieth century, the ten largest industrial countries accounted for over four-fifths of the world's trade in manufactures.[16] On the other side, a United Nations study has estimated that in the early 1970's the developing countries as a whole supplied only 6.3 per cent of the total imports of manufactured products of twenty-one of the most developed countries.[17]

Given the dichotomy which has evolved between the developed, manufactured export nations and the underdeveloped, primary export nations, one influential economist, Alfred Maizels, has proposed a system of classification with interesting and important implications for Canada. He suggests that countries may be divided into three groups – industrial, semi-industrial, and non-industrial – based on the value of their production of manufactures per head of population and the proportion of their exports consisting of "finished" manufactures (products not normally subject to a further manufacturing process). In 1955, most industrial countries had at least one-third of their exports as finished goods. Up to 15 per cent of the exports of semi-industrial countries were similarly finished. For non-industrial countries the proportion was under 5 per cent.[18]

Table One gives a picture of the export performance of individual countries assigned a classification by Maizels. Data on these countries has been brought up to date and has been supplemented by a record of their current imports of finished manufactures. In the quarter century since Maizels originally studied this question, international trade in manufactured products has intensified, as Table One indicates. In the industrial countries, finished manufactures currently account for at least half of their total exports; in the semi-industrial countries, 10 to 25 per cent; and in the non-industrial countries the

TABLE ONE

Degree of Industrialization and Finished Manufactures as a Proportion of Trade: 1913, 1929, 1955, and 1980 (per cent of total trade)

	Exports				*Imports*
	1913	*1929*	*1955*	*1980*	*1980*
Industrial Countries					
Japan	31	43	64	71	11
Italy	31	41	47	61	28
Germany (Federal)	46	54	65	60	34
Sweden	23	26	33	53	45
United States	21	37	48	52	38
Great Britain	58	49	62	50	39
France	44	47	38	50	35
Canada	5	14	11	32	59
Semi-industrial Countries					
India	13	19	31.0	23**	27**
Brazil	—	—	0.4	22***	29***
Argentina	—	—	0.4	14**	49**
Australia	—	—	6.0	10	54
Turkey	—	—	0.4	7***	39***
Non-industrial Countries					
Egypt	—	—	3.0	4.0***	35***
Zaire	—	—	0.8	0.6**	48**
Burma	—	—	0.4	0.3*	55*

*1976; **1978; ***1979.

SOURCES: A. Maizels, *Industrial Growth and World Trade* (Cambridge: Cambridge University Press, 1963), pp. 59, 64; United Nations, *Yearbook of International Trade Statistics,* vol. 1, 1980.

figure is below 10 per cent. As a corollary of his proposition that high exports of finished manufactures indicate high levels of industrialization, Maizels suggested that the larger industrial countries were less dependent on imports of manufactures than the smaller industrials, semi-industrials, and non-industrials.[19] This is indeed reflected in the striking contast between the positive trade balances in finished manufactures held by all the industrial countries (except Canada) and the negative trade balances which appear to be characteristic in both other groupings.

Considered only from the perspective of exports, it could be debated whether Canada more properly belongs among the semi-industrials of Maizels' classification. Historically, our proportion of exported manufactures has fallen significantly short of the average for industrials. Moreover, we have endured a very large negative trade balance in finished goods. Of course, the relatively high value of Canada's per capita production, the other element in Maizels' scale, rescues us from such a fate. Interestingly, for Maizels, the deciding factor was the extremely close relationship between the Canadian and United States economies, a relationship so close that "in many respects, the two countries can effectively be regarded as a single economic system."[20]

An optimist might argue that Canada has made dramatic progress in the last quarter century by increasing threefold, from 11 to 32 per cent, the proportion of her trade composed of finished manufactures. Unfortunately, this advance is less significant than it appears for a number of reasons. First, and most obviously, most of Canada's competitors have been pressing ahead as well. We remain at the bottom of the industrial heap, substantially below the 50 per cent line that marks the other developed countries.

In addition, direct comparisons between these two periods are suspect because of the peculiar effects of the Auto Pact, a United States-Canada trade agreement which allows for free trade in automobiles and parts between the two countries. Since 1965, when the Auto Pact was inaugurated, the Canadian proportion of exports of finished manufactures has risen dramatically. In the early 1960's, finished exports had stood at approximately 13 per cent of total exports. This jumped to nearly 38 per cent by the early 1970's but, as we have observed, settled back to about 32 per cent of total exports by the end of that decade.

Although it is true that the Auto Pact has stimulated Canadian exports of manufactures to the United States, its net advantage in our total trade picture is less than clear because it has been an even greater stimulus for U.S. manufactured exports to Canada. In only three of the sixteen years of Auto Pact operation (1970-72) has Canada been in a surplus position in this trade, and then only slightly. The cumulative deficit over the life of the agreement now stands at $14 billion, nearly half of this suffered in the last three years alone.[21]

For the purposes of our inquiry, a strong case can be made for excluding Auto Pact exchanges from Canada's external trade picture.

As we have spoken about it, the ratio of finished manufacture exports to total exports has meaning only because it is a rough indicator of a nation's ability to compete industrially within the world economy. The Auto Pact, however, tells us nothing positive about Canada's position as an industrial exporter as it provides basically for intra-firm transfers of goods which incidentally pass over an international frontier. This may mean nothing more than the exchange of vehicles of different sizes, models, or colours from a Canadian subsidiary to its U.S. parent company. Furthermore, as we have noted, Canada has a large deficit in these exchanges. If, then, an adjustment is made to remove Auto Pact exchanges, Canada's proportion of finished manufactures falls to 22 per cent of total exports in 1980. This leaves us squarely in the company of Brazil and India.

Finally, progress in Canada's industrial trade during recent decades seems even more illusory when we consider our failure within the machinery and transport goods sectors. These sectors, it will be remembered, played a key role in making manufactured goods this century's most dynamic department in world trade. In recent years, while exports of machines and transport equipment from the other industrials have averaged in excess of two-fifths of their total exports, Canada, after the removal of Auto Pact trade, can only manage to place about one-sixth of her total exports in this category. Not only is this just slightly above the levels achieved by the semi-industrials, but Canada also shared with these countries large negative trade balances in these important commodities.

Canada's export impotence is more than just a statistical irregularity. In fact, it has considerably aggravated two of the country's most persistent economic policy problems – balance of payments policy and employment policy. In only four of the thirty-two years between 1950 and 1981 has Canada been able to manage a surplus on the current account of her international balance of payments. This means we are in a virtually constant state of deficit when all of our international transactions – such as merchandise trade, investments, and services (consulting fees, royalties, travel, etc.) – are considered. Although these deficits are a result mainly of high carrying costs of foreign investment, trade in manufactures has made a significant and growing contribution to our balance of payments difficulties. During the 1970's, our trade deficit in fully manufactured end products totalled $87.6 billion, $60.6 billion of which was suffered in the last five years of the decade. As the economic downturn deepens, the picture for the 1980's can only be viewed with alarm. In the first two years of this decade, our end product deficit totalled $38.5 billion.[22]

Our manufactured export shortfall has also had a negative impact on employment policy. In general, resource industries are capital-intensive, while manufacturing industries are relatively labour-intensive. Put simply, this means that historically Canada has sacrificed many potential jobs by emphasizing resource extraction rather than trade in industrial products. As a result, the country stubbornly maintains an unemployment rate near the top of the highly developed OECD countries. It also has a lower than typical percentage of her workforce in manufacturing employment.[23]

Toward a Political Economy of Canadian Industrialization

The reader may feel the need for some clarification at this point. On the one hand, it has been argued that Canada has a privileged centre location in the world order with a developed economic, political, and social structure. On the other, it has also been made apparent that there are a number of disturbing points of convergence between Canada and the semi-industrialized underdeveloped countries in regard to export trade. When we look in the mirror, which image should we see?

Perhaps the easiest way to throw light on this question is by turning our attention to how the search for solutions to the serious policy problems of balance of payments and employment might proceed differently in Canada as compared to a truly semi-industrialized nation. Peripheral status in this instance would be indicated by a country's inability, by itself, to significantly improve its terms of entry into the world economy without some form of extraordinary upheaval such as a revolution. As we have already observed, however, Canada shares with the periphery neither its limiting structures of economic underdevelopment nor its typically rigid social and political institutions. This means that the benefits of reform within one sector of the basically autocentric Canadian economy – through, for example, a thoroughgoing program of industrial renovation – would likely spill over into other sectors and not be confined within the disarticulated and extroverted economic channels of foreign domination that characterize underdevelopment. This also means that in Canada social pressure for such economic reform is likely to be mediated through the political process in a qualitatively more complex fashion than the application of a repressive dose of coercion (as in a dictatorship or through a military coup) with the straightforward object of preserving the status quo.

If these observations are held to provide an essentially correct description of Canada's contemporary situation, it is the contention of this book that their principles may be used to understand the puzzling evolution of our manufactured export capacity from its late nineteenth-century origins. Our inquiry will outline the complex interplay between the economic constraints and opportunities Canada has faced in the last century because of her unique position as a centre nation attached, in turn, to the British and American Empires. It will also highlight the decisive factors influencing the choices, conscious and accreted, about industrial strategy made within the overall political process as well as at the level of the individual firm.

It probably is worth reiterating that what is being attempted here is not a comprehensive theory of Canadian economic or industrial development. Rather, a political economy method of inquiry is being applied to a detailed examination of the failure of our manufacturers to take advantage of their twentieth-century opportunities in world markets. The truth is that a great deal more investigative work in many areas still needs to done before a general theory of this kind can be written. It is hoped that this study will make a contribution to the search.

To be sure, many attempts in the past have sought to "explain" Canada's industrial weaknesses. Unfortunately, most have lacked the global perspective necessary for the task and, accordingly, have slipped into near determinisms of either an economic/environmental or political/social type. These explanations include: our comparative trade advantage in resources which rendered an industrial specialization uneconomic; the unambitious character of our business elites and/or their willingness to betray the national interest to foreigners; our small domestic market which did not permit the production efficiencies necessary to industrial export; the protective tariff policies of successive federal governments which sheltered Canadian manufacturers uncompetitive in world markets; and, finally, external domination of the Canadian economy and state which chained the country to a resource hinterland role. While each of these interpretations has something to offer and will be more fully discussed in subsequent chapters, it will soon become clear that none is sufficiently strong to be considered the prime cause of export impotence.

Our study will proceed from a diagnosis of conditions in the womb of our modern industrial structure by examining the late nineteenth-century National Policy tariffs of Sir John A. Macdonald and the Conservative Party. Here, we will examine the selection of an industrial strategy that has shaped the development of Canadian manufacturing to the present day. Instead of adopting a policy of international specialization through the production for world markets of a number of technologically innovative lines, our state and economic elites chose a much less ambitious alternative strikingly similar to that known in the contemporary underdeveloped world as import substitution industrialization (ISI). This model relies on a tariff structure as an instrument for domestic manufacturers to capture primarily consumer-oriented sectors of the home market with a production process borrowed from foreign industrialists. Its two major components, import replacement and technological dependence, when fused, produce an industrial structure with little potential to grow beyond its domestic horizons.

With our conceptual model of ISI in hand and relying largely on previously unpublished material, we will explore four periods of industrial export failure. The first period parallels the astonishing developments in Canada's booming "wheat economy" at the beginning of the twentieth century. In the second period, Canadian manufacturers failed to turn the extraordinary export opportunities provided by the Great War to their long-term advantage. In the third period, the "roaring twenties," a segment of our economic and political elite dreamt of making Canada the industrial workshop of the British Empire. The final period of export blocking through foreign branch plant dominance of Canadian manufacturing takes us from the late 1930's through the 1960's.

Our principal source in these four chapters will be the observations and reports of the officials of the federal Department of Trade and Commerce. Mandated to stimulate Canadian export trade, the Department occupied a unique vantage point from which to record the course of the events we are studying. Its collective vision was at once wider than that of the individual business enterprises involved in export trade and more detailed and accurate than the impressions of other observers such as politicians, academics, and reporters.

This does not imply that the views of such observers merit only passing attention. On the contrary, the concluding two chapters argue that one of the primary reasons so little has been done to meet the challenge of transforming our stalling, sputtering, inward-looking manufacturing sector is precisely because our political and intellectual elites failed, until relatively recently, to acknowledge that something had gone seriously wrong with the export side of our industrialization process. Accordingly, our discussion addresses itself to an evaluation of how this awareness developed. We shall see that two main schools of thought have emerged on the issue of Canada's industrial development in the modern era. Each of these schools is associated with a radically opposed public policy alternative – one free trade and foreign investment oriented, the other protectionist and nationalist. In our concluding chapter, we will trace this fierce debate over industrial strategy during the last decade and identify those factors that will be crucial in its eventual resolution.

CHAPTER 2

Import Substitution: Strategy of Export Impotence

An examination of Canada's industrial export frustrations could not proceed on any other basis than from a rigorous probe of the late nineteenth- and early twentieth-century foundations of modern Canadian manufacturing. The key to this formative period, it is generally agreed, is the National Policy tariffs that began to appear in 1879. Early commentators focused on the material achievements of an industralization process they saw, either approvingly or disapprovingly, as being the artificial creation of the tariffs.[1] More recent analysis has highlighted the gaps and limitations in this strategy in order to account for the evolution of Canadian secondary manufacturing as an "inefficient, non-innovative, and backward . . . structure with a penchant for dependence on foreign technology, foreign capital, and state assistance as its sine qua non."[2] Our inquiry turns in this latter direction.

This critique of Canada's pre-World War I industrial strategy is not an attempt to find past scapegoats for present difficulties. Instead, our task is to piece together the logic of a decision process which in the end assigned a relatively low priority to the industrial side of our economic development. The leading actors of Canadian society found the industrial strategy that we will soon dissect both rational, from the perspective of profit and employment, and nationalist, within the nineteenth-century ideology of strengthening the British Empire. The pattern of expansion in our early secondary manufacturing fits an industrial strategy model – import substitution industrialization (ISI) – pursued much later in the underdeveloped countries. What sets Canada apart from the beginning is her favoured position as a young country of the centre. Accordingly, neither was the choice of ISI inevitable, in the sense that it was imposed by external economic or political structures, nor were the economic benefits of ISI to be confined within the disarticulated channels of underdevelopment. Rather, our relatively rich domestic market permitted ISI to proceed on a scale inconceivable on the periphery of the world economy and thereby to confirm the basically developed nature of the Canadian economy.

Import substitution industrialization is the industrial strategy most typical of the underdeveloped periphery. It is essentially simple, rapid, and painless in execution. This has accounted for its widespread popularity. At levels set high enough to make domestic production feasible, tariffs are placed on selected commodities which enjoy established markets formerly serviced by imports. This generally means consumer goods ranging anywhere from laundry soap to automobiles. Foreign technology (usually both machinery and processes) is freely employed by a domestic licensee or foreign-owned subsidiary to create an instant industry.

From the perspective of our study of manufactured exports, the limitations of the ISI model are clear. The new factories cannot compete on world markets as they have nothing distinctive to offer them. In addition, a condition of the use of the foreign technology is usually that production be restricted to the domestic market. Further, the ISI factory provides few backward linkages to the rest of the country's economy as it needs no domestic capital goods industry to keep it supplied with new processes and machines. In this regard, the continual demand for imported capital goods often creates new burdensome strains on the balance of payments accounts. Thus, the ISI manufacturing sector tends to stagnate as a mere supplement to other productive activities (usually resource extraction).

Not surprisingly, ISI appears to run contrary to the experience of such "late" European industrializers as Germany, Italy, and Russia, which initially stressed producers' goods over consumer goods.[3] While it is hazardous to oversimplify, the industrial strategy typical of such centre countries might be styled the specialized world competitive model. As we shall demonstrate later in this chapter, while Canada was following ISI in the early twentieth century, Sweden and Japan adopted a policy of developing world technological leadership in the production of a limited number of innovative lines. Although their domestic markets were used as a base, it was clear that efficient production runs required foreign customers. In turn, this demanded the local assimilation and adaptation of existing foreign technologies to the point where marketable technological breakthroughs made exports possible.

Occupying the Home Market

Having set out the essential characteristics of ISI, tariff-induced import replacement with extreme technological dependence, we are now prepared to examine the case of the National Policy. While the National Policy tariffs are familiarly, and correctly, discussed as a tool of national development policy, a device to increase government revenue, and as a measure to check the southward emigration flow by providing permanent employment opportunities, their relationship to import replacement and the balance of payments has been less well documented. In his 1878 pre-election speech to the House of Commons outlining the proposed new tariff of the Conservatives, Sir John A. Macdonald made it quite clear that Canadian industrialization would be based primarily on replacing imports in the domestic market.

> I believe that, by a fair readjustment of the tariff, we can increase the various industries which we can interchange one with another and make this union a union in interest, a union in trade, and a union in feeling. We shall then grow up rapidly a good, steady and mature trade between the Provinces, rendering us independent of foreign trade, and not, as New Brunswick and Nova Scotia formerly did, look to the United States or to England for trade, but look to Ontario and Quebec – sending their products west, and receiving the products of Quebec and Ontario in exchange. This is the great policy, The National Policy, which we on this side are advocating . . . .[4]

Later, we may assume, with the completion of the railway, the West was also to be brought into this domestic "union in trade."

S.L. Tilley, Conservative Minister of Finance, in introducing the National Policy legislation in 1879, explicitly tied the new tariffs to import reduction and balance of payments difficulties.

> Regarding the matter as I do, I think it is to be regretted that the volume of imports has not been materially reduced. I look upon the large imports, ever since the Dominion was organized, showing a large balance of trade against it, as one of the causes of the troubles with which we have to contend . . . . They have been decreasing to a certain extent, but are still very large, showing . . . that they ought still to be further diminished . . . .I think then, without entering into a discussion here of Free Trade and Protection, so far as it affects England and the United States, we may fairly conclude that the prosperity of the one country . . . is caused in great measure by the large surplus in its favour, and the depression in the other by the large deficiency. Under these circumstances it appears to me we should turn our attention to the best means of reducing the volume of our imports from all parts of the world.[5]

The "best means" of reducing imports was, of course, to increase home production.

From the manner in which he introduced the specific clauses of the tariff legislation, many of which came from the manufacturers themselves,[6] it can be shown that Tilley was not just making a theoretical point for the edification of the Honourable Members. For example, in imposing 25 and 35 per cent tariffs on various types of earthenware, Tilley observed "they [the government] did not anticipate any increase of revenue from the new duties, being satisfied that a large portion of the importations would be replaced by the home-made article."[7] In raising the tariff on candles and paraffin wax, Tilley said "it was very probable that a large portion of the candles formerly imported would [now] be manufactured from Canadian paraffin wax."[8]

It should be emphasized that the National Policy tariffs were not only designed to protect existing Canadian industries, but also to give manufacturers a chance to expand their operations or to establish a new plant to fill orders for goods which were formerly imported. Tilley stated that

> The policy of the Government had been that where an article was made in the country, where we had raw material in abundance here, it was considered desirable to give those industries not only such encouragement and protection to keep up those already in existence, but to encourage the establishment of others.[9]

Specifically, in imposing a tariff on clocks, Tilley observed "there were some manufactories in the country, the principal one being at Hamilton. The tariff would, no doubt, increase the production of this establishment, and probably might lead to the establishment of others."[10]

Eight years later another Minister of Finance used the same import substitution argument to justify his government's new tariffs on iron and steel imports. Pointing to the fact that there had been $288 million worth of iron and steel imports since Confederation, Sir Charles Tupper chided Canadians for allowing other countries to "reap this golden harvest that lies unconsidered at our feet." His answer? A tariff to "put this iron industry upon the same footing and foundation that you have put all the other industries of Canada, and you will sweep away to a large extent the balance of trade which stands against Canada up to the present time."[11]

One can readily find echoes of the logic of Tilley and Tupper in such business publications as the Montreal *Journal of Commerce.* In 1881, it mused:

> To us it seems somewhat extraordinary that, with raw materials near at hand, and every facility to manufacture, the bulk of the fabrics used in this country should continue to be imported . . . . The aim to promote home industry embracing the erection of factories to give employment to a large number of work people, must ere long greatly benefit this country. However persistently politicians preach agriculture as the proper vocation for Canadians, it is being more fully recognized that while our money is sent elsewhere to employ others to manufacture our articles of consumption our progress cannot be satisfactory.[12]

Manufacturers also looked on the tariff as a means of substituting domestic production for imports. As early as 1883, the *Canadian Manufacturer*, organ of a leading group of Ontario industrialists,[13] pressed for higher tariffs on iron and steel imports on the grounds that

> The N.P. [National Policy] is good as far as it goes but it has not yet been carried far enough. So far it has gone that we need not today import a single yard of gray cotton or a pound of refined sugar; we can make enough of both at home. But we are still sending to England and to the United States for iron that we ought to be making at home instead.[14]

Indeed, during the 1880's and the early 1890's the *Canadian Manufacturer*, in the context of this strategy of replacing imports, sang psalms of praise to the "home market" while downgrading the importance of export sales. For example, an 1883 editorial entitled "About an Export Trade" told readers that Canada's chances of exporting manufactures to the U.S. market were "about equal to those of getting to the moon by railway" and that the idea of selling surplus Canadian cottons or woollens "in any foreign market is about as visionary and impracticable as anything that could be conceived . . . . Both Old England and New England would meet us in every port and we would not have the ghost of a chance."[15] A similar sentiment was also expressed in 1885 by this periodical:

> In these days of over-production, when nation is fighting against nation for possession of markets, and when commercial war is hotter the civilized world over than ever it was before – what seems the most sensible course for us? Clearly this, we should say to hold our own – to keep a fast grip of the home market, the only one that we can hold, if we choose, against all comers.[16]

Like arguments were advanced in 1881 by the *Journal of Commerce* when it editorialized on the subject of Canadian trade in manufactured exports: "it is scarcely necessary to observe that it [export trade] has been and must long continue to be comparatively insignificant . . . . Canada can reasonably expect to do no more than supply her home market to a reasonable extent."[17] Two years later it derided an article in the Montreal *Gazette* which lamented that U.S. rather than Canadian manufacturers were establishing themselves in the Australian market: "So long as the United States manufacturers are able to supply our home market, notwithstanding heavy protective duties, it is vain to complain . . . . it is preposterous for them to expect to [compete] in the markets of the world."[18] In 1889, the *Journal of Commerce* again took note of the export successes of U.S. manufacturers, observing that they "certainly afford reflection for Canadians." However, the *Journal* cautioned that "nearby trade is all the more profitable and satisfactory owing to quicker returns, etc. . . . We do not advocate the abandonment of distant trade possibilities, but there is some danger of looking too far abroad and concentrating all our energies in one direction."[19]

By 1890, these practical arguments against developing foreign markets had been elevated to the level of economic theory. Readers of *Canadian Manufacturer* were told that "the nation that is self-contained, giving employment to its people and producing within itself all that the people require, may be enjoying the acme of prosperity, although it has never a ship upon the ocean and has no foreign trade whatever."[20] Later editorials more fully elaborated this autarkic theory.

> Before we worry ourselves about foreign trade in our manufacturing let us first fully occupy our home market. Let us make all such articles as we can manufacture to advantage at home, purchasing abroad only such things as we cannot produce here . . . . When we have done this it will then be time to consider the question of exporting our surplus manufactures, but not till then . . . . We should not desire to import any thing which we could manufacture to advantage at home, and we should not export anything which we ourselves could consume. This is the correct theory, and if it were elaborated and carried out to its fullest possible extent, our foreign trade might not be so large, but we would become richer and more independent. [21]

In accepting, indeed celebrating, the limited horizons of their domestic market, Canadian manufacturers were patterning a passive export model later adopted by industrialists in the periphery of the world economy. However, a minority of Canadian manufacturers, whose core was made up of agricultural implement producers, pursued the more aggressive export model typical of capitalists of the centre. One indication of this split can be found in the opposition of many leading agricultural implement manufacturers to the introduction of protective tariffs.[22] As late as 1876, Massey declared that "the existing tariff is satisfactory to us: perhaps even a little less would also be."[23] This unusual attitude was taken for at least two reasons. First, more than most Canadian manufacturers, agricultural implement producers were linked directly to prosperity in agricultural staples sales in world markets. Any drop in farmers' incomes due to tariff-related increases in the Canadian prices of other commodities could result in decreased sales of farm machinery.[24] Second, many of these industrialists were aggressive expatriate Americans who did not fear world competition and who, in fact, had not given up their dreams of access to the larger U.S. market. One such manufacturer had even gone so far as to work out a scenario for continentalizing the production of agricultural machinery in the event of free trade being negotiated with the U.S. He suggested that "there would not be so many manufacturers conflicting with each other here for we would strike out with particular branches of the trade, say in one or two articles, and after we had supplied Canada we would send the balance into the States."[25]

The difference in attitudes and emphasis toward export sales of the two groups of manufacturers is well illustrated by the reactions of *Canadian Manufacturer* to pressure placed by Massey-Harris on the Canadian government for a somewhat minor adjustment in the tariff. In order to protect his competitive position in world markets by maintaining low production costs, Massey threatened in 1894 to shift much of his enterprise to the U.S. if he was not given a refund on the tariff collected on imported raw materials which he re-exported as manufactured machinery.[26] *Canadian Manufacturer* originally supported Massey's eventually successful demands, but, significantly, when it became apparent that such tariff-free imports threatened the economics of import substitution production in the exempted articles, it reversed its stand. It noted that Massey-Harris had received $10,083 as compensation for 3,385 exported harvesters and angrily suggested that the interests of Canadian industry would have been better served if the government had simply handed the company a grant of $10,000. The effect of the tariff adjustment, it argued, was to force a drop in the Canadian price of the raw material to the lower U.S. level and, thereby, "to disorganize and demoralize the industry without one single compensating feature to any Canadian industry, except that of the Massey-Harris people."[27]

Canadian Manufacturer and the group of import substituting industrialists whose views it reflected did not really comprehend the desire of the agricultural implement manufacturers to maximize their sales by becoming internationally competitive in specialized lines. Their attitude toward export markets was, as we have earlier noted, basically passive – "while it is desirable to export our surplus products, that export should consist only of what we cannot possibly consume at home."[28] So it was that the agricultural machinery manufacturers were criticized for exporting before filling the "home market." For example, in 1901, *Canadian Manufacturer* was deeply troubled that $2 million of farm machinery was imported into Canada at the same time as this Canadian industry was exporting its products.

> We are not of that optimistic temperament which allows us to see anything particularly desirable in the fact that the foreign trade of Canada increased to the extent of nearly $2,000,000 a year by the imports of agricultural implements alone. It is said of the Massey-Harris Company that they are the largest manufacturers of agricultural implements under the British flag; and there are a large number of other such concerns in Canada, but they do not supply the home market however much they may strive to increase the volume of our foreign trade.[29]

Technological Dependence

On the basis of our discussion to this point, it seems reasonable to conclude that the National Policy tariffs were rather more than simply the protection of "infant industries" which were eventually to become internationally competitive. Rather, they reflected a preoccupation on the part of state and business elites with the capture of the "home market" by substituting domestic production for imports. Another component of the ISI strategy, as it was earlier outlined with reference to the periphery of the world economy, is extreme technological dependence. In order to determine whether this feature was shared by pre-World War I Canada, we will now examine the circumstances of both the branch plant sector, worth only approximately 9 to 11 per cent of the total capital invested in Canadian industry at this time, and the dominant Canadian-owned sector that controlled almost all of the remainder.[30]

A study of the relationship between technology and the development of modern industry in Canada must begin with the Patent Act of 1872. Before this date only Canadian residents could hold Canadian patents and the diffusion of foreign technology was accomplished by the theft of techniques, processes, and patterns and by the immigration into Canada of U.S. industrial entrepreneurs. Technology transferred in this manner was thereby assimilated by Canadian industry and adapted to local market conditions. The 1872 Act, however, made this learning process superfluous. It contained a "compulsory working" clause which allowed non-residents to hold Canadian patents on the condition that they or their representatives manufactured the article in question within two years of their submission of an application for patent protection. This liberalization came in concert with attempts on the part of many countries in the second half of the nineteenth century to rationalize their patent laws in order to cope with the flood of new technological innovations.[31] More directly, it was the result of many years of pressure on the part of U.S. industrialists and their government.[32]

The new Act opened the way to a deluge of imported techniques, which rapidly swamped Canadian industrial innovation. The proportion of patents issued to Canadian residents dropped from 100 per cent in 1870 to 35 per cent in 1880, to only 15 per cent by 1900. Not surprisingly, there was a corresponding increase in the proportion of patents issued to Americans – 70 per cent in 1900. In addition, in absolute terms, the total number of patents annually issued increased by a factor of fifteen between 1870 and 1900, while the number going to Canadians only doubled.[33]

The "working clause" of the 1872 Patent Act and the 1879 National Policy tariffs worked hand in hand to transfer U.S. technology and production to Canada. Much of this transfer was accomplished through licensing agreements with Canadian industrialists, as capital shortages often prevented direct U.S. investment in branch plants.[34] Notices, like the following, under the title of "A New Canadian Enterprise," frequently appeared in *Canadian Manufacturer* and demonstrate how the development of technological dependence was seen as a positive accomplishment of the National Policy.

> We always take pleasure in being able to draw the attention of our readers from time to time to new industries being started in our midst . . . .The party in power in Ottawa . . . showed their wisdom and foresightedness when they framed the National Policy and put it into force, and in proof of its success it has developed the country, increased its manufacturing interests to a large extent and covered the country with railways, so that we are in a more prosperous

condition today than any other country in Europe or America. It is significant and to the point to notice that the well known firm of Henry R. Worthington, of New York, manufacturers of pumping and hydraulic machinery, have been obliged at last to make arrangement to make their goods in this country to enable them to hold their own. They have, therefore, entered into an agreement with the old established and well known firm of John McDougall, proprietor of the Caledonian Iron Works, Montreal, to manufacture and sell them, and to be known as their sole general and manufacturing agents for the Dominion of Canada. [35]

For Canadian industrialists, the short-run advantages of entering into such licensing agreements with U.S. firms were very clearly superior to the more difficult task of developing their own technology. First, these agreements provided relatively cheap access to an already proven industrial process. Second, only minimum delay would be encountered in exploiting innovations. This was of importance because if a Canadian manufacturer were to consider choosing the longer course of working up his own process in a similar line, he would be aware that a competitor might frustrate his efforts by simply picking up the licensed technology. Finally, those Canadian industrialists who entered into licensing agreements often gained a patent monopoly in the Canadian market that provided as much, or more, protection from foreign and domestic competition as the tariff. For all these reasons, then, the impact of U.S. patents and licensing arrangements on Canadian industrial capital was so great that, as early as 1892, W.K. McNaught, president of the Canadian Manufacturers' Association, was able to observe:

Anyone who has studied manufacturing in Canada must be aware that our factories are largely duplicates of American industries, a large proportion of which are carried on by the help of patents which secure to their owners an absolute monopoly of their own market. Our manufacturers of articles patented in the United States, and "their name is legion, for they are many" . . . .[36]

Preoccupied as they had become with "occupying" the domestic market, Canadian manufacturers demonstrated little concern for the disadvantages of technological dependence through licensing agreements. Perhaps the most serious of such faults is the risk that an industrial structure will lose the capacity to manipulate technology through the creation of its own marketable innovations if a serious effort is not made to adapt and transform at least a portion of the licensed technique. From the point of view of our study, however, the export barriers that typically accompany licensing agreements are of the greatest interest. M. Wilkins points out that manufacturing firms entering into licensing arrangements with U.S. firms during the pre-World War I era usually relinquished their export potential as they were allocated only a specified market territory by the licenser. U.S. General Electric is cited by Wilkins as a good example of an organization that carved up its international market by using licensing agreements. She notes that by 1914 U.S. General Electric had "associated" manufacturing operations in Canada, Great Britain, France, Germany, and Japan with ownership shares ranging from virtually complete to small minor holdings. Nevertheless, licensing agreements rather than ownership shares were the key factor in determining the marketing restrictions of the satellite firms. Wilkins observes that U.S. General Electric centred a network of exclusive rights, patents, and agencies that allowed it, effectively, to say to each affiliate, "You can't sell in a particular territory because we hold the patents – your patents, too – and have granted them to others."[37]

The source of new machinery going into industrial establishments can also be an important indicator of technological dependence or independence. In a typical ISI situation, it will be recalled, backward linkages to the domestic capital goods industry remain undeveloped while imports supply the necessary machine tools. Estimates by K. Buckley indicate that between 1900 and 1913, the key years in National Policy industrial expansion, nearly three-fifths of the total capital investment in plant were imported. The comparable proportion for the period 1914 to 1925 was over one-half.[38] By far the largest share of these imports was furnished by U.S. machine tool factories. In most years between 1885 to 1900 they supplied 80 to 85 per cent of this market. These figures increase to 85 and 95 per cent between 1901 and 1914.[39]

In this context, it is little wonder that Charles M. Pepper, a special agent of the U.S. consular service sent on a cross-Canada tour in 1905, was prompted to gloat:

> One striking fact is apparent, and this helps to explain why the imports from the United States have increased in spite of the steady development of Canadian industries and their partial success in supplying the home demand. Not a factory of any kind is built in the Dominion that the installation is not made very largely from the United States. This was the case with the steel works at Sydney and Sault Ste. Marie. The electrical works at Hamilton are a speaking catalogue of manufacturers of hoists, cranes and machine tools

> on this side of the border. It is the case with the flour mills . . . . It is also true of the lumber mills. In mining machinery the United States may almost be said to have a monopoly, and the great smelters are its contribution to Canadian progress. So long as Canada continues to build new mills and establish new industries, the installation of the plants will be done largely by the splendidly-equipped engineering works of the United States.[40]

According to Sir William Van Horne, chairman of the Canadian Pacific Railway, a considerable portion of this imported machinery may have been secondhand. *Industrial Canada*, the official organ of the Canadian Manufacturers' Association, quoted him as charging in 1908 ("with an authority that cannot be overlooked") that the use of machinery which U.S. manufacturers had "discarded" had resulted in a weakening of the competitive position of Canadian industrialists, even within their own tariff-protected market.[41]

Further, the approximate two-fifths of new machinery for industrial plants, which were Canadian in origin, cannot be assumed to represent an important sector of potentially competitive and technologically innovative production. In fact, a significant portion of Canadian machine tool manufacture during this period was undertaken by U.S. branch plants and licensed ventures.[42] In 1905, *Industrial Canada* surveyed the largely imitative foundations of the Canadian producers' equipment industry and the resistance to technical design innovation that kept it relatively backward:

> Up-to-date United States patterns are followed almost exclusively, but our machinery is built upon somewhat heavier lines, though not so heavy as the British. The combination is very suitable to the needs of a country where manufacturing is not conducted upon so large a scale as in the United States and where manufacturers are consequently not so ready to abandon old machines to adopt new ones slightly better.[43]

Admitting that most specialized machinery in Canada continued to be imported from the United States twenty-five years after the 1879 introduction of the National Policy tariffs, *Industrial Canada* excused this deviation from import replacement by arguing that "naturally the making of machinery is one of the last industries to be developed in a new country."[44] As late as the 1920's, the *Monetary Times* could report little growth in Canada's machine tool industry:

> It should be noted that much specialized equipment comes from

> the United Kingdom and the United States. Canada provides a sufficiently large field to permit the domestic manufacture of machines of such common use as small printing presses, concrete mixers, lawn mowers and gasoline engines. But for some of the more elaborate devices there are so few orders in a year that economical production in this country is impossible.[45]

By this point, it should be clear that the establishment of Canada's modern industrial structure was almost completely dependent on U.S. manufacturing for reproduction (through patents, licences, and machinery) of its means of production. Lacking any real commitment to the development of a more independent technological base by assimilating, adapting, and innovating on the basis of what it had borrowed, Canadian manufacturing from its point of origin was never in a position to become a competitive force in the world economy. Indeed, as we have seen, the possibility of international specialization had been rather scornfully rejected in favour of a more autarkic industrial model.

It is now appropriate to investigate the special role of U.S. direct investment in enhancing Canadian technological dependence during the formative years of our industrialization. An interpretation that would minimize the significance of the approximate 10 per cent of Canadian industrial capital controlled by U.S. branch plants is quite misleading because it fails to identify the sectors in which this investment was concentrated. In the pre-World War I period, a "second" industrial revolution was laying the base for modern industry in the United States, Germany, and Great Britain. Historian E.J. Hobsbawm identifies three major "growth industries" of this era: electrical industries, chemical industries, and industries based on the application of the internal combustion engine.[46] In the previous chapter we noted that the technologically advanced and highly finished products of these "growth industries" led the way in making manufactured goods this century's most dynamic department in world trade. We have just concluded a discussion of the barriers to Canadian industrial trade that typically accompanied licensing arrangements. Since U.S. branch plants were concentrated in these three "growth" sectors, then the negative possibilities of export blocking for Canada as a result of this more direct form of technological dependence can be readily deduced. Let us examine each sector.

Two electrical companies dominated production in Canada at the start of the First World War. One, Canadian Westinghouse, was a branch plant of a U.S. firm. The other was Canadian General Electric, nominally owned by Canadians but in fact bound securely in the orbit of U.S. General Electric through licensing arrangements. Some of the other U.S. branch plants manufacturing electrical goods in Canada by 1914 were Crouse-Hinds, Northern Electric, and Wagner Electric.[47]

U.S. branch plants were also well represented in the broad field of chemical production. In industrial chemicals we find American Cyanamid, Bird-Archer, and Canadian Explosives (a Dupont and Nobel joint venture which later became C.I.L. Chemicals); in medicinal drugs, W.K. Wampole and Parke-Davis; in paints, Sherwin-Williams, Pratt and Lambert, and Glidden. Imperial Oil was already a leader in petroleum production. Goodyear Tire and Rubber was one of Canada's most important manufacturers of rubber goods.

From its outset, automobile production in Canada centred on the U.S. industry. Ford and Studebaker both had branch plants in Canada by 1914. One of the founding members of U.S. General Motors, Reo Motor Car Company, also had a branch plant here. Another important link with General Motors was instituted in 1908 by R.S. McLaughlin, who entered a licensing arrangement with Buick to import engines for bodies he was producing in Oshawa. Later, of course, his firm was absorbed by General Motors. In the same year, Canadian Cycle and Motor Car Company, which had prospered originally as the result of a licensing agreement with a U.S. bicycle manufacturer, began production of the Durant under licence. Finally in this sector, although Canadian manufacturers of agricultural machinery dominated production in Canada, U.S. branch plants such as International Harvester, Case, and John Deere had captured a significant share of the market.

While much can be inferred from the pre-1914 presence of U.S. branch plants in these critical sectors, unfortunately there are no statistics that would allow us to assess accurately the extent to which they had captured control of the "growth industries." We do, however, have a breakdown of the nationality of capital investment in Canadian manufacturing just after the Great War.

It would seem that the special requirements of wartime production stimulated a significant expansion in the value of U.S. investment in Canada as it reached approximately 30 per cent of the national total by the conclusion of World War I. An analysis of Table Two indicates that this U.S. investment was indeed concentrated in the "growth industries." In all these sectors, the level of U.S. investment is higher than its share of total capital investment in manufacturing (with the exception of agricultural implements in 1921). In automobile production, as well as in paints, drugs, and chemicals, U.S. capital is clearly dominant. If we accept that Canadian General Electric was a quasi-branch plant, then U.S. capital would also be dominant in the electrical

TABLE TWO

Origin of Capital Investment in Selected Industrial Enterprises in Canada, 1920 and 1921

Industry	*Per cent of U.S. ownership*		*Per cent of Canadian ownership*	
	1920	*1921*	*1920*	*1921*
Electrical apparatus	45	42	43	42
Paints, drugs, chemicals	60	55	33	35
Petroleum refining	63	36	36	63
Rubber goods, boots, shoes	36	40	52	53
Automobiles, auto accessories	69	78	31	22
Agricultural implements	39	24	50	52
Total	**31**	**28**	**58**	**61**

SOURCE: Dominion Bureau of Statistics surveys published in the *Financial Post*, December 1, 1922, pp. 17, 20, and October 19, 1923, p. 16.

sector. Only in agricultural implements, petroleum refining, and rubber manufactures is U.S. capital not dominant, although a strong base for later expansion had been established.

Industrializing within the Empire

To this point, our inquiry has argued that a particular set of individual and collective choices was made in late nineteenth- and early twentieth-century Canada by both politicians and businessmen, choices which, when put together, fit the ISI model of import replacement with unchallenged technological dependence. The growing power of the branch plants toward the end of this period merely further institutionalized ISI as the dominant mode of domestic industrial production, rather than signifying the liquidation of an independent, aggressive, export-oriented Canadian manufacturing sector. In order to better understand why these choices seemed appropriate to those who made them, we now shift our focus to an examination of the environment that conditioned them. This will require us to scrutinize the field of post-Confederation economic development with a much wider lens than we have previously employed.

The opening of the West, the building of a transcontinental railway, large-scale immigration, and the establishment of an integrated domestic economy through industrialization – all these were the objectives of Canada's ambitious, even visionary, national development scheme of this era. In this respect, our political and economic elites achieved no mean measure of success, thereby confirming both their entrepreneurial spirit and skills. How did these objectives emerge and what was the place given to industrial strategy among them? As we address this crucial question, it will become apparent that, more than any other single factor, Canada's attachment to the British Empire at this historic juncture seems to have structured the view of Canadian decision-makers as to the economic and political opportunities and constraints of their circumstances.

Let us survey first the economic context of Canadian industrialization. From the late nineteenth century until World War I, Canadian wealth was rooted in agricultural production for export to Britain. That country absorbed fully half of Canada's exports between 1875 and 1914, most of them agricultural. To illustrate, between 1900 and 1913 about four-fifths of Canada's exports to Britain were agricultural products. The importance of this trade to both countries can be seen in Table Three.

From the perspective of British capital, Canada's main function in the Empire was as a supplier of food products. Canada, India, and Australasia were dependable sources of cheap food and it was both for immediate profit and for future strategic security that British

TABLE THREE

The British Market for Canadian Agricultural Products, 1870-1913

Years	*Canadian agricultural exports to Britain as a percentage of total Canadian exports*	*Percentage of total British imports of wheat and wheat flour supplied by Canada*
1870-79	23	7
1880-89	29	4
1890-94	37	5
1895-99	43	7
1900-02	41	9
1903-06	43	10
1907-09	47	16
1910-13	39	n.a.

SOURCES: Canada, House of Commons, *Sessional Papers*, 1916, no. 6, pp. 12-15; Great Britain, House of Commons, *Papers*, "Food Supplies (Imported)," 1903, no. 179, and 1910, no. 278.

capitalists were eager to develop them agriculturally. Although the United States, not Canada, was Britain's main supplier of foodstuffs during this period, Canada was a principal imperial producer of some important staples, including meat and grains. Her contribution in this regard was greatly enhanced by the opening of the West. For example, in the first decade of this century, Canada accounted for two-fifths of Empire imports of wheat and wheat flour into Britain and nearly 16 per cent of Britain's total requirements by 1909.

While the Canadian bourgeoisie was becoming ever more dependent on British markets to digest its exports, it was also increasingly dependent on British investors to finance the massive transport infrastructure needed to move agricultural products from the Canadian West to London. A comparison will serve to illustrate the remarkable extent of this capital assistance. By 1911, there was somewhat more British capital invested in Canada than in India. Measured in per capita terms, it is apparent that as a young country of the centre, Canada was figuratively swimming in development capital. Reflecting the different regimen prescribed by British financiers for different parts of their Empire, the gap was dramatically wide – almost fifty-two pounds invested for every Canadian and less than 1.5 pounds per Indian.[48]

For those involved in directing Canada's economic development in this formative era, the availability of these massive infusions of British investment was at once an economic opportunity and a constraint. It was an opportunity in the sense that a dynamic capitalist accumulation process of economic expansion and transformation could run on extraordinarily rich fuel in pre-World War I Canada. Fortunes were being made and the country was booming. At the same time, it must

TABLE FOUR

British Investment in Canada, selected years, 1870-1914

Year	*Value (million pounds)*	*Percentage of total British foreign investment*
1870	20	2
1885	113	9
1902	205	n.a.
1911	373	11
1914	515	n.a.

SOURCE: A.K. Cairncross, *Home and Foreign Investment, 1870-1913* (Cambridge: Cambridge University Press, 1953), pp. 182-6.

be realized that this boom was being directed toward a very particular destination. By its nature, the swollen investment demand of resource staple extraction set a limit on the energy available to fuel other economic activities.

When we look at the record here we find that Canadian investment in the resource extraction sector dwarfed capital formation in the industrial structure even during the period of manufacturing's most rapid expansion before World War II, 1901-1915. Based on Buckley's estimates, total rail investment during these years sucked up approximately 27 per cent of gross capital formation in Canada. Prairie farm investment represented an additional 15 per cent of domestic capital formation. After everything else was considered, this left only 7 per cent to be directed into industrial, electrical, and mining machinery and equipment – the means of manufacturing production. To place this small share in its proper perspective, it was only very marginally greater than that being invested at the same time in farm machinery.[49]

We are led inescapably to the conclusion that in comparison to the staples focus of both trade and investment, industrialization was placed basically in the position of being an afterthought of capitalist expansion in Canada. In the light of the near-monopoly of effort in the direction of resource export, the choice of a less thoroughgoing industrialization strategy, with a greater similarity to the ISI of the periphery than to the world competitive model of the centre nations, is hardly surprising. The economic objective of the majority of industrial adherents appears to have been merely supplementary to the main field of battle, resource extraction; namely, the creation of an "instant," technologically dependent, manufacturing sector to tap Canada's relatively rich domestic market. In proceeding in this manner, Canadian political and economic elites demonstrated little awareness of the long-term implications of their choice of investment priorities. In opting for limited, but above all rapid and cheap, industrialization they believed they were contributing to the creation of a more integrated and balanced national economy. They saw this as vital to Canada's economic development because the nation had to hold out the promise of industrial employment if it was to attract and keep immigrants in competition with its more developed southern neighbour.

This brings us directly to the issue of how the political opportunities and constraints of the Empire connection structured the views of Canadian decision-makers on industrial development. From our vantage point in the late twentieth century, it is possible to forget that the British Empire, for most of its inhabitants, was not simply stuffy pictures of Queen Victoria and pink blotches on a flat map of the world. Rather, it was a very nasty piece of repressive business which systematically subjugated hundreds of millions of people in the quest for world power and economic advantage. Typically, within the colonies, challenges to the economic domination of British commerce were thoroughly smothered by an unyielding application of legislative and administrative measures on the part of British authorities.[50]

Canada's National Policy industrialization presented just such a challenge. To Britain, Canada was not only a market for British manufactures but, as we have noted, was also a producer of raw materials for British factories and homes, as well as an outlet for investment capital. If the tariff assisted Canada to reach industrial maturity, she would no longer need to import British manufactures, would increasingly monopolize her own raw materials to serve her expanding industries, and would be searching for investment outlets and markets for her manufactures in competition with Britain. Indeed, National Policy industrialization was to hurt British exporters. Between 1880 and 1914, the British share of Canadian imports dropped from one-half to one-fifth.[51]

Yet, if the National Policy tariffs of 1879 were a "Declaration of Economic Independence," as suggested by F.H. Underhill,[52] it is curious that they provoked only mild disapproval from official Britain. The cabinet of the day sent a telegram to the Canadian Governor General informing him that "Her Majesty's Government regretted to observe that the general effect of the Tariff was to increase duties already high, but deemed that the fiscal policy of Canada rested, subject to treaty obligations, with the Dominion Legislature." Even the *Times* conceded that there was nothing Britain could do when it observed that "the election was the constitutional manifestation of the popular will, and that popular will must be obeyed. It must rule in Canada, and we have long since abandoned all power, even if we cherished the wish, to interfere with its supremacy there."[53]

To understand the reasons for the mildness of this response from the same Imperial lion that was preparing to swallow large parts of the continent of Africa, we must briefly contrast Canada's position in the Empire with that of other British possessions during the last half of the nineteenth century. After 1776, Britain became cautious of recreating the circumstances which had led to popular rebellion within colonies peopled by her "kith and kin." Thus, political and economic arrangements in the remaining white colonies tended to be more flexible than in the rest of the Empire as these colonies progressed through stages of representative and, then, responsible government, which featured home rule over domestic matters.

The 1837 Rebellions demonstrated that this policy of appeasement must be vigorously pursued in the Canadas if independentism was not to become a threat. Accordingly, the British reacted with caution to the growth of a movement among the Canadian bourgeoisie supporting annexation of the provinces to the United States after the destruction of their markets for agricultural produce in Britain with that country's introduction of free trade in 1846. The Governor feared that unless access for Canadian resource exports could be obtained in the United States, "there is nothing before us but violent agitation, ending in convulsion or annexation."[54] By conceding the ensuing Reciprocity Treaty of 1854, in which the Canadas were allowed to impose duties more favourable to a foreign country than to Britain, a precedent was established for the development of an independent Canadian tariff policy.

This precedent was extended by new tariffs in 1859, 1879, and 1887 in the face of angry storms of protest on each occasion from British industrialists who demanded that their government intervene to disallow this legislation on the grounds of "high economic and State reasons."[55] However, the British government did nothing more than frown. Sir Robert Herbert, Permanent Under-Secretary for the Colonies during much of this period, wrote that he was "satisfied that we (Colonial Office) shall have to give up all pretension to dictate, to such a country as Canada now is, the fiscal policy which is most acceptable to British manufacturers."[56] The British had little choice here. In the last half of the nineteenth century, Canada could not be held by military occupation. A serious rupture with Britain over trade policy could have led to rebellion and/or union with the United States. This had been made perfectly clear as early as 1859 by A.T. Galt, then Minister of Finance in the Macdonald-Cartier government, when he set the stage for a Canadian revolt by writing to the Colonial Office:

> . . . in the imposition of taxation, it is so plainly necessary that the Administration and the people should be in accord, that the former cannot admit responsibility or require approval beyond that of the local legislature. Self-government would be utterly annihilated if the views of the Imperial Government were to be preferred to those of the people of Canada. It is, therefore, the duty of the present Government distinctly to affirm the right of the Canadian Legislature to adjust the taxation of the people in the way they deem best, even if it should unfortunately happen to meet the disapproval of the Imperial Ministry. Her Majesty cannot be advised to disallow such acts, unless Her advisers are prepared to assume the administration of the affairs of the colony irrespective of the views of its inhabitants.[57]

So it was that, in administering a colony of settlement, Canadian political and economic elites enjoyed far greater opportunities to shape their own economic development strategy than that which was permissible in most of the Empire. Nevertheless, it is apparent that the politics of Empire also framed constraints around our economic planners, even if these were largely self-imposed and more in the realm of ideas than material forces. It can be reasonably argued that the ideology of imperial nationalism (or, in the language of the time, imperialism), common to the discourse of the era, validated a Canadian ISI strategy and thereby stifled visions of a more thoroughgoing world competitive industrialization.

Let us consider the manner in which the Canadian government did all it could to soften the blow of its industrial strategy to the British. While not for a moment considering abandoning the protective tariffs, it at least dressed them in imperial clothes. Two lines were pursued in explanatory communications to Britain. The first was that the tariffs were necessary because they were the only available method of raising needed government revenue. The second, and more important, put forward the position that the tariffs were principally aimed at foreign, that is U.S., suppliers of Canadian imports. For example, Galt stated in 1859 that "We have in Canada tradesmen who make goods similar to the Americans, but not to the Sheffield: and if our duty operates as encouragement to manufacturers, it is rather against the American than the English manufacturers, as any one acquainted with this country well knows."[58]

Tilley was even more encouraging in 1879, stating that the National Policy's "general effect must certainly be to decrease importations from the United States . . . while if it materially alters the measure of trade with Great Britain, it must be on the side of increase."[59] Tupper, in 1887, observed that U.S. iron and steel imports were gradually displacing British imports to Canada, and, therefore, his new tariffs on iron and steel products were trying to decrease Canada's "dependence on foreign sources" and were "on the whole in favour of British as against foreign industry." "In ceasing to be dependent on foreign sources . . . and by the development of her great natural resources," he told the Colonial Office, "Canada may hope to attain a more prosperous position and become a source of strength to the British Empire."[60]

One is tempted to dismiss these imperialist concerns as so much cynical rhetoric designed simply to defuse the criticisms of British capitalists. We have already noted, for example, that a primary purpose of the National Policy tariffs was to encourage the "foreigner" either to replace his export trade by licensing his product to a Canadian capitalist or to establish a branch plant in Canada. But in the curious world of turn-of-the-century Canadian nationalism, what can appear to us now as inconsistent or illogical may actually have conformed to the somewhat paradoxical world view of our state and business leaders. We know that during this period Canadian nationalism meant both a strong adherence to the Empire and an equally firm rejection of things American.[61] Therefore, was it not possible to assist the Empire by transferring to Canada the production of U.S. commodities, particularly those in the "growth industries" in which Britain herself was not adept?[62] And, following this logic one more step, could not Canada serve imperial interests further by becoming the Empire purveyor of these "foreign" manufactures? In fact, as we will document in subsequent chapters, this rather befuddled strategy of import substitution for the Empire was to achieve an ever greater prominence until the Great Depression of the 1930's.

Industrialization outside Empire

It could be objected at this point that one need look no further than to the factors of time and size to explain why Canada's political and economic elites chose to emphasize the development of resource extraction and staples trade over manufacturing. Put simply, this argument would hold that our late start in the industrial race meant that we entered too far behind the leaders to be able to close the gap and effectively compete. In addition, any attempt to catch up was doomed by the inefficiencies of short production runs inherent in Canada's relatively small domestic market. With a total population of only 5.3 million in 1900, Canadians were outnumbered approximately seven to one by Britains, ten to one by Germans, and fourteen to one by Americans.

This line of reasoning has intuitive appeal but crumbles under the weight of an examination of the experience of two other late industrializers, Sweden and Japan. As we will see, the economic and political elites of these two nations, somewhat more removed from the considerations and temptations of Empire than their Canadian counterparts, selected industrial strategies founded upon the achievement of a significant level of technological independence and export competitiveness.

Sweden, with only 5 million inhabitants in 1900, was an economic backwater in Europe throughout the nineteenth century. Almost 70 per cent of her population remained agricultural as late as 1880 and living standards were depressed when compared to those of her larger, more successful northern European neighbours. In this period, Sweden's industries were concentrated in the traditional iron and timber resource export trades which dated from the Middle Ages.

Sweden's "take-off" into modern industrialism, like Canada's, peaked between 1895 and 1920. Here, too, this period of rapid expansion of production appears to have been linked to the completion of a state-financed program of railway construction undertaken to improve internal communications in the latter half of the nineteenth century. Total rail kilometrage increased more than eleven-fold between 1860 and 1880.[63] The enactment of tariff legislation in the 1890's also seems to have had some beneficial effect on the expansion of the domestic market.

For our purposes, of particular interest in Sweden's "second" industrial revolution is the rapid and early development of her high-technology engineering industries. To a certain extent, Swedish producers may have enjoyed a slight head start on Canadians in this key manufacturing sector as they had been able to satisfy a portion of the machinery demands of their iron and timber producers during the earlier part of the 1800's. Nevertheless, they were incapable of supplying the modern processes, techniques, and machines necessary for the "take-off" into modern industrialism. As in Canada, the greater part of this new technology initially had to be imported from more advanced centres.

Nor was it seen to be an easy matter to catch up to Germany, Great Britain, and the United States. Swedish machinery manufacturers understood that, despite tariff protection, their home market was "inadequate as a base for advanced, large-scale industrial operations."[64] However, the satisfaction of the demands of foreign markets, especially Russia, for specialized high-technology manufactures was seen from the first as a means of expanding their production runs to world competitiveness. The support of leading financiers associated with the timber and iron trades appears to have been a crucial factor in mobilizing the investment capital necessary for the intensification of manufacturing.[65] As one observer has noted, "these wholesalers, being both importers and exporters, had an international outlook. They saw the needs of the foreign market and reacted rapidly by founding or cooperating at the founding of new export enterprises."[66]

On the basis of this aggressive, outward-looking industrial strategy, Swedish engineering plants borrowed foreign manufacturing technologies and techniques; copied, assimilated, and adapted them; and rapidly came up with a number of innovations and inventions that were competitive on world markets – dairy separators, ball bearings, diesel engines, primus stoves, electric motors and generators, and others. The outcome was a growing volume of production in engineering goods after the turn of the century, which both largely supplied the home market, thereby reducing Swedish dependence on foreign imports of advanced technology and machines, and developed considerable foreign markets.

In less than twenty years, Sweden moved from import dependence in advanced high-technology manufactures to a position as net exporter, selling abroad nearly four times as much as she purchased in foreign markets in 1917. Overseas sales of engineering products reached 16 per cent of Sweden's export income in 1916.[67] The reader will recall that in this same era the official organ of the Canadian Manufacturers' Association was suggesting to its readers that "naturally the making of machinery is one of the last industries to be developed in a new country."[68]

Japan is perhaps the most dramatic example of a successful late industrializer. In 1887, nearly 80 per cent of the population still worked in the agricultural sector and only 10 per cent in industry. Here, as in Sweden, the key to success on the part of its economic and political elites was to link technological independence with the development of modern manufacturing. Here, too, the cultivation of foreign markets for industrial products held strategic importance from the beginning.

Held rigidly in check by a traditional feudal aristocracy, Japanese manufacturing was either extremely backward or nonexistent in virtually all sectors until the collapse of the old regime in 1868. As a consequence, the Japanese bourgeoisie in formation was forced to rely completely on foreign technology in order to begin the construction of its modern industrial base. This was to mean the import of foreign specialists, the purchase of foreign machine tools, production under licensing agreements, and even a limited degree of direct foreign investment in pivotal sectors such as automobiles and machinery.

However, it was conscious government policy, in close co-operation with the growing manufacturing oligopolies, to utilize this borrowed technology to build up an independent Japanese technological capability. This translated into the adjustment and adaptation of foreign technology to meet local conditions requiring the labour-intensive production of cheap and often shoddy goods. The state established model factories and experimental stations using foreign machines and processes in order that Japanese manufacturers might imitate and adapt the technology they found useful. As one study has pointed out, this "process of imitation not only helped improve the understanding of the working of the technology involved but considerably strengthened, on account of the trial and error involved, the design and engineering capability of domestic machinery manufacturers."[69] The slogan used to highlight this policy was "the first machine by import, the second by domestic production."[70]

This approach rather quickly transformed the structure of Japanese industry. At the end of the nineteenth century traditional industries like foods, textiles, and forest products were dominant, with over 70 per cent of total manufacturing production, but by 1935 the modern machinery, chemicals, and metals industries made up more than 50 per cent of the total.[71] Imports of machinery equalled only 10 per cent of gross domestic output of these goods in 1936.[72] A "decidedly protectionist" tariff policy aided in the construction and consolidation of these modern industries.[73]

Foreign markets for Japanese manufactures held a strategic importance in this remarkable success story. In order to pay for the import of the raw materials and capital goods necessary to fuel industrial expansion, Japan had to sell the products of her industries abroad. In fact, both merchandise exports and imports were to expand more than forty-five times between 1887 and 1935. Here, too, state policy was of some assistance. The government encouraged the formation of export combinations, as well as providing technical assistance and commodity inspection.

The achievements of state and business export policies soon manifested themselves. By 1930, approximately 25 to 35 per cent of the entire product of Japanese industry was being exported. This represented nearly 20 per cent of Japan's gross national product. According to one source, while only 2 per cent of Japanese exports could be considered "wholly manufactured" in 1870, by 1930, over 50 per cent could be so classified.[74]

Conclusion

This chapter has employed a number of different directions to cut into the critically important formative years of modern Canadian industrialization which followed the proclamation of the National Policy tariffs of 1879. In so doing, we have confronted many of the more familiar interpretations of the failure of Canadian manufacturing to become competitive in the world economy. Our examination of the Swedish and Japanese cases helps to illuminate a number of the traditional explanatory myths which have surrounded the discussion of the issue. Clearly, by themselves, factors such as a late start, a small domestic market, a tariff-coddled production process, a high initial degree of technological dependence, and lack of comparative advantage in manufacturing cannot account for the failure of Canadian industry to climb out of its domestic market. Nor, in this early period, has foreign ownership yet become the crucial variable.

Neither do explanations that search for scapegoats among the business and government leaders of the era hit their targets. To illustrate, the post-Confederation Canadian bourgeoisie has been blasted for its alleged anti-nationalism, lack of entrepreneurship, and divisive intraclass rivalries between manufacturers and merchants. However, we have seen that the pre-1914 expansion and intensification of the resource export economy to include the West was, at once, nationalist, within the nineteenth-century perspective of Empire development; highly ambitious and successful as an entrepreneurial project; and, finally, a scheme that united, rather than divided, Canadian capitalists.

The concept of import substitution was injected into our discussion not to explain the course of Canadian industrialization but to help describe it. ISI serves as a framework to direct our attention to those internal and external factors that formed the investment decisions of individual members of the Canadian bourgeoisie into a collective strategy. The intent of the policy-makers, both inside and outside the state apparatus, was to build an industrial structure that would provide a supplement to the resource export economy – a quick and profitable return on minimal capital investment and a base for urban employment. A secure domestic market would be captured for local producers by means of a tariff-induced replacement of imports. Significantly, capturing the home market was not to be accomplished while becoming internationally competitive in specialized lines (with a few exceptions). Instead, an extreme and unchallenged dependency on foreign technology was to preclude from the beginning any serious attempt to move into foreign markets.

It has been suggested that Canada's position within the British Empire had a significant effect on the decision to pursue a more passive industrial strategy than typical in a centre country. We observed that political and economic considerations related to the Empire were important in influencing the decision to place maximum energy and investment in building a staples economy based on the production of western wheat. ISI, as a supplementary activity, was a strategic choice rooted in the logic of Canada's position in the Empire which, when made and carried out, became a constraint on future industrial development. It was to become progressively more difficult, even irrational, for individual Canadian manufacturers to swim upstream by risking investment capital in taking a more independent, export-oriented direction. This became especially the case as the branch plant sector, for which import substitution was the raison d'être, gradually expanded into a dominant position in Canadian industry.

CHAPTER 3

"We Don't Need the Marts of Europe"

The perplexing story of the failure of Canadian manufacturers to take advantage of their opportunities in world markets during the twentieth century could probably best be told directly from their own mouths. Unfortunately, this is unlikely to happen for a number of reasons. First, there are so many who could speak that the voices would deafen, forcing us to listen only to a sample. Since the fortunes and circumstances of firms vary so greatly over the hundred years of our investigation, it would be nearly impossible to select those few who could pronounce with authority for all. In addition, the perspective of individual firms, caught up in their own affairs, is typically too narrow for them to appreciate how they fit into the more general pattern we seek to describe. Then, too, we could not count on their record-keeping over such a long period of time to be anything more than fragmentary on the kinds of export policy questions we are addressing. Finally, firms are not different from individuals when it comes to revealing their own weaknesses. We could expect to find this to be particularly the case in an area as sensitive to national economic development as export trade. The temptation to stress minor successes in the face of more meaningful failures would very likely be irresistible.

Our method of inquiry, then, must of necessity be somewhat indirect. Rather than surveying the performance of individual manufacturers, we will excavate the historical record of their collective activities layer by layer. As we will discover, the core of these deposits can be extracted from the business publications of the time, and, more importantly, from the well-recorded interface between manufacturers and the branch of the federal state apparatus specifically charged with the responsibility of stimulating the foreign sales of Canadian industry, the Trade Commissioner Service of the Department of Trade and Commerce. This focus on government will also prove valuable at a later stage. It will lay the foundation for a theme to be explored more fully in our last two chapters, the evolution of state export policy as a central aspect of an overall Canadian industrial strategy.

Export Promotion in the Post-National Policy State

In the last chapter we concentrated on the formative years of our modern industrialization. During that time, we argued, our political and economic leaders chose to direct their principal efforts and investments toward the expansion and intensification of the staples trade to the detriment of industrial development. Manufacturing was organized primarily as a supplementary activity with little sustained effort to cultivate an internationally competitive export capability built on a significant degree of technological dependence. The reader might reasonably wonder how the Canadian government came at all to form a policy of stimulating manufactured exports during this early period. Indeed, as we will soon discover, it was far more on the basis of "muddling through" than rational planning.

Shortly after the re-election of his Conservative government in the midst of a worldwide depression in 1887, Sir John A. Macdonald introduced legislation to create a Department of Trade and Commerce. Influenced by the demands of business for more direct input into policy-making, Macdonald intended to split the functions of the existing Department of Finance, leaving it with the technical accounting duties and giving the broader national and international economic policy concerns to Trade and Commerce. However, by the time the Act was finally proclaimed in 1892, plans to grant such weighty responsibilities to the new department had been scrapped. Instead, Trade and Commerce was provided with an external trade orientation as it inherited a patchwork quilt of overseas part-time trade agents and subsidized shipping lines from Finance.[1]

At first, neither the new department's purpose nor its clientele seemed clear. Manufacturing interests had petitioned the government, from at least the mid-1880's, to furnish them with a foreign network of state export agencies such as those that had been available for at least a hundred years to capitalists in Great Britain and the United States.[2] Equally important in the introduction of overseas export agencies were the representations of land-based transportation companies, such as the Canadian Pacific Railway, as well as a number of influential Canadian merchants. These interests supported parallel program of state subsidies to steamship lines which would connect Canada and a few selected foreign markets. The railways hoped to stimulate the use of their facilities for through traffic and the merchants were anxious to intercept the flow of Canadian resource exports that found their way to foreign markets through U.S. ports. Terminals of these subsidized lines were often selected as the sites of Canada's first external trade offices in order to drum up business for the shippers.

At the turn of the century, some manufacturers began to complain about the meagre quality of export services they were being offered by the few, mostly part-time agents placed in the haphazard manner just described. The reorganization and expansion of the Canadian Manufacturers' Association (CMA) in 1900 provided these industrialists with a platform from which they could air their grievances. Forming themselves into the "Commercial Intelligence Committee" of the CMA, they pressed the government to provide them with an expanded overseas service organized along the lines of "what is recognized as the most complete consular system in the world, that of the United States." They denounced then current Trade and Commerce efforts as "notorious . . . inadequate and disappointing."[3]

Criticism was focused on three principal areas: the poor quality of agents and their conditions of service, the meagre transmission of trade information between agents and manufacturers, and the small number of overseas trade offices. To begin, the committee argued that the system of part-time agents was inadequate as such men had "most of their time and interest taken up with private business." Consequently, Canadian "consuls" should be hired on a full-time basis. It was also recommended that these positions be given to candidates qualified in the field of export promotion and be removed from the patronage system that dominated public service appointments in this era.

On the question of information that agents were to gather on behalf of Canadian industrialists, it was proposed that they should be given more adequate funds for travel within their countries of posting and be periodically returned to Canada in order to bring them up to date on current business conditions. The committee contended that Trade and Commerce issued the reports of their agents too slowly to be of immediate use to manufacturers and suggested that in future the preparation of intelligence summaries should be more frequent and systematic.

Finally, it was recommended that Trade and Commerce establish "consular" offices in London, Sydney, Cape Town, Yokohama, Kingston (Jamaica), Paris, Hamburg, Rio de Janeiro, Calcutta, and Shanghai. They estimated that this new system would cost the government $75,000, fully four times greater than the established level. This substantially increased expenditure was justified along precisely the same lines used when the matter of state export agencies had first been raised by the industrialists of 1885.

> We do not believe in relying too much on Government support or Government interference in trade matters. At the same time we feel that in a work of this particular kind success can only be secured through active Government co-operation. The practise of the whole world recognizes the correctness of this attitude.[4]

The Commercial Intelligence Committee was quite accurate in its assessment that government co-operation was essential to the advancement of Canadian manufactured exports. Had the committee's enthusiasm for trade matters been more widely shared by the general membership of the CMA, government intervention in this case might have been less crucial. However, it was far in advance of the majority of its colleagues. For example, the committee, wishing to mark the inauguration of a new government-subsidized shipping line from Canada in 1902, was forced to scrap a plan to send along a representative of its own to promote Canadian products in South Africa. After canvassing the membership of the CMA for financial support for this project, it could only find twenty-five interested firms, which collectively anted only one-fifth of the cost. In this indifferent environment, state assistance would seem the only logical alternative.

Largely as a result of this committee's efforts, the trade promotion facilities of Trade and Commerce were very significantly upgraded in the period before World War I. Although changes did not immediately follow on the heels of the committee's demands of 1900, the number of overseas postings of full-time agents was gradually built up. By 1905, the reports of these trade commissioners began to be published on a weekly basis. Continuing complaints about the quality of appointments brought a system of merit selections of university graduates in 1914.

The "Side Show"

Although evidence can be found in these representations to Ottawa of a desire to export among some manufacturers, for the great majority the home market remained almost their total focus of activity. This was the clear conclusion of a 1907 report of the Commercial Intelligence Committee on the subject of membership use of the CMA 's own export services. Three programs were surveyed: requests for the reports of foreign commercial houses, applications for translation services, and the appointment of correspondent agents for the use of CMA members in "the principal cities of the world." As Table Five indicates, only a handful of manufacturers used either of the first two services. Because of general disinterest, the third program lapsed.

Throughout this report, the neglect of these export services by Canadian manufacturers was unfavourably compared to the performance of their more accomplished U.S. rivals. To illustrate, it was pointed out that members of the National Association of Manufacturers had requested over 26,000 translations during 1906-07. With obvious frustration, the committee's secretary determined that little could be done to improve the export scene "under present conditions, with our domestic trade expanding at a rate which is taxing the capacity of many of our factories to the utmost, and with the consequent indifference displayed by many of our manufacturers to export trade."[5]

In 1912, the Commercial Intelligence Committee publicly conceded that the progress of Canadian manufactured exports in the previous decade had been slight because the rapidly expanding domestic market had made the "average" industrialist "indifferent" to foreign trade. Stress was placed by the committee on the many exporting opportunities which had been neglected during these years. "Enquiries from abroad for Canadian merchandise have been distributed by the score," they lamented, "only to be met in most cases with the response that the parties addressed were too busy with domestic orders to quote on foreign business."[6]

Industrial Canada, the official organ of the CMA, had been forced earlier to conclude that "few manufacturers are willing to go in for

TABLE FIVE

Membership Use of Canadian Manufacturers' Association Export Services, 1904-1907

	1904-05	*1905-06*	*1906-07*
Reports of foreign commercial houses			
no. supplied	47	36	42
members served	30	26	16
Translations			
no. supplied	n.a.	57	43
members served	n.a.	18	14

SOURCE: Public Archives of Canada, MG 28, I 230, vol. 36, nos. 154-163, Canadian Manufacturers' Association, Minutes of the Commercial Intelligence Committee, July 16, 1907.

an export business" after learning the results of an "experiment" undertaken in 1909 by the Commercial Intelligence Committee.[7] Each of the nearly 2,200 members of the CMA was asked for its co-operation in collecting information for the use of the government trade commissioners stationed abroad. No expense was involved for the individual firms as all that was requested was that catalogues and price lists be sent to the CMA for transmission. "Yet less than a hundred were interested enough to comply with the request," the journal reported.

Industrial Canada speculated on the reasons for the failure of more than 97 per cent of its organization's members to respond to this appeal. Big manufacturers had their own export facilities, it suggested, while the smallest companies were simply uninterested. Medium-sized firms were wary of foreign markets because "many feel that the same money and pains put into the local field would bring them just as ample and much quicker returns."[8] This was hardly an original conclusion. The home market bias of capital investment in Canadian industry and its negative effect on export trade had been earlier described in the pages of *Industrial Canada* by H. Watson, secretary of the Canadian Section of the Imperial Institute in London:

> Nearly all Canadian industrial enterprises were originally established for supplying the wants of the domestic market without, in most instances, any particular attention to the possibilities of export . . . . As a result, whereas capital has naturally been forthcoming for ventures from which local markets promised an immediate and profitable return, investment in other industries the product of which is more particularly suitable for outside markets has been, until recently, restricted.[9]

For its part, *Industrial Canada* frequently attempted to stir manufacturers to action, arguing that it was a short-sighted strategy to neglect export business

> merely because the unexampled prosperity Canada is enjoying gives them all they can do to fill home orders . . . . some day the manufacturers of Canada will be sorry that they regarded export business as a "side show", to be taken in when the other show was not running well.[10]

A sense of lost opportunities for Canadian manufacturers in foreign markets and a foreboding of a future in which Canada had missed the exporting boat permeated all the other important business journals of the era. The *Monetary Times* warned that "there is a danger of losing a chance to get into foreign markets . . . so long as prosperity remains, the purchasing power of Canada is high and the absorption strength of the home market is increasing."[11] Twenty years earlier, the *Journal of Commerce* had similarly observed that

> At present, possibly, the requirements of the home market are sufficient to absorb the whole of our Canadian industrial production. But this will not always be the case . . . . Would it not, then, be wise to exploit this new outlet for our wares [Australia] in time: so that we may have a secure foothold there against the day when it may be of vital importance for us to secure it . . .?[12]

Such indirect appeals to action appear to have had little effect in altering the extreme domestic orientation of Canadian industrialists. Typical were these sentiments of J.P. Murray of the Toronto Carpet Manufacturing Company, an important CMA militant. Murray argued that the "most profitable market for a manufacturer is his home market" and that spending money on immigration was as important as spending money to break into foreign markets. Exports were to be considered only after domestic requirements had been filled.

> We cannot hope to have much of a standing in foreign markets until we are able to supply in a greater way our own requirements. To do this properly we must manufacture much more largely, and we are not warranted in doing so unless we have a larger home market. Until we have reached that stage we cannot hope to export successfully.[13]

Readers should take heed of the sharp contrast between this statement and the outward-oriented Swedish industrial practice of the same era outlined in the previous chapter. There, it will be recalled, exports were, from the beginning, used as a means of lengthening production lines and thereby making them more efficient.

When we consider export developments in these years, we should not lose sight of the fact that the general membership of the CMA was preoccupied with extending their reach only as far as the new markets of Canada's western territories and the Yukon. For example, in 1903, over 100 manufacturers, including the president and other executive members of the association, chartered a train to the West Coast to survey business conditions for themselves. The train was decorated with such slogans as "Build up our Home Markets" and "Canadian Goods for Canadian People," and *Industrial Canada* boasted that it was "the heaviest passenger train ever handled by the C.P.R."[14] Not surprisingly, this popular poem of Pauline Johnson was heartily appreciated at many CMA banquets:

> We don't need the marts of Europe,
> nor the trade of the Eastern isles,
> We don't need the Yankees's corn and wine,
> nor the Asiatic's smiles.
> For what so good as our home-made cloth,
> and under the wide blue dome,
> Will you tell me where you have tasted bread
> like the bread that is baked at home.[15]

Abundant evidence that this poem was an accurate reflection of the viewpoint of the majority of Canadian industrial capitalists was readily available to both the business press and the general public in the published reports of the overseas representatives of the Department of Trade and Commerce. In fact, the trade commissioners frequently commented on the problem. "Nearly every letter from Canada in respect to propositions for new business here," one wrote, "has been a regret that the writer is unable to consider any foreign trade at the present time, as the improved demands in Canada require his full capacity."[16] Another government agent in Argentina was mystified by the industrial strategy of Canadian capitalists and their almost neurotic abhorrence of exporting.

> From the inquiries received from Canada to date, it would not appear that much interest was being taken by manufacturers in this part of South America. One reads that factories are choked with orders for the domestic trade, which is highly satisfactory, but having assured a market at home, it would seem all the more reason that they should commence to show some interest in the foreign field. It is an inexplicable thing, but many manufacturers appear to fear the very thought of the export trade; they apparently harbour the delusion that it is full of pitfalls for the unwary, full of unknown risks, and that once embarked upon it there can be no return to domestic trade.[17]

All could not be put down to fear derived from ignorance, however. Even manufacturers who were well travelled told much the same story in regard to exports.

> A manufacturer from the Maritime Provinces passing through [Japan] lately . . . was asked if he did not wish to look into the market here with the view to export to this country . . . . Being pressed, he

said, well the fact was that unless things had gone wrong since he left home, his company had enough to do in their line to supply the home market .... Another Canadian manufacturer, largely interested in textiles, literally travelling for his health said ... the demands of a rapidly developing home market were such that they could not pretend to offer business to Japan.[18]

Export Performance of the Manufacturers

In such a background of general apathy, it is hardly surprising that the *Weekly Reports* of the trade commissioners are vivid catalogues of the many follies of Canadian industrial exporters. To begin, most manufacturers seemed to have attached so little importance to developing a foreign trade that they habitually neglected to answer letters from potential overseas customers in any meaningful fashion. Canada's first full-time agent, after two years in the Australian field, wrote:

> The greatest impediment to the success of the work here is in Canada. A few firms have a knowledge of what is necessary to be done to get entrance to this market, but the majority do not and writing seems to make small impression. On behalf of an [Australian] house, I recently wrote to a number of Canadian firms for information respecting their goods and of all the replies that I received, but one answered the questions in such a manner that would determine whether business could be done or not.[19]

Experiences in New Zealand and in other markets were even more graphically communicated to Canadians by the trade commissioners.

> In Auckland a large commission house wrote to eight Canadian paper mills soliciting their agency. One reply was favourable, the other seven stated they were selling all they could make at home at better prices than could be got in New Zealand. In Wellington, a firm had received but three replies to forty-two letters written to manufacturers of various lines, in only one of which was there a promise of trade. In Christchurch, a firm in a large way in boots and shoes, leather and leather goods had received five replies to over fifty letters.[20]

As we might expect, given the demonstrated reluctance of Canadian industrialists to reply to their correspondence, it was a rare occasion indeed when they would dispatch a salesman to directly canvas a foreign market. This sin of omission generated a good deal of critical heat from the trade commissioners who made frequent and unfavourable comparisons with the performance of the firms of other industrialized countries in this matter. These comments were typical in this regard.

> Manufacturers' representatives from Great Britain make periodical trips and interview the business men and they invariably secure substantial orders. The resident agents of firms in Great Britain, Germany and the United States have regular customers upon whom they call at stated intervals. Canada is at a great disadvantage in this respect. There have only been two instances within the past year when a direct representative of a Canadian firm has appeared in New Zealand, although the result justified the expense.[21]

Even in the much closer Bahamas, a Canadian salesman was said to be "a rara avis indeed, while from the United States he is a familiar object."[22] In Barbados, it was claimed that Canadian trade had not expanded as rapidly as that of Britain or the U.S. "due largely to the fact that Canadian commercial men do not visit the Island."[23] The trade commissioner in South Africa warned that unless direct representation was established in that country, Canadian manufacturers would continue to "receive the leavings of United States manufacturers, and tend to confirm the opinion of local business men that we do not take our export trade seriously."[24] The Manchester posting reported that U.S. commercial travellers were "constantly pushing trade and canvassing orders for hot water heaters, furnaces, radiators, and plumbing supplies "in marked contradiction to our Canadian manufacturers, who are not represented and are totally unknown, hence the trade goes to their United States competitors, though the English dealer would prefer to trade with Canada."[25]

Unfortunately, even when the mountain journeyed to Mohammed, in the form of foreign sales agents eager to place orders in Canadian factories, our manufacturers frequently remained aloof. A Trade and Commerce agent in Australia recounted one such visit.

> A number of Sydney houses sent representatives to visit Canada last year; those who have returned express disappointment at the results of their trip. They state that few firms seem to be interested in export trade, and fewer still were willing to make the sacrifice requisite to make a success. Some agreements were entered into which will lead, it is hoped, to business, but in the majority of cases little can be anticipated from their visits. They complain that even where contracts were entered into they have not been observed.[26]

Among those few enterprises that did make some attempt to break into foreign markets, participation was often token as it was limited to sending out copies of their Canadian order catalogues. This provoked a further set of complaints from the trade commissioners. As no revisions to the Canadian catalogues had been made, goods advertised in them were often completely unsuitable for sale in the markets to which they had been forwarded. For example, the Barbados agent recounted an early version of the "refrigerators to Eskimos" chestnut:

> On more than one occasion, catalogues and price lists have been furnished by a Canadian manufacturer . . . without the least suspicion apparently . . . that a different description of stove might be required in the tropics from that used in the north. Not only have illustrations shown stoves too large in size and therefore too hot to be successfully used, but even furnaces and radiators for heating houses and descriptions of hot water systems have sometimes accompanied them.[27]

These catalogues were not usually accompanied by price lists of which the potential customer could make any sense. Instead of quoting the cost of goods landed in foreign ports, Canadian factory prices were provided. More than one trade commissioner reported that "dealers will not even pay ordinary attention to such scant unaccustomed information."[28]

When a Canadian manufacturer did decide to make a serious attempt to enter a foreign market, the reason could very often be traced to causes within the domestic market. A precedent for overseas dumping of surplus stock in the face of a soft local demand or overproduction was established within the first few years of the introduction of the National Policy tariffs. The *Journal of Commerce* had noted at the time that "in spite of the glowing accounts of mill managers, every consignment sent to Chinese ports had to be sold at a loss."[29] From this point, the practice of dumping continued, as reported by *Industrial Canada*, "not infrequently."[30] It was so universally denounced by the various trade commissioners that *Weekly Report* took the unusual step of publishing a strong editorial blast. "To create the impression that Canada is merely coquetting with foreign markets would be most pernicious to our national reputation," it fumed.[31]

Trade and Commerce reports also related numerous incidents of the export of substandard or obsolete products from Canadian plants. One agent, stationed in Mexico, appealed to the higher sensibilities of the offending manufacturers in pleading that they discontinue the practice. "Any, who from personal motives, do not hesitate to send out an inferior article should," he maintained, "at least from patriotic motives refuse to do so."[32]

The lengthy delays that overseas customers encountered in getting Canadian firms to fill their orders also received their share of attention from Trade and Commerce agents. In 1910, the trade commissioner in Australia estimated that only one-fifth of orders shipped outside of "established trade" were filled within a "reasonable" time.[33] Even if one received a Canadian order without unnecessary delay, one could rarely be certain of the condition in which it would arrive. Apparently, many manufacturers failed to pack their goods for export any more carefully than they might for shipment between two Canadian cities. A trade commissioner in Argentina suffered personally from this habitual oversight. In a report detailing the "large" Argentinian market for imported furniture, he admitted that he was not "very sanguine" about the possibility of Canadian firms seizing this opportunity.

> The writer has recently had some experience of Canadian methods. The whole of the furniture for this office was purchased in the Dominion, from three separate factories, the idea being that . . . it might be an advertisement for the manufacturers . . . . the goods, although promised by a certain date, were late in shipment, or some of them, and were unaccompanied by the proper documents . . . . These things were not so serious, but on arrival the cases were found to be of old and inferior wood, and much damaged, and the packing to have been nothing short of disgraceful. The things appear to have been thrown in haphazardly . . . . As a consequence, the articles were in a shocking condition, requiring the service of two men for a week, to put them in repair, and even then it was impossible to restore all to their original condition.[34]

In the last chapter, we suggested that the technologically dependent structure of Canadian industrialization placed important barriers in the way of developing a trade in manufactured exports. Licensees, we discovered, were often forbidden to export as a condition of utilizing a foreign patented process in the Canadian market. U.S. branch plants, then as now, had to be content with a division of the world market determined by the priorities of their parent firms. It would now be appropriate to examine the extent to which the overseas agents of Trade and Commerce became aware, in their everyday work, of the structural barriers to export which, we have argued, were at once a cause and an effect of the almost exclusively domestic orientation of Canadian manufacturing.

It must be admitted from the outset that there is not as much discussion of the problem of export blocking in the trade commissioners' reports as one might initially expect, given the considerable extent of technological dependence. Certainly, all of the follies detailed above are far more pervasive themes. Yet, this is perhaps natural, given the perspective of these men. Physically removed from the Canadian scene, they were far more likely to comment on the concrete performance of industrialists with whom they had direct contact, rather than with any set of what were often highly invisible export restrictions imposed at the Canadian source.

Nevertheless, there is sufficient evidence to suggest that a number of the trade commissioners encountered the problem frequently enough to become aware of its negative effects. For instance, occasionally cases of direct export blocking, such as the following, were reported:

> During the past few years several Canadian enterprises have commenced the manufacture of skewers and have worked up a certain amount of British trade ... in several instances, no sooner had a regular trade been established ... than the Canadian manufacturer sold out to the United States Skewer Trust and no further supplies have been available from that particular source. Chiefly from that cause Canada has not obtained anything like the share of the British skewer trade which might otherwise have been secured .... Only recently a couple of Canadian concerns which had concluded arrangements with United Kingdom firms – and in one case made contracts ahead – have sold out their plants and gone out of business. [35]

That this may have been a fairly common pattern is indicated by a similar account originating in Australia.

> One of the difficulties in getting good agents to take up [Canadian] lines is the fear that after they have gone to the expense of building up a trade their Canadian principal enters into an agreement which prevents them from shipping goods to Australia. Two cases of such hardship occurred in our trade. United States firms finding their Australian trade cut into, went to Canada and purchased the rival factories and put an end to Canadian export in these lines.[36]

In this regard, there is some evidence that the constantly heard cry of "home demand" may have simply been a popular euphemism for export restrictions. One trade commissioner narrated the story of an Australian buyer who had made supply arrangements with several Canadian firms.

In one case, after he had done this he received a reply that the home orders were increasing and the firm had concluded not to attempt an export business just yet. In a second case, he received information that they were unable to go any further, as they had been negotiating for some time with another firm in Australia and could do nothing until a conclusion could be reached in such negotiations. In both of these cases the firms were branches in Canada but owned abroad and the possibility is that the branches had been stopped in their proposition to do an export trade from Canada.[37]

Some notice was also taken by the trade commissioners of the undesirable consequences of licensing arrangements on Canadian industrial exports. Under the title of "cannot export," one observed that "a number of large factories in Canada are operated on arrangements with patentees or others which prevent their exporting to Australia, though the article may not be patented here."[38] Two years later the same agent pointed the finger at Canadian manufacturers of electrical goods "able to export" but forbidden to do so because of their "arrangements."[39] Another trade commissioner, working in Japan, also demonstrated his awareness of the territorial limitations of Canadian licensees.

The practical nothingness of the Canadian bicycle trade here is consistent with the impression that I received in Canada before leaving; that the bicycle trade, like the wire trade and doubtless others, was not free but bound; that it had its allotment of territory or its measure of output, and must rest and be thankful, which is an industrial condition very well understood now-a-days.[40]

Industrial Capitalists and the Trade Commissioners

With all that has been recorded to this point, it stands to reason that the disinterest, incompetence, and even dishonesty of Canadian industrial exporters gradually eroded the enthusiasm of many trade commissioners with some years of service, often leaving them discouraged, frustrated, and cynical. In 1908, J.S. Larke, perhaps the most diligent of the early appointees, lamented that the dismal record of Canadian exporters in Australia had made it "more difficult to sell Canadian goods today than it was ten years ago." He cited these examples of how past performance had destroyed future prospects:

I have endeavoured to get firms interested on behalf of two Canadian exporting houses. One firm wrote that he would not com-

> municate with Canadian houses, as he, unfortunately, had had the experience of the uselessness of so doing. Another, a prominent manufacturers agent, who was very desirous a few years ago of taking on Canadian lines, stated that he did not care to touch the Canadian trade. He had been so disappointed in what he had tried to do through mistakes made in shipping and failure to meet conditions or even to reply to correspondence that he did not wish for any further experience.[41]

A Trade and Commerce representative in South Africa also deplored the "half-hearted business methods" of Canadian firms, which made much of his work futile:

> Any firms desiring to compete in a new market should study the trade statistics which appear in the Weekly Report . . . . customs duty, preference if any, c.i.f. prices, the particular kinds of articles required, the methods of marking and packing, terms of payment, etc., all of this information can be received through the Government Trade Commission Service free of charge. But in spite of the valuable and disinterested information which is contained in the Weekly Report, instances occur time and again which indicate that this journal is never studied, much less read, by the manufacturing firms.[42]

The Japan posting was equally frustrated by the export apathy of Canadian manufacturers and their failure to use the information provided by Trade and Commerce to learn from past mistakes.

> The manufacturing interest of Canada has had the benefit, for nearly thirty years, of a system of tariff aid that must have come far short of its pretentions, since, upon their own confession, they are not yet in a position to offer business to so accessible a market as that of Japan . . . . After four years experience here, I know of nothing Canadian offered to this market at a price that would compete with similar products supplied by other countries, with the further fatal disadvantages of uncertain supply in the event of a demand being worked up. Although I have from time to time placed this same statement of fact, variously worded, before the Canadian public in these reports, I still find public opinion as expressed in parliament, and upon the platform, and echoed by the press, uninformed as to the situation, and continuing to cry out its surprise that Canada's share of the trade with Japan is not greater.[43]

That such critical remarks piqued some Canadian manufacturers is evident from a 1911 article in *Industrial Canada.* In it, exception was taken to the charges of the trade commissioners "over our apparent lack of aggressiveness in foreign markets." This CMA organ counselled patience, submitting that Trade and Commerce agents "should not grow discouraged if the results come somewhat slowly" because industrialists were now preparing the base for a move into world markets.

> . . . the great majority are utilizing their capital to the utmost to meet the demands of the Canadian market. Canada is growing rapidly. The West is developing more than any region in the world today . . . . So in most cases every effort is being made to cater to the home market and to meet the extraordinary demands which are being made upon producers in every line . . . there can be no cessation of the fight to maintain supremacy at home . . . . As, however, firms grow in strength and experience more and more will follow the lead of those companies which have built up a valuable export trade . . . . Meanwhile, the ground is being prepared by the investigations of trade commissioners . . . . [44]

Thus, in the space of a single decade, we have seen the CMA move from the offensive, in regard to the overseas services of the Canadian state, to the defensive. There can be little doubt, however, that during this period the Department of Trade and Commerce moved firmly into the orbit of industrial capital. As we have already learned, after 1900 the Commercial Intelligence Committee of the CMA became both increasingly active in formulating demands on Trade and Commerce and successful in translating these demands into policy outputs. In addition, it would seem that Trade and Commerce progressively developed its services in the field of stimulating manufactured as opposed to primary exports. To illustrate, R. Grigg, who made a tour of inspection of the department's European offices prior to his appointment as director of the trade commissioner service, concluded that little could be done by Trade and Commerce to assist the sales of Canada's "natural products such as wheat, flour, cheese, timber etc." Greatly pre-dating the establishment of the department, the trade in such staples had long possessed its own channels. It was, Grigg stated, "the universal opinion among the highly competent body of men" who conducted it that there was no need of "help" from the trade commissioners. He suggested that a more useful role for the department could be developed in pushing industrial exports in "rising markets either in the Far East or in non-manufacturing countries such as South America, Australia, New Zealand, South Africa, and Russia."[45]

Import Substitution for the Empire

There was one quarter in which some Canadian industrialists expressed genuine export interest during this era and even lobbied for government action to further their cause. These enterprises sought Ottawa's assistance in gaining preferential tariff entry into the markets of the other white Dominions (and even Britain if it could ever have been persuaded to abandon free trade). These markets held a number of unique qualities that generated considerable excitement among Canadian manufacturers, especially U.S. branch plants and licensees. First, these countries had little domestic production of their own to compete with Canadian products. As early as 1894, *Canadian Manufacturer* noted that export possibilites in Australia and South Africa were favourable because "in their market our manufactures would not suffer from home competition."[46]

This, of course, was also true of much of the world at that time. What made the white Dominions particularly attractive to Canadian manufacturers was their position near the top of the international hierarchy of wealth. In the same article, *Canadian Manufacturer* contrasted the "limited" markets of the less prosperous parts of the Empire with the fact that the white Dominions were "large consumers." The *Monetary Times* posed the problem more bluntly:

> What can the millions of Hindoos whose labour brings only a few cents a day buy from Canada?. . . They would not take our manufactures, for they can buy British on better terms. When the elements of trade exist, distance can be overcome; but when you reach poor customers, at whatever distance, you will find a million of them go a very short way compared to an equal number of more prosperous people.[47]

Thus, while the colonies of occupation were less important in the preference plans of our industrial exporters, they did not completely ignore them. The rich harvest reaped by their resident colonial masters made a lucrative target. For example, a 1902 "Mission of Inquiry" to the West Indies led by the president of the CMA noted that

> It is always necessary to remember the class of people in the islands and their purchasing power . . . . The black is lazy and independent . . . . He is generally a contented man and his requirements are

few . . . . At the larger islands the wants of the white population are, however, important, and in the large stores the range in all lines of goods is very wide.[48]

Clearly, as rich non-industrialized markets, the white Dominions held many natural enticements for Canadian industrialists. However, their strongest attraction may have been the taste these countries had begun to acquire for U.S.-manufactured products. Licensees and branch plants in Canada sensed an opportunity to undercut their U.S. and European rivals in these markets if a system of Empire tariff preferences could be instituted. *Canadian Manufacturer* expressed the strategy in this manner:

> With the . . . possibility of a preferential commercial policy amongst the colonies, there is every likelihood of an expansion which may yet be deemed marvelous. Lacking that great impetus to commerce, the United States has built up an [Australian] trade of $20,000,000 a year. With it, there is no reason why Canada should not establish herself as a successful rival of the Republic in many lines and a successful middleman in others.[49]

This imaginative form of ISI by proxy which Canadian industrialists dreamed of introducing to the white Dominions and Britain was, as we outlined in the last chapter, tightly wrapped in the Union Jack. Canadian manufacturers used self-interested sentimental appeals directed toward Empire unity to justify their campaign.[50] In the face of fierce competition from the more technologically advanced U.S. and German manufacturers, concern was also raised over the failure of Britain to hold her position in the international trade of the sophisticated products of the "second" industrial revolution. R. Munro, 1902 president of the CMA, told the annual meeting of his organization that "Where Great Britain has held the bulk of the trade, her percentage is being attacked at every point and that by the most scientific methods. Canadian manufacturers can do much to retain in British hands the trade of other British possessions."[51]

Canadian manufacturers felt that their government should use the fact that Canada had granted an unconditional preference on certain classes of Empire goods in 1897 as a lever to persuade the other white Dominions to offer corresponding concessions. For example, the Tariff Committee of the CMA in 1907 requested that Ottawa negotiate, "at the earliest possible moment," a preferential treaty with Australia:

> . . . by virtue of the fact that Canada was the first to raise the

> standard of Imperial preference, we ought to be accorded equal privileges in the Australian market with our fellow-subjects from Great Britain. Given such a preference we could secure a large share of the business that is now going to the United States, as the lines which these two countries produce is almost identical and are of a kind that Australia requires. [52]

Australia, however, did not follow until the 1920's the examplc established in 1904 by New Zealand and South Africa in extending to Canada the privilege of their British preferential rates.

Unfortunately, a number of Canadian manufacturers rapidly fouled their own preferential nests in these white Dominions. A New Zealand correspondent of *Industrial Canada* reported in 1907 an increase of the tariff preference on a number of U.S. manufactures in which Canadians might now be able to substitute their products. However, "will manufacturers now avail themselves of their opportunity," he asked, "or are they going, as has been done before, to raise their prices so much that practically the whole of the preference goes into their pockets?"[53] Some months later his question was answered when Canadian clothing manufacturers, with a preference of 20 per cent, were caught *raising* their prices to the level of their competitors. As a consequence, the New Zealand government removed this particular preference and

> the business is going back to the United States. Even if Canadian manufacturers reduce their prices again to the level of the foreign manufacturer the business will go past them as merchants are disgusted with the manner in which the Canadian manufacturers have appreciated a benefit which was given to them, not for the purpose of filling their own pockets, but to keep the foreign manufacturer out.[54]

International Competitiveness

This chapter could not properly be concluded without some mention being made of the small minority of Canadian industrialists who seriously pursued export trade. These firms, which did not accept the logic of the mass of their compatriots who argued that the home market must always come first, became the darlings of the trade commissioners. Contrast, for example, the tone displayed here in complimenting the aggressive tactics of one Canadian firm with that found in the comments we have previously reported.

> After a determined and tactful effort made by the direct representative of a leading Canadian corset manufacturing company to introduce their goods – hitherto unknown, this line has been successfully introduced to Australian wholesale importers. Large initial orders are going forward . . . in a line which competition is most marked . . . [and] are attributable to the exceptional ability of the travelling salesmen in overcoming the prejudices of conservative buyers.[55]

The agricultural implement manufacturers were the leading force in this minority, although it may be noted that they, too, on occasion provoked complaints from trade commissioners about sloppy performance in some less important markets such as Mexico.[56] In Australia, however, these firms were so aggressive that, by 1910, Canadian agricultural machinery held the largest share of the import market. According to the Trade and Commerce agent, the manufacturers had achieved this success as the reward for establishing Australian sales subsidiaries with ample stock, good salesmen, and effective local management. They had also provided consistently high quality commodities adapted to local conditions in Australia. "The result achieved is an object lesson to Canadian manufacturers of other lines of merchandise," he submitted, "as to what can be obtained in distant overseas markets by persistent effort while holding an equally prominent position in the home markets."[57] In South Africa, the export performance of one agricultural implement firm was actually held up to favourable comparison with its U.S. and British competitors. "If one Canadian firm can make a success, why not others?" the trade commissioner demanded.[58]

Conclusion

The creation of a federal government agency charged with a specific responsibility for stimulating exports can be traced to the lobbying efforts of various business groups desirous of a Canadian equivalent to the consular services long enjoyed by their counterparts in other countries. Before 1914, the growth of this agency was fundamentally incremental in nature. It was greatly influenced by a steamship subsidy program, the creation of an independent organizational base in the Department of Trade and Commerce, and the close relationship it developed with industrial capital because of its redundancy in the staples trade. From the reports of the trade commissioners, it is clear that Canadian manufacturers had many export opportunities in this era but failed to take advantage of them. Numerous instances of disinterest, incompetence, and dishonesty were catalogued. Interest in upgrading the foreign services of Trade and Commerce appears to have been limited to a select few at the core of the Canadian Manufacturers' Association. Ironically, as the trade commissioner service became better organized, industrialists found it necessary to defend themselves from its criticisms of their export apathy.

Our examination of this period largely confirms the analysis of the nature of Canadian industrialization undertaken in the last chapter. Although it could be alleged that a general lack of entrepreneurial spirit was operative here, it is more likely that the ISI milieu of Canadian manufacturing, with its limiting world view of import replacement and unchallenged technological dependence, was at fault. In this context, we should bear in mind that other relatively small nations, such as Sweden, were having considerable success during this same era in establishing a more export-oriented and technologically independent industrial strategy.

Among those few manufacturers who did export, three levels of intervention in overseas markets were identified: import substitution for the Empire; dumping of surplus production during depressed domestic conditions; and international competitiveness in specialized lines of production. Regrettably, this latter group was no more than a fragment of Canadian industrial capital.

CHAPTER 4

War and Peace: Opportunities Averted

Statistics, we are often reminded, never tell the entire story. So it was with the export performance of Canadian manufacturers during and directly after World War I. On the surface, it appeared that our industrialists took advantage of the unusual circumstances of these years to improve dramatically their standing in world markets. To illustrate, for almost all of the pre-war era covered by the preceding chapter, only 3 or 4 per cent of Canada's exports could be considered "finished" manufactures. By contrast, in the period we will now consider, this category jumped to approximately 25 per cent of total exports.[1] Nevertheless, as we will soon see, these achievements neither heralded a fresh outward orientation nor yielded many long-term benefits for Canadian industry.

Nearly all of the remarkable increase in exports just described can be attributed to the sale of war munitions. During 1916 and 1917, almost one-third of Canadian manufacturing output resulted from the production of shells and explosives. By the conclusion of hostilities, total exports of these weapons were valued at more than $1 billion, a figure equivalent to approximately two-thirds of the total Canadian war expenditure.[2] Prime Minister Sir Robert L. Borden reported that in early 1917, at the height of wartime manufacturing, 630 Canadian firms with a total labour force of over 304,000 workers were involved in making munitions. As a result, Canada was then producing more munitions than had any country before the Great War except for Germany and was supplying over a quarter of all the artillery shells used by the British armies.[3]

To a considerable extent, these impressive export successes must be credited to the federal government. Ottawa's heavy involvement here included the procurement of foreign contracts, the financing of war credits needed by overseas purchasers, and even the production of some vital components through the establishment of "national factories." The Department of Trade and Commerce, however, was only marginally drawn into all of this activity.[4] The reader may well wonder at this. After all, have we not documented how the department grew into its role of representative, spokesman, and agent for the export concerns of Canadian industrialists by 1914?

The answer to this little puzzle signals the reason why the massive wartime trade did not stimulate a reversal of the manufacturers' introverted outlook. As it unfolded, the munitions trade had little use for the specialized services painstakingly developed by Trade and Commerce after 1900. In fact, it was an export trade *in destination only*. Contracts were allocated within Canada to firms through official state agencies – the Shell Committee before November, 1915, and, subsequently, the Imperial Munitions Board – on the basis of orders submitted by the British Ministry of Munitions.[5] Canadian industrialists, therefore, did not face the difficult task of cultivating overseas contacts in order to make sales; competition was mainly with domestic rather than foreign producers, products did not have to be adapted and advertised to suit exotic tastes, and deliveries were generally to Canadian points.

"A State-induced and State-regulated Business"

Let us examine this munitions trade more closely. As we might have anticipated from our discussion of the pre-war period, the initial interest of Canadian manufacturers in overseas arms contracts owed a great deal to soft demand in the domestic market. A severe depression had erupted in 1913 and unemployment was still high in some regions in early 1915.[6] Not surprisingly, then, Ottawa was bombarded with requests for munitions contracts. Prime Minister Borden complained in mid-1915 of the "continuous pressure from companies and firms desirous of undertaking this work."[7] Typical was this appeal by the Imperial Steel and Wire Company of Collingwood: "We would not be so insistent if we had other business to look forward to but unfortunately, we have a large plant lying idle with heavy overhead expenses and little prospects of new business owing to the general depression in the country."[8]

Even though munitions work was greatly coveted by the manufacturers, a considerable number were unwilling to risk their capital in retooling for production. This is highly consistent with the reluctance to invest in export opportunities that we noted in the last chapter. For example, the Ordnance Adviser to the Shell Committee reported that

> when the Minister of Militia and Defence induced the manufac-

> turers of Canada to consider shell manufacture several of them would not undertake the risks involved while others were prepared to do so although with some reluctance. It was a new class of work for the manufacturers, the execution of which involved expenditure of money in new plants and risks of rejection of materials until their employees became skilled.[9]

Many manufacturers demanded that the government provide guarantees that they would not lose money before they were willing to invest in the necessary machinery. J.R. Shaw, president of Canada Furniture in Woodstock, promised Borden that he would increase his firm's shell-making capacity tenfold "if any definite assurances could be received in respect to the continuance of demand." He claimed that he had discussed the matter with "half a dozen gentlemen controlling large engineering plants" who were also ready to expand their wartime operations "only provided they can receive definite contracts for definite deliveries which will warrant them turning their plants into this work."[10] That this hesitant approach was pervasive is confirmed by these remarks of F. Nicholls, president of one of the foremost industrial enterprises in the country, Canadian General Electric. He recorded that he had offered at the beginning of the war

> to invest two million dollars in a special plant to manufacture munitions provided we received a moderate guarantee of orders spread over a term of five years, but the Government did not entertain this proposal on account of the financial responsibility, although they were not asked to take any capital financial responsibility but only to accept delivery of the goods.[11]

Some smaller concerns unsuccessfully requested advances to purchase the equipment required for munitions manufacture, "as these special machines would be of practically no value, except for this particular work, and would simply be so much junk at the expiration of the contract."[12]

The weakness of Canadian industrial technology was also highlighted in wartime arms production. Work proceeded in two stages. In the first year, almost no finished shells were fabricated by Canadian firms because their capabilities did not extend beyond the provision of simple empty casings. Because of the intricacies of fuse and cartridge manufacture and the high cost of acquiring the necessary production equipment, manufacturers sought U.S. supply sources for these components. After mid-1915, however, the British refused to accept deliveries of any more unfinished shells and Canadian manufacturers were forced to secure the more complex skills and machinery.[13]

It would appear that many, if not most, of the machine tools required for both stages of production, as well as the specialized techniques necessary for their use, had to be acquired in the U.S. Writing some years after the war, the Shell Committee's Ordnance Adviser observed that Canada simply "had not the equipment and had not the facilities for its supply." Nevertheless, from the beginning of the war, U.S. machine tool factories "expressed" their products to Canadian manufacturers "with a commendable speed."[14]

In spite of this dependence on foreign technology, by the end of the war technical advances had been made in a number of fields. Still, many of the most complex processes (including the manufacture of airplanes, fuses, and explosives) were carried on in seven "national factories" established for war production in Canada by the Imperial Munitions Board. When the U.S. entered the war in 1917, some of the technical knowledge developed in Canada was shared with American manufacturers, although Canadian firms continued to purchase specialized machinery in the U.S. Thus, while munitions production may have increased the size of Canada's industrial establishment, it did not seem to have provided the stimulus necessary to induce Canadian manufacturers to sink independent technological roots. Time constraints were obviously an important consideration here, but it seems reasonable to suppose that fewer innovative spin-offs were achieved than might have been the case if Canadian industry had possessed the capability of producing its own capital goods at the start of the hostilities.[15]

In summary, the munitions trade provided Canadian manufacturers with uniquely painless export opportunities. It was a "state-induced and state-regulated business"[16] in which the buyers sought them out in a period of slack domestic demand. There was also little need to disturb the established patterns of minimum capital investment and extensive technological dependence in order to make a success of the trade.

Other Wartime Exports

Export orders for other military supplies (including clothing, bedding, soldiers' kits, etc.) did not fall quite so easily into the hands of Canadian manufacturers. The Allies tended to look first to the U.S. rather than Canada for their import requirements because, as one trade commissioner put it, "the greater out-put capacities of her industries makes her position more elastic for meeting exceptional demands, while her export experience and organization are superior."[17] Consequently, in striking contrast to the munitions experience, Canada was generally overlooked in the establishment of direct purchasing agencies for these other war materials. As a result, Canadian industries had to deal directly with Allied governments in Europe or with their purchasing commissions in the U.S.

In this quite different situation, the export expertise of Trade and Commerce was quite naturally called upon by the interested firms. Trade and Commerce Minister Sir George Foster sent Borden a forceful letter in mid-1915 which communicated the unhappiness of the manufacturers that no satisfactory purchasing agencies had been appointed in Canada by the Allies. Industrialists complained that representations to Allied procurement bodies in the U.S. had met with the obstacle of paying "hosts of middlemen," each seeking a "comfortable commission" before orders could be secured. They submitted that they "ought not to be reduced to the alternative of getting no business from these countries or of taking it through middlemen and jobbers." In London, Foster stated, manufacturers reported "long delays" and a "certain averseness to doing business with Canada." As a result, many had returned empty-handed.[18]

In the first months of the war, manufacturers were desperate for these orders because of the unhealthy condition of the home market. For example, the Canadian Clothing Manufacturers' Association asked Foster to intercede on their behalf to procure orders from the British War Office because "our factories are at present either entirely at a standstill, or at best working from 20 to 30 per cent capacity." This "general depression" had thrown "thousands" out of work.[19] For their parts, Borden, Foster, and Sir George Perley, Canada's High Commissioner in London, pressed the case of the manufacturers to the Allies at every opportunity. Canadian firms, they argued, should be given patriotic preference over those of the "neutral" Americans. Borden told one wartime meeting in London that "nearly everything that comes from the U.S. could also be produced in Canada at prices which would bear favourable comparison . . . . All that Canadian manufacturers desire is that they may be given a reasonable opportunity of producing goods so far supplied from the U.S."[20]

In spite of these representations, little progress appears to have been made during the remaining years of the war. To a considerable extent, Canadian manufacturers may have been the authors of their own misfortune. Not only did they fail to show initiative in expanding upon the export opportunities resulting from government efforts,[21] they also burdened themselves with a reputation for producing shoddy goods. At the conclusion of the war, Borden's office compiled a report detailing many of the negative experiences suffered by Allied purchasers of Canadian industrial goods. The sloppy performances recorded there are consistent with what we already know about the poor export habits developed before 1914: numerous cases of failure to respond to orders or to fill promised orders; lengthy delays; and the shipment of defective and substandard goods. Comparisons with the export performance of U.S. firms were almost always unfavourable. In fact, they were quite likely at the root of the "certain averseness to doing business with Canada" of which the manufacturers were complaining to Foster. For example:

> There have been many complaints as to the unbusinesslike methods of packing, shipping, etc., and although the most precise instructions have been sent out as to what is required, the [British] War Office states that they are not followed. The Contracts Department contrasts their experience with Studebakers [U.S.] and with the Canadian manufacturers. The former have always delivered to time, have so packed, shipped and advised the consignments, that a boy could undertake the distribution to the various depots, and the quality of goods has, with one exception, been all that could be desired.[22]

During this period, Canadian manufacturers continued to demonstrate their reluctance to accept the ordinary business risks of the export trade, often viewing it as an abnormal activity forced upon them in times of depression, something which could be safely abandoned when domestic market conditions strengthened. A good illustration of this attitude can be found in a letter from G.M. Murray, secretary of the CMA, to Foster in early 1916.

> Mr. King, in common with other Canadian manufacturers of boots, complains that the manner of handling this [war export] business heretofore has been so unsatisfactory that he would not care to interest himself in the business further unless a firm offer were made to him. On previous occasions the time that was allowed to elapse between the invitation to tender and the closing of the contract was unduly long: tenders submitted on the basis of current market quotations for leather could not be lived up to with profit to the manufacturer if his tender were not accepted until three months later, by which time the price of the leather had materially advanced. Moreover if other business became available in the meantime manufacturers accepted it and were consequently unable to guarantee deliveries.[23]

We will now turn to an examination of the wartime export trade carried on by Canadian industrialists outside of the provision of munitions and other military supplies. For its part, Trade and Commerce was very optimistic in 1914 that the war would shake the manufacturers out of their exporting torpor. Foster, in an editorial in his department's *Weekly Report,* called on Canadian firms to launch what amounted to a holy crusade to capture those export markets now cut off from German industry.

> Whilst a comparatively small number of our manhood fights the battle for Imperial existence and control of our ocean highways, those who remain should with spirit and energy throw themselves into the task of taking possession of the markets from which our enemies have been driven and supply them with the products of our own fields and factories. Here is a peaceful field of operation in which we can carry on a bloodless but most effective and profitable warfare . . . . Here are markets for hundreds of millions of dollars of products, the making of even a portion of which will keep our industries going and give employment to hundreds of thousands of our people.[24]

The CMA also expressed some interest in moving into markets Germany had been forced to quit, particularly South America. It printed a number of informative articles on the subject in *Industrial Canada* with material provided by Trade and Commerce. In addition, the CMA offered assistance to its members in forming "syndicates" of non-competitive manufacturers to share the expense in sending a sales representative to scout South America. However, since "comparatively few" industrialists responded, it abandoned the project.[25] The CMA leadership was also alert to the potential of former German markets in Russia. They persuaded Trade and Commerce to place a "Commissioner with two or three assistants . . . on the ground" to study that country's commercial possibilities.[26] However, the interest there, as in South America, was to prove to be mainly academic.

Undaunted, during the early years of the war the department spared little ink in pointing out the considerable value of markets lost to the Germans and the opportunities thus afforded for Canadian initiative. At the end of 1914, it published a 110-page report that reprinted articles on this subject. In addition, the trade commissioners frequently noted the excellent prospects of replacing specific German goods in the published market reviews of their posts.[27]

In general, Canadian manufacturers showed themselves to be incapable of seizing any extensive advantage from these favourable circumstances. They excused this failure by pleading transportation difficulties and the pressure of wartime production.[28] An examination of the trade commissioners' reports, however, indicates that this, like the plea of "home demand" which had preceded it, may have been in many cases simply a convenient apology for avoiding export business.

To begin, Canadian firms continued to shun the practice of sending out salesmen to establish direct representation in foreign markets. In contrast, U.S. enterprises had, in the words of one Trade and Commerce agent in South Africa, "flooded the country" with commercial travellers during the war.[29] Some time later, this same individual warned that it was vital for Canadian manufacturers to establish an active presence in foreign markets, even if only token for the duration of the war, so that a base for future expansion could be secured. "It is true that the conditions of extra business in many of the Canadian plants may prevent all possibility of immediate business," he reasoned, "but surely the management must give an occasional thought to future trade."[30]

This declaration captures a frustration experienced by many trade commissioners. To illustrate, the Bristol posting recited from a similar chapter and verse:

> Although Canadian manufacturers of the various kinds of steel products are busy with the filling of orders arising from the exigencies of war, yet this would appear to be the time to look into the opportunities for the sale of their products in the United Kingdom after the war. The United States firms are making energetic efforts to secure the trade in bolts, nuts, screws, nails, wire, etc., and . . . almost every boat entering the port of Bristol from the United States carries large quantities from that source.[31]

Even such exotic markets as India were showered with attention from U.S. industries during the war, while "Canadian commercial travellers were never seen." The readers of *Weekly Bulletin* were informed that as a result of an aggressive wartime sales campaign on the sub-continent "very strong American vested interests . . . are growing up among the importers, and unless Canadian producers take early steps to cultivate this market by personal visits and systematized propaganda work, they will find that it will be impossible to secure their fair share of the trade later on."[32]

Not only did Canadian manufacturers seem uninterested in matching the more venturesome sales tactics of their U.S. competitors, they continued to prove themselves unenthusiastic about even replying to mail from potential foreign customers. The trade commissioner in New Zealand transmitted the unhappiness of a number of importers in that country, previously agents for German firms, who, when the war came, were anxious to switch to Canadian enterprises "even at a slightly higher price." Initiatives from New Zealand were, nonetheless, met with silence from Canada. In this case, "the difficulty is not to secure orders but to get them filled . . . after exhaustive letters are written, no reply is received."[33] The problem became so acute in Great Britain that in 1917 one Trade and Commerce representative maintained:

> The neglect of correspondence on the part of Canadians has been mentioned by English firms more than any other feature in connection with their trade with Canada . . . . As an instance of neglect of correspondence the manager of a Bristol firm who . . . represents high class Canadian firms and yet could not get even an acknowledgement of letters enclosing remittances of money for goods sold. During the months of May, June and July he sent 107 letters to Canada, about 90 of which required answers. He has received only 32 answers, 15 of which were received from one firm which always answers its letters. The other concerns practically ignored all correspondence. This is just one instance of many. It is realized that many Canadian houses have been extremely busy on war orders, but if they wish to build up a trade for the future there is no excuse for this neglect of correspondence.[34]

The columns of *Industrial Canada* also carried regular complaints on this subject. On one occasion, toward the end of the war, its editors became so exasperated that they indignantly lectured their readers: "Even if you don't wish to engage in export trade or are unable to carry out suggested arrangements, at least have the decency to say so, politely and cordially. Let Canadian manufacturers at least have the reputation for courtesy."[35]

During this period, Canadian manufacturers continued to lose export business because of the stubborn unwillingness of many of them to quote the prices of their goods landed in foreign ports. Deviating from the procedure customary among the exporters of other countries, these firms quoted only in Canadian or U.S. dollars at their factory gates. The trade commissioner in Paris suggested that Canadian firms were missing opportunities in France because "to ask a Frenchman to buy his goods in America or Canada in dollars is like squeezing blood from his very heart." The Birmingham post concurred that Canadian-dollar price quotations made it "almost impossible to transact business" in Great Britain. While British purchasers held a sentimental preference for Canadian over U.S. exporters, this was largely negated by the more "accommodating" U.S. attitude in matters such as these.[36]

Buy Canadian

In spite of the unusual opportunity that came in the wake of the wartime disruption of German trade, we must conclude at this juncture that there was little positive improvement in the apathetic export behaviour of most Canadian industrialists. Even *Industrial Canada* was moved to criticism. "But after all," it editorialized, "it is an old story. Ever since *Industrial Canada* started publication there have been complaints that the Canadian [manufacturers] have been slow to bestir themselves. The war might have been expected to wake up the tardy ones but it does not seem to have had that effect even yet."[37] Near the conclusion of the war, it probed the psychology of Canadian industrial capitalism in an attempt to discover an explanation for this export lethargy. "We must confess," it submitted, "that we have not developed the mental avidity which is the necessary accompaniment of vigorous and overmastering action."[38]

As might have been anticipated, however, *Industrial Canada's* criticism of the continued home market obsession of Canadian manufacturers was far less forceful than its defence. This CMA organ, reflecting the views of its membership, saw more opportunities for the replacement of German goods in the Canadian market than in foreign markets. An illuminating contrast can be drawn from a comparison of Foster's earlier noted war editorial in *Weekly Report,* in which he called for a crusade to capture Germany's external trade, and *Industrial Canada's* war editorial which trumpeted a "Buy Canadian" crusade.

> This is no longer a commercial appeal .... It is the duty of Canadian citizens to spend every possible dollar at home during the war. Sending money abroad in payment for foreign goods indirectly helps the enemies of Britain, because such action weakens ourselves.... It is evident that a flood of goods, from neutral countries deflected from the ports of belligerent nations, will threaten to overwhelm our markets .... This is no time to indulge whims, prejudices, or fancies in favour of foreign manufacturers .... Fight the enemy by buying at home.[39]

In what could have been a response to Foster's early September, 1914, call to export action, *Industrial Canada's* October, 1914, issue counselled Canadian firms to be very cautious in moving into the foreign markets Germany had been forced to vacate. Citing the numerous difficulties of export trade – intense competition, capital shortages, transportation delays, and language barriers – the journal argued that a threatened influx of imports from the "neutral" U.S. into Canada made it essential that industrialists give first priority to domestic trade and to replacing imports formerly made in Germany.

> The exclusion of goods formerly imported from nations at war goes hand-in-hand with determined efforts to flood our home market with the manufactures of neutral nations. We can begin to manufacture some goods formerly imported, but the processes are difficult to master and establish. We can try and capture foreign trade, but the obstacles in the way are serious, though by no means insurmountable. Canadian manufacturers are performing a great feat by merely holding their own under existing conditions.[40]

The industrialists were soon to lobby Ottawa for assistance in more effectively substituting domestic production for the excluded German imports. In early 1915, an "influential deputation" urged Borden and Foster to organize exhibits of foreign goods that could be inspected by manufacturers interested in import substitution.[41] As a result, Trade and Commerce mounted a show of German toys in Toronto in the spring and summer of 1916. This was followed, in the fall of that year, by a six-city tour of over 8,000 Austrian and German commodities borrowed from the British Board of Trade. Trade and Commerce was even able to arrange with the railways to grant reduced fares to manufacturers who wished to visit the display. By the war's end, a more permanent exhibit of replaceable foreign products had been situated in Ottawa.[42]

Fear of Flying (alone)

As the war progressed, Canadian manufacturers began to worry openly about a collapse of their export trade at the conclusion of the war. For example, in mid-1916 the Tariff Committee of the CMA correctly noted that the recent vast increases in overseas sales of industrial goods were largely due to shipments of munitions and other war supplies. "When the demand for these articles ceases at the conclusion of peace, how will the present volume of exports be maintained?" this committee wondered.[43]

By 1917, these concerns had crystallized into a resolution passed at the annual meeting of the CMA calling for a government inquiry into the "best methods for conserving and increasing our domestic and overseas trade, to the end that our present prosperity may not unduly suffer when the stimulus resulting from orders for munitions and other war supplies is removed."[44] After appointment to the Senate in 1917, F. Nicholls, one of the nation's leading industrialists and a life-long CMA militant, took it on himself to ensure that this resolution was acted upon in Ottawa. In his maiden speech before the Upper House, he pleaded for a "systematic method of state aid" for Canada's industrial exporters. To him, this meant the establishment of a peace-time government agency to continue the job done during the war in bringing "export" orders to the doors of Canadian factories. Such an agency, according to Nicholls,

> would actually sell Canadian products in foreign markets and distribute the orders received amongst Canadian producers .... A Government department as a sales agent would carry more weight than an individual corporate body could. It would also be able to finance trade credits on a much lower basis of interest and thereby create a trade that it would be impossible for the individual to develop.[45]

Nicholls was able to secure the appointment of a special Senate committee to study the problem of post-war trade and was successful in getting it to recommend many of his proposals to the cabinet.

The Canadian Industrial Reconstruction Association, drawn from a most illustrious list of prominent capitalists, also placed pressure on Ottawa to pick up once again the export ball on behalf of the manufacturers after the war was finished.[46] In mid-1917, its president, Sir John Willison, suggested that each individual Canadian industrialist "acting alone cannot hope to get such a foothold in foreign markets or such a share in the reconstruction of the devastated portions of Europe as may be had by co-operation and organization." He recommended that Canadian manufacturers act with "vigor, foresight and courage" to form trade cartels if they hoped to compete with their rivals from Germany, Great Britain, Japan, and the United States. Further, since the governments of these countries "freely afforded" many valuable services to their exporters, "the movement which Hon. Frederic Nicholls has inaugurated in the Senate for a Canadian Trade Corporation should have liberal aid from the Government and the active, organized support of the industrial and financial interests."[47]

The institutional machinery eventually settled on by the Borden cabinet to handle European reconstruction trade held many important similarities to the Nicholls plan. In late 1918, a Canadian Trade Mission was headquartered in London. It was charged with "the purpose of securing for the agricultural and other productions of Canada their appropriate share in the markets of the world during the period of reconstruction."[48] Any orders obtained in Europe were to be funnelled to the parallel Canadian Trade Commission in Ottawa. This Ottawa body, in turn, was to pass these foreign orders to the appropriate Canadian firms to submit bids.

Scarcely a week after the formation of the Canadian Trade Commission, Finance Minister Sir Thomas White, who was left in charge in Ottawa with Borden and Foster in London to prepare for the Peace Conference, chaired two meetings of a Reconstruction and Development Committee. This committee was made up of a number of important industrial and transport capitalists. White was warned of serious disruptions to occur as a result of the collapse of the munitions trade. These business leaders pleaded for various types of subsidy schemes to assist them in making the transition to peacetime trade. F.H. Whitton, president of the Steel Company of Canada, was more direct than most, but his comments fairly reflect the imperious tone of these meetings. He stated that

> as Canada had contributed to the war in Europe, we had a right to demand a share in the reconstruction business that would follow. If Canada's prices were too high on this business, our manufacturers should have the right to call on the Government to make up the difference . . . and boats must be provided at once in order to get our goods delivered overseas.[49]

White was clearly shaken by what he heard. The day after these meetings were completed he fired off a cable to Borden in London passionately urging immediate action on behalf of the manufacturers.

> It is of utmost importance to Canada that you should immediately and strongly impress upon the British Government necessity of having new orders placed in Canada for manufactured products required for overseas reconstruction purposes replacing the volume of munitions business which is now being rapidly demobilized. Within six weeks over one hundred thousand operatives will be dismissed. We are taking every step to provide for their absorption but overseas orders for our manufacturers imperatively necessary to prevent unrest and discontent over the war.[50]

Reconstruction Trade

Meanwhile, those in London were discovering that post-war Europe was by no means the captive market it had been during the hostilities. Soon after arriving to take up his position as chairman of the Trade Mission, L. Harris, an industrialist himself, warned that "business over here is not going to come as easily as the munitions business came, and the manufacturers must not expect that we are going to get immediate results."[51] Foster and Harris both concluded from an early point that in order to capture any significant share of the continental reconstruction trade, the Canadian government would have to extend purchase credits. Harris was particularly cheered by possibilities in the less industrialized markets of Rumania, Serbia, and Greece and spoke of the "splendid results" that could be anticipated if credits were extended to these countries. "They require so many things," he opined, "that it would be possible to keep Canadian industries busy for some months to come."[52]

Finance Minister White, who had long supported the idea of Canada extending reconstruction loans, was concerned nevertheless that the weak financial position of the Balkan countries might result in defaults. From the beginning, White had also insisted that credits should only be extended for manufactured goods as Canada's raw materials and agricultural products would "probably find a market for themselves" in Europe.[53] Consequently, when credits of $25 million were eventually extended to France, Belgium, Rumania, and Greece, it was on the condition that more than half the money be spent on Canadian manufactures.

In spite of the extraordinary state efforts to assist Canadian manufacturers in developing their post-war export trade, it appears that the results obtained were less than satisfactory. By the end of 1919, for example, almost two-thirds of the export credits remained unclaimed by European purchasers.[54] The manufacturers themselves may have been at least partly to blame for this state of affairs. Harris complained to the CMA that the traditional sloppy business tactics of Canadian industrial exporters, including their unwillingness to send catalogues overseas or even to reply to their foreign correspondence, had cost them reconstruction sales. In addition, Harris accused a number of manufacturers of missing opportunities through delays caused by their attempts to adjust prices to take advantage of the strong European demand for certain commodities. To illustrate, Harris related the case of a British trade inquiry which he had channelled to a Canadian firm through the Canadian Trade Commission in Ottawa. The manufacturer cabled London to say "anxious to get order, ascertain price we have to meet and cable quick so we can answer Ottawa on your inquiry." Harris concluded disapprovingly that "if a man has got stuff to sell surely to God he ought to have a price on it. Some of our people just want all the traffic will warrant."[55]

The state structures put in place to handle the reconstruction trade were also unsuitable. While centralizing the acquisition and distribution of wartime munitions contracts may have been highly effective in the munitions trade when it concerned only a small number of government purchasers, such centralization proved unnecessarily cumbersome for the more varied and flexible requirements of peacetime trade in which bureaucratic delays could prove fatal. After a year's experience in the field, Harris advised Borden that following each of the necessary steps between the Trade Mission in London and the Canadian firm consumed so much time that "before we could get prices and deliveries back to London other sellers were able to secure the business."[56]

Almost certainly aware that state assistance here was proving to be counterproductive, White cabled Borden in April of 1919 that it was wise to pass once again the initiative in the reconstruction business to the private sector. "The sooner we compel business houses to rely more upon themselves and less on government the better," he argued. "Our business firms and banks can do much more to help themselves than they are doing."[57] White felt secure in making such a recommendation because the predictions of economic disaster which had been placed before him in his previously discussed meetings with industrialists in late 1918 had failed to materialize. The domestic market was strong and sales of manufactured exports had not totally collapsed due to the exceptionally strong reconstruction demand. Although exports of manufactures were nowhere near their wartime volume, at least until early 1920 there was evidence of a significant gain over pre-war levels.

This mini-boom in industrial exports provoked considerable chest-thumping among manufacturers. T.P. Howard, president of the CMA during 1919-1920, proudly informed his convention that in spite of the halt in munitions exports "we have held the greater part of our export trade, and instead of unemployment, we are now experiencing a shortage of labour."[58] Conditions appeared to be so favourable that one CMA official was prompted to compose an "Answer to the Critics" of the past export performance of Canadian industrialists. He stated that

> in the two years since the signing of the Armistice there has been more money spent by Canadian manufacturers in endeavouring to

develop export trade than in any ten years previous to the war. Not only has more money been spent, but more people have been engaged. Where there were probably between two hundred and three hundred manufacturers doing considerable amounts of export trade before the war, this figure will now easily exceed one thousand.[59]

Self-congratulatory remarks of this kind proved to be premature as exports of Canadian manufactures were to sink in the early 1920's to a level not strikingly in excess of pre-war averages. The reconstruction trade, like the munitions trade before it, was based in the exceptional circumstances brought on by a world war. Although some firms undoubtedly made progress, evidence that the majority of industrialists had not yet undertaken the needed fundamental adjustments can be found in the reports of the trade commissioners. Even in the midst of the reconstruction boom, export trade once again was sacrificed on the altar of the home market. Take, for example, this report from the important Australian post:

> In recently interviewing some of the departmental buyers for the largest wholesale dry goods importing warehouses in Sydney and Melbourne, stress was laid upon their inability to obtain anything like prompt execution of orders placed in Canada. The reasons given by the manufacturers in the Dominion were that the domestic demand was so active, and their inability to secure the necessary mill and other operatives. Under the conditions outlined, the buyers (who prefer to obtain "made in Canada" goods) are compelled to place orders of great magnitude with countries which make prompt shipment.[60]

After the war, as during it, Canadian manufacturers continued to allow their competitors to foreclose their future export opportunities in new markets. To illustrate, sixty U.S. firms, some of major size, established direct representation in China in 1919, according to Canada's long-time resident trade commissioner in that country. In marked contrast, he testified that Canadian manufacturers had *never* made any serious attempt to obtain orders in China.

> Canada has had direct steamship communication with China from the port of Vancouver for more than thirty years, yet in all that time not a single Canadian business firm have established themselves or had agents in this country; and very few Canadian business men have evinced any but the most perfunctory interest in this

market, or thought it worth the trouble to visit it and investigate conditions for themselves. The most that was done was to write letters in the hope of selling goods, and when this method failed in results – which it was bound to do – (for in the meantime some live agent from another country was here with his samples, and of course secured the business), they condemned the market as being of no value.[61]

The trade commissioners were not alone in their unhappiness. Another state enterprise, the Canadian Government Merchant Marine, had its own cause for complaint about the reconstruction performance of Canadian industrialists. As we will recall, the manufacturers had blamed a portion of their export sloth during the war on their inability to obtain ocean transport. Pressure from the CMA, the Canadian Industrial Reconstruction Association, the railways, and staple producers led the government to form a state merchant marine to carry Canadian exports during the reconstruction period. Fully sixty-three vessels were built to service all parts of the world.

However, overcapitalized and underutilized in an international context of excess shipping capacity, the line began to run aground after 1920. C.C. Ballantyne, Minister of Marine and Fisheries, singled out the manufacturers for particular blame. In 1920, he made a "public appeal to the Canadian manufacturers to bestir themselves and show more interest in the export trade of Canada than they have shown during the past years."[62] The following year saw him express his "disappointment" that industrialists had not heeded his "urgent appeal." "Canadians must not only look after the home trade but must reach out aggressively for foreign markets," he argued.[63]

For their part, the manufacturers saw little need for concern. Reasoning that the government merchant marine should be written off as a "trade builder," they counselled patience. *Industrial Canada* asked rhetorically, "What does it matter, if, by running the lines at a slight operating loss for a few years, an expanding market is obtained for Canadian products which by the traffic it creates will ultimately make the actual carrying profitable?"[64] Nevertheless, faced with staggering losses, the Canadian Government Merchant Marine decided in 1923 that it had no alternative but to dispose of almost half of its fleet.[65]

Conclusion

World War I and its aftermath presented Canadian manufacturers with a unique opportunity to establish a strong and permanent base for future expansion of their export trade. Yet, on the whole, they failed to seize the occasion. Other industrial nations were not so short-sighted. It must be remembered that, in these early formative years, every decade Canada fell further behind made it all that much more difficult for her ever to catch up.

While massive and vital to the war effort, the munitions trade in shells and cartridges produced few long-term benefits. Any significant structural improvement to the base of Canadian manufacturing was vitiated when its proprietors followed their traditional course of minimum capital investment and maximum technological dependence. In addition, since munitions purchasing was carried out within Canada by a state agency operating in a context of feverish demand, industrialists were not forced to sharpen their competitive skills by making direct representations in international markets. Indeed, rather than being stimulated to strike out on their own after the war, the manufacturers pleaded for the creation of a new government body to generate their peacetime "export" orders. This effort, predictably, was doomed.

If anything, outside of the munitions trade the picture appears even more dismal. In supplying other war materiels for the Allies, Canadian manufacturers injured their future prospects in foreign markets by dispatching considerable quantities of shoddy goods. Activity in ordinary export channels was equally lethargic. Specifically, it would seem that few serious attempts were made to match the active, comprehensive U.S. campaign to prepare for post-war trade in overseas markets. Even when foreign customers sought out Canadian industrialists during the war, many habitually declined to reply to their correspondence.

There are many indications that the vision of the majority of manufacturers in this era did not extend far beyond substituting domestic production for excluded German imports. Although they argued that transportation difficulties and the intense demands of munitions production prevented them from giving serious attention to export development during the war, their uneven performance in the subsequent reconstruction period largely confirms our thesis concerning their extreme home market orientation.

CHAPTER 5

Import Substitution for the Empire

The rhythm of our narrative greatly changes as we enter the interwar period. The firing of the last Canadian shell in 1918 signalled a new growth plateau for our industry. With production both deepened and intensified, its future development seemed secure. In addition, as explained in Chapter 2, foreign owners were poised to capture, if they had not already, the export dynamic "growth industries" of our century: electrical industries, chemical industries, and industries based on the application of the internal combustion engine.

Until now, our investigation has paid testimony to the unhappy inability of the mass of Canadian manufacturers to field internationally competitive products capable of gaining a foothold in the rapidly expanding world markets of their era. For most, an unchallenged technological dependence and an obsession with the home market were to preclude a serious attempt to export. So it was, then, that their forays into foreign markets were either dilettantish or non-existent. Only a minority of our industrialists could be said to be making an organized effort to reach broader horizons.

To be sure, incompetence and lack of interest continued to characterize the external relations of many manufacturers.[1] But this steadily became less significant in the more general pattern we are trying to trace. Canadian-owned amateurs, hampered by the innovative vacuum which typified their licensee production facilities, are no longer the main story. Between 1914 and 1960, foreign capital tripled its share of control over Canadian industry, moving from one-fifth to three-fifths of total investment. Accordingly, our attention will be focused on the new order. In this chapter, which roughly covers the 1920's and 1930's, we will scrutinize the branch plant export strategy of imperial import substitution. In the next chapter, which takes us from World War II into the modern era, the relationship between foreign firms and the blocking of Canadian-manufactured exports will be probed.

A "Permanent Basis" for Manufactured Exports

In Chapters 2 and 3, we outlined the export strategy we have styled import substitution for the Empire. With it, U.S. branch plants and licensees in Canada hoped to gain preferential tariff entry into British Empire markets so as to gain price advantages on their American and European competitors. Imperial sentiment, we noted, was the basis of their preference appeals. Manufacturers also argued that their Canadian-based firms could strengthen the Empire by compensating for Britain's weakness in exporting the sophisticated "growth industry" products. They persistently pressured the Canadian state to become involved on their behalf because only the government could provide the institutional framework and legitimacy necessary for the conduct of trade negotiations with other Empire governments.

Ottawa and the manufacturers achieved some early success in this area, gaining tariff access in 1904 on British preferential terms in New Zealand and South Africa. In addition, a reciprocal trade agreement that included some Canadian manufactures was concluded with a number of the smaller West Indian islands in 1912. The Great War, however, brought the question of a wider extension of Empire preference to the fore. In 1916, worried by the prospect of a post-war collapse of their munitions export business, the Tariff Committee of the CMA called on the federal government to pursue "wisely arranged preferential tariffs." They were particularly keen on Australia.[2]

Shortly after the conclusion of the war, the manufacturers applied more pressure in the form of a letter to Finance Minister White "unanimously endorsed" by the executive of the CMA. In this remarkable communication, the strategy of imperial import substitution was argued to hold three principal benefits for Canada: it would advance the goal of Empire unity, broaden Canada's industrial base, and provide a "permanent" foundation for industrial exports. All of this was set forth in the most enthusiastic and visionary terms.

> The noblest aspirations that animate the intellect, for the vitality and honour of one's country, can be satisfied by a system of reasonable tariff preferences within the Empire . . . . As regards Canada, under such a system, there would be immediate and extraordinary increases in industrial production. It would ensure the large expansion of Canadian exports on a permanent basis. Before deciding whether or not to establish branch factories in Canada a number of United States industries are waiting for British countries to determine their policy on this subject. Were British preferential tariffs the rule, great numbers of United States in-

dustries would have to establish large works in this country in order to hold their export trade with British countries.[3]

The manufacturers were soon to see many of their prayers for a framework of Empire tariff preferences answered. In 1919, the British government extended preferential treatment to a number of Canadian-manufactured products. During the early 1920's, the 1912 agreements with the West Indian colonies were considerably augmented by expanding both the list of commodities covered and the number of islands included.

This left Australia, the richest white Dominion market excepting Canada, as the only major holdout. The industrialists continued to lobby Ottawa for action. A CMA deputation reminded the cabinet of Prime Minister W.L.M. King in early 1922 that "a large proportion of the goods supplied to Australia by the United States could have been supplied by Canada" if preferential tariff rates had been secured.[4] King responded by dispatching J.A. Robb, his Minister of Trade and Commerce, to Australia to see if some progress could not be made in obtaining tariff concessions. Nevertheless, it was not until mid-1925 that agreement was reached on a limited number of items.

On paper at least, 1932 was the high point of the imperial import substitution export strategy. By then, Canada had established some form of preferential agreements with Great Britain, the other Dominions, and Ireland, as well as with the scattered outposts of Empire including the West Indies, the Rhodesias, the Malay States, Cyprus, Ceylon, Malta, Hong Kong, and even Fiji. This had been the work of the Imperial Economic Conference of that year in Ottawa. Here, Prime Minister R.B. Bennett promised Canadians a way out of the Great Depression through what he called "family" arrangements for Empire preference in the exchange of both manufactured and primary products.

Canadian industrialists were particularly keen for such agreements; they sought a mechanism not only to revivify their collapsed enterprises, but also to renew their temporarily lapsed tariff privileges in the New Zealand and South African markets. Bennett left no doubt that he was in complete sympathy with their objectives. His announcement of the Ottawa accords echoed what the manufacturers had been saying for decades.

> Canada is the only part of the British Empire with the factories equipped to manufacture for export to the United Kingdom many of the manufactured articles heretofore supplied to that market by foreign countries. The possibilities of increased activities in Cana-

> dian factories and transportation routes with corresponding decrease in unemployment, as a result of these preferences, is unlimited. We should not fail to note the additional advantage of transferring to Canada the industries formerly carried on in these other [foreign] countries . . . .[5]

As the interwar period got under way, the fruits of imperial import substitution appeared delicious to its proponents. In 1919 alone, nearly 200 U.S. firms established branch plants or acquired an interest in existing Canadian industries.[6] While most of the new branch plants were set up to exploit the domestic market, many also hoped to engage in export trade within the Empire.[7] Under the stimulus of imperial preference, foreign enterprises contributed the largest share in a new surge of "finished" manufacture exports from Canada. This category doubled its share in overall Canadian trade during the 1920's and reached over 10 per cent of Canada's total foreign sales. Approximately half of these finished exports consisted of transport equipment, mainly automobiles and their parts.[8]

With these boom conditions, it is hardly surprising that the political elite of the time became convinced that an industrial stategy combining U.S. branch plants and imperial preference had indeed rendered a "permanent basis" for Canadian manufactured exports. In 1923, Trade and Commerce Minister Robb argued that not only were manufactured exports making the structure of Canadian trade more diversified, but that these improvements were fully in step with developments in the United States. Breaking down Canadian trade by a formula which was to become commonplace for decades to come, he concluded that

> the exports of raw materials of the United States were 39 per cent, and of Canada 44 per cent. Of partly manufactured products the exports of the United States were 11 per cent, and the exports of Canada 14 per cent. Of manufactured products, the exports of the United States were 49 per cent, while those of Canada were 41 per cent . . . . Canada is not only a large exporting nation of agricultural products, but she is becoming an exporting nation of manufactured goods.[9]

A later Minister of Trade and Commerce went so far as to predict in 1928 that Canada would eventually become the world's second largest producer of manufactured goods.[10] In reviewing this situation, Prime Minister King, as well, was prompted to deliver a glowing account of Canadian industrial success:

> the percentage of wholly manufactured commodities which we have been exporting is continually increasing. In other words, we are getting away from the stage of a country which is simply selling its raw materials to the stage where as a country we are developing a large manufacturing industry as well . . . . we have reached a higher stage in our manufacturing development in Canada, having regard to the age of the country and its population, than has, I believe, any other country in the history of the world.[11]

As previously noted, the branch plants contributed the most to the increasing importance of manufactured exports. While partisan differences between the Liberals and Conservatives developed during the interwar period on the degree of processing the branch plants should be induced to undertake in Canada, there was little suggestion from either party that the branch plant political economy brought with it limits to industrial expansion or trade. Prime Minister Bennett's hopeful confidence, as expressed in these 1931 remarks, was typical of the era:

> All young or underdeveloped nations have been dependent on large capital investments by outside countries for the development of their natural resources and for assistance in the establishment of the diversified industry necessary to all-round national development. Without such assistance, industrial progress would be slow and desperately difficult . . . . Fear has sometimes been expressed that these outside nations by starting industries in this country . . . are obtaining a menacing position in our economic life. The facts of the case reveal these fears to be entirely unfounded.[12]

Industrial export progress in the 1920's was so remarkable that even contemporary detractors of foreign investment, who might otherwise criticize Bennett's naivete here, have been dazzled. For example, J. Laxer recorded the massive trade in automotive products that resulted from Empire preferences. By 1929, he observed, Canada was capable of building over 260,000 vehicles and exporting over 100,000 of these. "A nation of under ten million people out-produced all the great nations of Europe including the United Kingdom, France and Germany," he concluded with some apparent pride.[13]

In spite of the fact that many indicators point to the success of import substitution for the Empire as an export strategy, it will soon be demonstrated that appearances were very deceptive. A close examination of the evidence (most of which was readily available to the decision-makers of the era) indicates that not only were the achievements of this export strategy superficial, but its duration was certain to be temporary. With its collapse, first noticeable in the late 1920's, we can witness the destruction of this CMA vision of a "permanent basis" for industrial exporting. As our downcast condition in the 1980's testifies, no effective alternative was subsequently to take its place.

Canadian Content

Far less actual manufacturing took place in Canada because of imperial import substitution than at first might be imagined. At the beginning of the 1920's, many U.S. firms found it convenient to establish rather primitive assembly operations in Canada to take advantage of Empire tariff preferences. Under these schemes, they were only required to demonstrate that 25 per cent of the factory price of their commodities was composed of Empire labour. When firms experienced difficulty in reaching this target with actual production costs, it was not unheard for them to inflate Empire content by adding various Canadian "administrative" charges.[14]

There is considerable evidence that many, if not most, of the branch plants engaged in preferential trade worked at the margins of Empire content regulations. Whenever these labour quotas were raised by Britain or the white Dominions (for reasons which will be discussed later), Canadian trade was considerably disrupted. One notable case involved the export of photographic equipment. After Britain increased its Empire labour requirements for these goods to 75 per cent in 1927, the value of Canadian camera exports plummeted from 130,000 pounds in that year to just over 2,000 pounds in the following year.[15]

When Britain raised her general Empire labour requirement to 50 per cent in 1933, Trade and Commerce was deluged with scores of inquiries from both the CMA and individual manufacturers seeking the most lenient possible interpretations of the new regulations. The CMA itself prepared "hundreds" of Canadian content cost analyses on behalf of its members.[16] Unquestionably, the export business of some firms was curtailed. For example, Goodyear Tire and Rubber complained that they had "an opportunity of doing a considerable business in shipping tire molds to England and could qualify quite easily under the twenty-five per cent rule but the fifty per cent requirement makes it extremely difficult."[17] Still, not all U.S. branch plants were unhappy with the new 50 per cent level. Those who could already meet these requirements hoped to gain an advantage over their competitors. Those who could not were angry. One threatened that "any increase in the quota would result in withdrawal of fully half of these plants from Canada" because it would be "unprofitable for them to operate in the Dominion."[18]

The standard-bearer of Canadian-manufactured exports in this epoch was the automobile. Its industry group dominated sales to the Dominions. The actual level of Canadian content in these products was uneven and greatly depended on the policies of individual firms. Ford, both the largest exporter and Canadian producer until 1926, also had the highest share of Canadian content. It claimed its products were over 75 per cent domestically produced as early as 1920. Controlled directly by the Ford family, Ford Canada was technologically dependent on the U.S. operation for patents, designs, and engineering. This dependence appears to have acted to reduce the level of Canadian input toward the end of the 1920's as models grew in complexity.[19]

The branch plants of the other U.S. automakers in Canada were unable or unwilling to match Ford's attempt to manufacture locally the largest share of their products. Many of their operations were simply sophisticated assembly plants which added a Canadian body and minor parts to a U.S. chassis and engine. As a consequence, while Canadian automotive export sales were quite formidable during the period, imports of these commodities were also massive. Table Six demonstrates that only in two years, fiscal 1924 and 1925, did Canada manage a slight surplus in her automotive trade. In 1929, Canada's best foreign sales year, imports were running at almost twice the level of exports. In that year, imports of parts and engines alone exceeded total automotive exports by just under $7 million.

The assembly nature of the automotive trade became a source of both foreign[20] and domestic embarrassment to the Canadian government. This became an important factor in King's major automotive tariff adjustments of 1926. Finance Minister J.A. Robb explicitly stated that his new regulations were designed to "compel the manufacturers of automobiles to cease having simply assembling plants in Canada. If they are in Canada to enjoy the advantages . . . of the British preference . . . then we submit it is only fair they should manufacture at least 50 per cent of their products in Canada to be entitled to that concession."[21] King spoke contemptuously of the "so-called Canadian manufacturers of automobiles." The new tariff provisions, he claimed, told them "if you wish to enjoy the advantages which our tariff gives you of getting into the British Empire market, then produce in Canada fifty per cent of your car with Canadian labour from Canadian products."[22]

While the intent of the King cabinet may have been clear in its own mind, the policy instruments it used to accomplish its objectives were,

TABLE SIX

Canadian Trade in Automobiles, Trucks, and Parts, and its Relationship to Gross Value of Domestic Production in these Commodities, 1920-1938

Year	*Exports ($million)*	*Imports ($million)*	*Exports (percentage of domestic production)*	*Imports (percentage of domestic production)*
1920*	19.2	36.1	(n.a.)	(n.a.)
1921	18.5	29.1	—	—
1922	9.4	24.3	—	—
1923	29.5	32.0	—	—
1924	37.0	33.3	—	—
1925	31.0	28.6	—	—
1926	43.1	48.2	—	—
1926**	38.5	61.4	26	42
1927	32.0	75.7	22	53
1928	36.2	101.2	20	56
1929	47.3	93.7	23	45
1930	20.6	49.3	17	41
1931	6.7	26.7	9	37
1932	7.1	17.4	13	31
1933	9.9	16.0	18	29
1934	19.7	26.8	20	27
1935	24.4	33.3	18	24
1936	23.2	36.9	17	27
1937	27.0	54.7	15	30
1938	25.1	39.9	16	26

*fiscal years; **calendar years.

SOURCES: Canada, *Trade of Canada*, and *Canada Year Book*, various years. Parts include engines but exclude rubber tires.

at best, somewhat obscure. To begin, the general tariff on automobile imports was significantly reduced, especially for the popular lower-priced models. Further, duties on a number of imported parts were either reduced or eliminated entirely. These moves, according to Robb, would stimulate the export sales of Canadian automakers in the following indirect manner. Since the domestic retail prices of Canadian automobiles were considerably higher than U.S. prices for similar models, and since for customs purposes in Empire markets Canadian cars were assessed on their "fair market value" in Canada, the preference advantage had been "practically wiped out on some Canadian cars."[23] The lower Canadian retail price resulting from these tariff reductions, it was hoped, would restore Canada's advantage.

In a related attempt to lower the "fair market value" of Canadian automobiles, while at the same time encouraging the branch plants to increase their Canadian content, a 25 per cent rebate on duty paid on imported parts (domestic drawback) was offered to Canadian manufacturers who could establish at least 40 per cent Canadian content before April 1, 1927, and 50 per cent after that date. This domestic drawback was available for all cars sold in the domestic market, provided the content requirements were met, and was not dependent on re-export. Interestingly, no attempt was made to impose a similar content restriction on the more directly relevant 99 per cent export drawback which Canadian automakers had enjoyed since 1920 on foreign parts which they assembled and re-exported.[24]

The offending automobile manufacturers, spurred on by these Canadian drawback regulations and higher Empire content quotas in Australia and New Zealand, gradually increased the Canadian component of their products. This is reflected in the lower percentage of the value of domestic production taken up by imports after 1932 (Table Six). According to claims made to Trade and Commerce, by that time nearly all firms had reached the 50 per cent mark (Table Seven). However, most cars were still one-third to one-half foreign manufacture and no firm was producing a product that was even three-quarters Canadian.

There are indications that Canadian content claims such as these may have been exaggerated. For example, investigations of British customs at the Oshawa plant of General Motors revealed that this company had misrepresented the Canadian content of some of its vehicles as being over 50 per cent in order to qualify for preference.[25] Even if this particular incident was exceptional, automobile manufacturers certainly had a strong incentive in the domestic drawback requirements to inflate their content claims. To some extent, this tendency was encouraged by liberal customs regulations. Parts purchased in Canada could have up to 25 per cent foreign content and still be considered all-Canadian. Administrative charges and 75 per cent of the duty paid on imported materials could also be included as Canadian costs. Entire plant production was the basis of content calculations, not individual models.[26] The scope for flexibility under these regulations was illustrated by testimony of an executive of Hudson and Essex Motors before the Advisory Board on Tariff and Tax-

TABLE SEVEN

Manufacturers' Claims to Canadian Content in their Automobiles, 1931-1932

Company	*Model*	*Canadian percentage*
Chrysler	Plymouth	50
	Chrysler	50
	Dodge	50
	DeSoto	50
Dominion	Frontenac	50
Ford		66
General Motors	Chevrolet	40-67
	McLaughlin Buick	32-47
	Pontiac	59
Studebaker		50
Willys-Overland		71

SOURCE: PAC, RG 20, vol. 94, no. 22693:E, August 15, 1932.

ation at the end of the 1920's. In considering whether to establish a Canadian branch plant, this company had determined that economic production was only possible with an actual Canadian content of 32 per cent. However, if "some of the [domestic drawback] laws were looked at broadly and perhaps stretched a bit without breaking them, we could come up to 38 per cent."[27]

In summary, a significant portion of Canada's exports under Empire preference were actually re-exports of U.S. goods which had been subjected to varying and often minor degrees of Canadian processing and assembly. Certainly, this was the conclusion reached by many in Britain and the white Dominions. For example, it was this understanding which led one Labour member of the Australian House of Representatives to object to a preference for Canadian imports. He informed his colleagues that he had

> studied this business fairly closely, and I find that business people in the United States of America are investing capital in Canada and

> opening up factories there, where parts of machinery manufactured in the United States of America are assembled in order to get the benefit of the preferential tariff granted by Britain to Canada. As soon as the Americans know that preference is to be granted to Canadian goods by Australia, this country will be flooded with articles of Yankee origin.[28]

This widely held opinion led the Australian government to fix its Empire content requirement at 75 per cent for goods from Canada.[29]

Resentment over the issue of Yankee-Canadian re-exports was also at the root of New Zealand raising its Empire content standard from 25 to 75 (later lowered to 50) per cent in 1924. The New Zealand Minister of Customs stated that the 25 per cent quota was "too easily complied with, and that articles of an essentially foreign character are treated as British for tariff purposes when only a comparatively small part of the manufacture has taken place within the Empire." This point was illustrated with a specific reference to the case of Canadian automotive exports.

> The chassis, which may be considered as the really important part of the car, may be made in a foreign country. Suppose it costs 150 pounds: by the addition to it in England or Canada of a cheap body, costing as little as 50 pounds, making the total cost at 200 pounds, the complete car qualifies for tariff preference.[30]

Not only was the degree of Canadian content an issue in the Dominions, but the mere fact that many Canadian exporters were U.S. branch plants was enough to raise suspicions that the principle of Empire preference was being abused by the Canadians. J.A. Robb, while Minister of Trade and Commerce, discovered the strength of these feelings on his unsuccessful 1922 mission to Australia to obtain preferential concessions. He reported to King:

> There seems to be an organized campaign through the public press against Canadian trade, the principal argument being that Canadian industries are controlled by United States capital, and that any concession granted to Canada is indirectly a concession to the United States against whom there is a very strong feeling throughout Australia.[31]

As an example of Australian hostility to the import substitution for the Empire strategy of Canadian industrial capital, Robb appended an editorial, "English Sovereigns or American Dollars," from the Sydney *Sun.* This newspaper opposed an extension to Canadians of the Australian preference already granted British manufacturers because

> Today American money dominates Canadian industries . . . . Preference given to Canada at the expense of Great Britain, therefore, mostly means pouring good Australian money into American safes, already choked with gold; while England will be that much poorer and that much less able to help Australia if war should come in the Pacific.[32]

Similar logic was frequently employed by the Australian legislative opponents of tariff preferences for Canadian manufacturers. One, who was later to become Minister of Trade and Customs, suggested that much of the benefit of a Canadian preference would "largely go to the United States of America, and the money may be re-invested there in other businesses that may compete with British manufacturers."[33]

Canadian manufacturers were stung by these criticisms that they were acting as Trojan horses for their U.S. parents, but they were unable to counteract such accusations effectively. For their part, English industrialists encouraged the spread of this idea in order to influence favourably the purchases of their more public-spirited customers. T.A. Russell, president of Willys-Overland, complained to the Toronto Export Club in 1928 of "a very offensive type of propaganda" prevalent in Britain. This suggested that "a car was not British unless assembled in the British Isles from materials acquired there." "In other words," he continued, "it denies to the product of this country classification as British."[34]

Despite such protests, Canadian manufacturers appear to have made little headway in convincing consumers of their "British" standing. Over the years, Trade and Commerce documented the widespread public resistance to this notion. For example, the English distributors of Moffat ranges reported that in "ninety-nine cases out of a hundred the consuming public in Great Britain classify Canadian products as being of United States origin." Wahl Evershape Company of Toronto stated flatly that "the British public do not regard Canadian products as British . . . . Retail shops particularly are inclined to regard Canadian goods as American."[35] Unfortunately for Canada's interests here, and the interests of our bona fide exporters, this impression was grounded in a reality which transcended uninformed prejudice. As late as 1950, Trade and Commerce agents were to report "certain shipments of so-called Canadian merchandise" which were being presented for entry under imperial preference. It was observed that "these are nearly always American goods which find their way to Canada, perhaps to some subsidiary company there, who decide to re-export them to the United Kingdom."[36]

Imperial Preference and National Self-interest

We have witnessed how Canadian manufacturers had to struggle to convince everyone save themselves that imperial import substitution was an act of patriotism on their part. Emotional acceptance of this strategy in their intended Empire markets was limited both by the assembly nature of Canadian production and by the considerable dimension of its foreign ownership. In addition, certain miscalculations by the manufacturers in the early years of the 1920's, notably, quoting their prices in U.S. funds, may have exaggerated these problems.[37] The ultimate collapse of the strategy, however, cannot be blamed entirely on its inability to rally Empire sentiment. Other, more fundamental weaknesses located in the economic structures of Britain and the Dominions doomed the project from its inception.

British acceptance of the theory of imperial preference was both delayed and partial. In the last half of the nineteenth century, free trade had been the economic orthodoxy in Britain. The easy access to markets and raw materials promised by that theory has often been in favour in nations confident of their ability to dominate world trade. Imperial preference, with its return to a type of tariff-protected mercantilism, only gained currency when British industry began to run out of steam. In conceding a very limited degree of imperial preference after World War I, the British government hoped to arrest some of its economic reverses. According to the "Imperial Visionaries" in that government, British prosperity could be ensured by a determined effort to rejuvenate the Empire. The extension of a preference to the Dominions by Britain was a principal feature of the vision. As a response to the already existing network of Dominion preferences for British goods, it was a price that had to be paid to ensure that these governments would remain willing to accept the continued export of surplus British capital, labour, and manufactures. This vision assumed a natural division of labour within the Empire. Britain would produce manufactures and the Dominions and colonies would supply mainly primary materials.[38]

This British idea of imperial preference bore little relationship to the scheme of Canadian manufacturers to become the Empire purveyors of goods that might otherwise be imported from the U.S. Britain was not necessarily opposed to Canadian industrialization. Nevertheless, it is clear that the imperatives of national self-interest as well as pressure from her own industrial capitalists would lead her to reject Canadian attempts to become the workshop of the Empire. The Labour Party in particular opposed British preferences on manufactured imports and revoked them when they held power during 1923 and 1924.

An excellent illustration of the attitude of the British state toward the pretensions of Canadian manufacturers can be found in the rebuffs they received when seeking orders from the purchasing agents of the colonial administrations. Not surprisingly, an informal code seems to have dictated that contracts were to be given whenever possible to firms located in Great Britain. Trade and Commerce compiled a thick dossier dealing with the frustrations encountered by Canadian companies who tried to bypass this rule by arguing that they, too, were "British."[39] P.C. Larkin, Canada's High Commissioner in London, attempted to assist Canadian industrialists in this matter, only to conclude it was hopeless. He wrote:

> if anyone imagines that the people here who control Indian affairs will allow a contract for as much as a nail which they can obtain in this country to go to Canada they are mistaken and Mr. Butler [president, Canadian Car and Foundry] is quite right when he says "that the policy of inter-Empire trade is a myth in which our Mother Country has no real sympathy." She certainly has no sympathy with contracts being given out of this country which can be executed here . . . . I have no doubt that every contract given out by India that will be made impossible for us to tender for will be made so.[40]

Like Britain, when the white Dominions embraced the principle of imperial preference, it was with their own economic self-interests fixed firmly in sight. Following Canada's 1898 lead, they unilaterally extended tariff concessions to Britain in the early years of this century. Like Canada, they held hopes of eventually persuading her to grant them reciprocal privileges on their agricultural exports. Because Britain absorbed the bulk of these goods, it made economic sense to create goodwill by doing all that was politically feasible to encourage the sale of British goods in their domestic markets.

In contrast, the economic incentive for granting the same preference to Canadian manufacturers was simply not there. Not only did Canada accept a very minor portion of the trade of the other white Dominions (as she needed few of their products), but all were in a deficit position in their trade with Canada, as we can see in Table Eight. Significantly, these deficits were swollen by the import of pre-

TABLE EIGHT

Canadian Trade with Selected Areas of the British Empire, 1920-1939 ($million)

	Imports to Canada		*Exports from Canada*	
	1920-29	*1930-39*	*1920-29*	*1930-39*
Australia	28	77	164	193
British Africa	14	71	105	138
New Zealand	48	46	128	98
Great Britain	1,069	1,197	3,870	2,834

SOURCE: Canada, *Trade of Canada*, 1939, vol. 1.

cisely those commodities in which Canadian industries sought favoured treatment.

Decisively, these other Dominions were eager to initiate their own import substitution industrialization in the products Canada was exporting. And, they hoped to begin as soon as their internal markets had grown to the point where they could support such enterprises. Canadian politicians had been given notice of the temporary nature of Canada's intermediary role as early as 1893. During that year, our first Minister of Trade and Commerce, Mackenzie Bowell, had journeyed to Australia to investigate trade prospects in that country. On his return, he wrote that the Australians were

> day by day growing strongly protectionist . . . . When I was met with the argument that they were putting on such high duties in order to enable their people to manufacture such articles as we could send them, I simply replied that they were quite justified, but until they were in a position to supply their own wants we wanted to sell to them instead of having the Yankees do so. To this they made no objection.[41]

When the Australians eventually conceded a preference to Canada in 1925, it was on the clear understanding that its benefits would last only as long as it took them to organize domestic production. In bringing forward the preference legislation, the Australian Minister of Trade and Customs observed that Canada was now being granted concessions on imports worth some 18 million pounds,

> of which motor chassis account for more than half . . . unfortunately [they] are not at present made in Australia . . . Canada's trade in

> motor chassis with this country, until we begin to make motor chassis for ourselves, should be looked upon with favour by all those who believe in inter-imperial trade.[42]

As a first step in undertaking the complete local assembly of imported vehicles, the Australians had already adjusted their tariff four years previously to induce the manufacture of auto bodies in that country. The success of this venture was observed with great interest in South Africa. By 1925, its government was ready to adopt a similar course of action. It discontinued its preference on completed vehicles and lowered its tariff on chassis imported to be fitted under bodies built in South Africa. Some were eager for even stronger measures to induce local assembly, but the government counselled patience could be profitable. The South African Minister of Finance spoke to his legislature of negotiations with a foreign manufacturer (probably Ford) interested in import substitution:

> The representatives of a firm, which came here some time ago to establish a motor car assembling station, pointed out to us that they were very anxious to increase their operations, but whereas they sell 30,000 cars in Australia, here they sell only 4,000. We import only 15,000 cars of all makes per year, so any firm which desires to establish assembling stations here will have to spend a lot of money. While we are not going as far as Australia has gone, we will see how things go and perhaps we may revise our policy later on.[43]

Progress in ISI proceeded far more rapidly in the Dominions than almost anyone had expected. By the mid-1920's, a number of U.S. automakers had warehouse-assembly branch plants in operation in these countries. Many products previously imported from Canada were now manufactured locally with predictably negative effects on Canadian trade. As a consequence, Canada slipped from second place in world automobile production during the 1920's to fifth in the early 1930's.[44] This ISI-related decline in export sales was an important contributor to the industry's disastrous collapse during the Great Depression. In 1932, it was only working to approximately 15 per cent of its capacity.[45] Although export sales were again to pick up after 1933, they never approached their earlier peak (see Table Six). Average sales in the years before World War II were only two-thirds of those of the previous decade's boom between 1923 and 1929. As well, the industry did not progress very far up the technological ladder. Almost 90 per cent of its exports in 1938 were complete vehicles, while parts still dominated imports.

While demand in the Dominions for "made-in-Canada" vehicles remained relatively strong in the late 1930's, the reprieve could only be temporary. There, in the midst of worldwide depression, ISI was proceeding with remarkable vigour. After the early bust years of the decade, substantial growth was experienced in the manufacturing sectors of New Zealand, South Africa, and Australia. New Zealand recorded a 50 per cent increase in production from 1928 to 1938; South Africa, 75 per cent. Between 1929 and 1937, the Australian volume of manufacturing rose by 40 per cent. By way of comparison, in these same years, Canadian manufacturing suffered a decline of some 8 per cent.[46]

State Policy and Branch Plant Exports

How did Canadian political leaders react to the flaws we have discovered in imperial import substitution? In general, as we witnessed at the beginning of the chapter, they remained optimistic that the CMA could deliver on its pledge to use this strategy to build a "permanent" base for Canadian industrial exports. Trade and Commerce Minister J. Malcolm came as close as anyone to being a critic. He believed that Canada was destined to become the world's second largest exporter of manufactures. Still, he blasted the warehouse-assembly nature of much Empire production as not being "of very much consequence to Canada."[47] Not surprisingly, then, Malcolm was a strong supporter of the 1926 domestic drawback legislation which, it will be recalled, gave tariff rebates to manufacturers who could produce vehicles with at least 50 per cent Canadian content.

Malcolm's predecessor in Trade and Commerce had taken a somewhat less aggressive stance. In 1924, T.A. Low had received a delegation of the Canadian presidents of Ford, General Motors, and Willys-Overland. These important industrialists were dismayed over rumours that the Dominions were preparing to raise their Canadian content requirements to 75 per cent. Low's assistance was requested in lobbying for a reduction to "some amount not exceeding 50 per cent." They also wanted the most lenient possible interpretation of what constituted "raw materials" for the purposes of determining Canadian content so that they could remain free to import a large portion of their parts from the U.S. In assuring these manufacturers of his "very best" efforts in pursuing "the interests of your industry in this connection," Low appears to have found nothing objectionable in their approach from the standpoint of the national interest.[48]

Malcolm's successor, H.H. Stevens, also became involved in attempting to ease the Empire content difficulties of the automobile manufacturers. In 1930, the colonial administration of Trinidad issued a new regulation that required all civil servants who obtained government car loans to purchase vehicles "entirely the product of the British Empire." In effect, this meant that only products of Great Britain were eligible. The trade commissioner in the field warned his department that the regulation was a "menace to the sale of Canadian cars" because it might lead to the cancellation of private orders from patriotic British residents of the territory. Stevens hotly protested to the British that the requirement was "unfair." "It is obviously impossible for us to state that our cars are 100 per cent British manufacture," he commented; "the cars manufactured in Canada run from fifty to eighty per cent British manufacture." Stevens' intervention was rewarded by a lowered 50 per cent rule. However, even this was not sufficient to satisfy all the Canadian suppliers. The trade commissioner reported "a great deal of disappointment that the figure has been set so high."[49]

These two examples serve to highlight a more general issue. Instead of attempting to lower content quotas on behalf of the manufacturers, to what extent could the Canadian state have used them as a lever to coerce the branch plants to undertake more processing in this country? It would appear that this policy option was never seriously entertained. The effectiveness of the one move undertaken in this field, the domestic drawback regulation, is questionable. Its Canadian content quota was set at a rather low 50 per cent, it was not applied to re-exports, and it came much too late to quiet Empire criticism.

The rhetoric of the Conservative Party during this period suggested that they would seek a better standard of performance from the manufacturers. Bennett was certainly aware of the content problem. In 1928, he declared that

> with decreasing exports we are assembling [automobile] parts to a greater extent than ever before. That means less work for Canadians – less manufacturing and an increasing tendency towards the assembling of parts. Now what is the aim of the Conservative Party? It is to endeavour to make this country economically independent . . . . If we are obliged always to go abroad for all our machinery, what will happen supposing, in a moment of caprice, that foreign supply is cut off.[50]

When their turn to govern came in the early years of the Depression, however, the Conservative industrial strategy was revealed as nothing more original or challenging than jacking up the tariff. This expedient, of course, was always in favour with the ISI manufacturers, whether branch plant or Canadian-owned.

As for the Liberals, high tariffs held few attractions. It will be recalled, however, that they coupled lower automotive tariffs in the 1920's with drawbacks for manufacturers who could build 50 per cent Canadian cars. This helped cement King's low-tariff farm and Progressive Party support.[51] But there were also political costs. The protests of the automotive industry and its workers, which included a brief closure of a General Motors plant and a rally of 3,000 workers in Ottawa, forced King to modify some aspects of the legislation. Automakers were particularly irked by the Canadian content provisions, although they reluctantly learned to live with them. Only the Canadian auto parts manufacturers and Ford, which sensed a competitive advantage because of its unusually high domestic content, would have been likely to support a Liberal move to increase content quotas.[52]

Faced with this hostile reaction from one industrial sector, the Liberals would naturally be wary of ever offering the drawback incentive in others. In addition their general laissez-faire orientation would have made the more drastic step of regulating a higher Canadian content unthinkable, save in the most terrible of circumstances. When all was considered, the political difficulties that would have resulted from probing these questions too deeply were far outweighed by the potential advantages of emphasizing the government's role in what was, on the surface, apparent export progress on the part of the manufacturers.

Besides, apart from the content question, King's administration was not a great believer in the ability of the manufacturing interest, with imperial preference or not, to deliver any extensive benefits to the nation through its export trade. Instead, they looked for succour to the sale of Canada's abundant resources in its "natural" market, the United States. So it was that King delivered this comment on Bennett's attempt to help Canadian industry to "blast" its way into world markets:

> If the tariff can be used as an instrument of national policy by raising duties to help the manufacturing industry of this country, why might it not also be used as an instrument of national policy to help the great primary, basic industries of the country in their production by lowering the duties? . . . what is most needed is a tariff which will help us export commodities, rather than a tariff that will help to prohibit importations.[53]

Through trade agreements with the U.S. in 1935 and 1938, King was to prove as good as his word. In exchange for American concessions on Canadian resources, the tariff door was once again propped open for the freer entry of U.S. industrial products.

For our purposes, more problematic than either the tariff or content issues was the whole notion of relying on the branch plants to motor the export strategy of Canadian manufacturing. After all, what was being created here was not a manufacturing sector capable of standing on its own technological feet and developing a line of products competitive in world markets. Rather, the strategy's success was predicated on U.S. firms being willing and able to transfer a certain portion of their foreign business to Canada. While many U.S. firms in the interwar period saw it to be in their interest to do so, many more did not. Table Nine demonstrates that even in the case of the coveted white Dominion markets, imperial preference was not a sufficient incentive to divert the lion's share of U.S. trade to Canada. In the crucial period of the 1925-29 economic boom, U.S. sales were running at more than twice Canada's level in New Zealand, five times Canada's average in South Africa, and eight times greater in Australia. Although some moderate closure of this gap was experienced during the Depression, particularly in Australia, this was to hold no long-term significance.

The trade commissioners were often far more clear-headed on this issue than were their political masters. Because these were men of practical field experience, they tended to recognize the dangers of remaining dependent on the branch plants to furnish Canada with

TABLE NINE

Dominion Imports from Canada and the United States, 1920-39 (per cent of total)

	*Australia**		*New Zealand*		*South Africa*	
	U.S.	*Canada*	*U.S.*	*Canada*	*U.S.*	*Canada*
1920-24	22	3	16	5	15	3
1925-29	24	3	18	8	16	3
1930-34	16	4	15	6	14	3
1935-39	16	7	12	8	18	4

*fiscal years

SOURCES: Australia, Bureau of Census and Statistics, *Year Book;* New Zealand, Department of Statistics, *Year Book;* Union of South Africa, Union Office of Census and Statistics, *Year Book,* various years.

its industrial export strategy. For example, in late 1919, one trade commissioner told the Windsor Chamber of Commerce that

> American firms establishing in Canada secure the advantages of free sites, taxation exemption, cheap power and good laws. Many such branches are established over here and in other parts of the Dominion for the purpose of doing export trade within the British empire. However, in many cases the selling organization is in the United States, and there is no authority in Canada to do an export trade within the empire. [54]

Over the years, the trade commissioners were to report many instances of export blocking on the part of U.S. firms in commodities as diverse as automobiles and bedsteads.[55]

Yet another snag in relying on the branch plants to produce Canada's manufactured exports also worried the trade commissioners. As we have already indicated in the case of the automakers, even when U.S. firms did choose Canada as their entrepot to the Empire, such decisions were vulnerable to being rescinded later and production shifted elsewhere. When such a shift in production was contemplated, it would appear that Canadian branch plants frequently requested the advice and assistance of the trade commissioner stationed at the prospective site. This posed a thorny dilemma. To what extent should Trade and Commerce carry out its mandate for overseas service to Canadian industrial capital in these cases, when it knew that it might be damaging to the long-term interests of Canadian trade? The department compromised. Trade commissioners were instructed to avoid "encouraging" such migrations "because it has not been considered that Canada can spare the export of capital for this purpose." All assistance short of official approval, however, seems to have been rendered. One widely experienced Trade and Commerce official noted that "we have, of course, given the best advice possible as to labour conditions, raw materials, factory regulations and the like, and have tried to avoid any precise advice."[56]

On occasion, the trade commissioners appear also to have believed it a normal part of their duties to act as a lobby for the branch plants with the governments of the countries where they were posted. This was particularly true of the Canadian content controversy. In 1926, the agent in New Zealand wrote his branch director in Ottawa of his activities in this regard:

> I am enclosing herewith two clippings which appeared in the Wellington papers recently, relating to the annual meeting of the New

> Zealand Association of British Manufacturers, from which you will see that . . . a direct insinuation was made that Canada is now controlled economically by the United States, so far as the motor industry is concerned . . . . I think you will agree with me that this is . . . a matter for continual work to overcome whatever prejudices may be created . . . . I may say that an effort has been made in a very informal way to counteract any impressions which may have been left in the minds of the Cabinet Ministers concerned . . . .[57]

The Director of the Commercial Intelligence Branch was favourably impressed with this trade commissioner's initiative and replied approvingly:

> I think you would do well to endeavour to overcome, in every way you can, any prejudices which may exist in New Zealand against purchasing from Canadian plants . . . associated with American interests. In our efforts to increase the export trade of Canada, we cannot leave out of the picture branch industries of American firms.[58]

Conclusion

In the interwar period, our discussion reflects for the first time the growing importance of the branch plant industrial sector. By way of contrast to the earlier era in which Canadian-owned industry was dominant, a coherent export strategy was developed by a number of important branch plants – import substitution for the Empire. These enterprises transferred some of their export business from their U.S. operations to take advantage of the preferential tariffs that Canada enjoyed in Great Britain and the white Dominions.

We have seen that this strategy, while it may have served the short-term interests of the U.S. firms in question, did little to develop the long-term export potential of Canadian industry. It was superficial, temporary, and incomplete. Under it, Canadian manufactured exports were often merely the products of warehouse-assembly processing. The strategy was doomed to early collapse because of a number of ideological and economic barriers in its intended markets. As well, the other Dominions manifested a growing determination to begin their own ISI as soon as their domestic markets grew large enough to support economic production. Finally, a significant number of U.S. firms did not participate in this strategy. They forbade exports by their Canadian subsidiaries because they found it more profitable to centre foreign trade in the parent operation.

The collapse of the imperial import substitution strategy in this period marks the beginning of the modern era in Canada's inability to export finished manufactures. From this point, the familiar contemporary pattern of a fragmented domestic market filled with small, uneconomic producers incapable of being internationally competitive, even if their parents were to permit them export freedom, became firmly established. Canadians, with the exception of iron and steel production, retained ownership of only those industrial sectors which were to decline in world trade.

Despite the extremely high stakes, the state failed to act decisively during this period to put Canadian industry in a less vulnerable position. Although problems with the branch plant structure were recognized by the political elite, they were not judged to be fundamental. King, for example, in concert with what we shall discover in Chapter 6 to be the economic orthodoxy of his era, believed that Canada was inevitably progressing from a resource export stage to a stage in which manufactured exports would be dominant. Accordingly, little in the way of remedy was offered except a rather limp device to encourage the production of the 50 per cent Canadian car.

CHAPTER 6

Blocked Exports

Remarkable. Although an overworked word, it serves to capture the flavour of Canada's economic expansion in the quarter century or so that began with World War II. To illustrate, from 1938 to 1968 Canada's gross national expenditure rose by five times, the value of manufacturing output by six times, and the net value of capital stock invested in manufacturing by over four times (all figures adjusted to compensate for inflation).[1]

Equally impressive was the tremendous swelling of the capital stock of direct foreign investment in Canada during the post-Depression era. Two central economic sectors, manufacturing and mining, moved from a position of majority Canadian ownership to majority foreign ownership with two-fifths foreign control at the beginning of this period and three-fifths at its conclusion. In the two decades after the war alone, the book value of foreign investment increased sevenfold. As indicated by Table Ten, this expansion consolidated itself at these peak levels through the 1960's. Since the early 1970's, a moderate decline has set in. This has been the result of mergers, government takeovers, and a few controversial reclassifications by Statistics Canada of the nationality of some large corporations.

Taken as a whole, then, this period was marked both by striking advances in industrial activity and foreign control of the firms responsible for carrying it out. What was the relationship between the two phenomena? As we examine this era, we must never lose sight of the fact that those with political and economic power in Canada generally believed that foreign investment had *caused* this economic growth. One particularly forthright Ontario Minister of Trade and Development submitted in 1968 that "we'd still be chasing Indians if it were not for foreign investment."[2] It is a short step from this kind of identification of foreign investment as the force behind economic growth to a conviction that the promotion of foreign direct investment will produce even more economic growth, which, in turn, will pay

TABLE TEN

Foreign Control of Canadian Manufacturing, 1970 and 1979 (per cent of total)

	Assets		*Sales*	
	1970	*1979*	*1970*	*1979*
Food	44	37	33	34
Beverages	32	31	30	35
Tobacco products	86	100	82	99
Rubber products	93	90	91	89
Leather products	22	20	20	18
Textile mills	53	56	49	56
Knitting mills	21	18	18	15
Clothing industries	14	14	11	12
Wood industries	33	20	23	17
Furniture industries	21	10	19	10
Paper and allied industries	45	39	47	38
Printing, publishing, and allied	15	12	13	11
Primary metals	43	14	41	17
Metal fabricating	45	37	43	39
Machinery	75	55	77	62
Transport equipment	85	73	90	87
Electrical products	68	59	66	65
Non-metallic mineral products	63	72	53	61
Petroleum and coal products	100	69	99	83
Chemicals and chemical products	80	76	83	77
Miscellaneous manufacturing	51	45	50	42
Total manufacturing	**59**	**49**	**56**	**53**

SOURCES: Statistics Canada, *Annual Reports*, 1971 and 1979; Corporations and Labour Unions Returns Act, Part I, March, 1974, and December, 1981.

large electoral dividends to the government or political party able to associate itself most closely with it. Those few outside the centres of state power who worried about the long-term consequences of foreign economic domination were accused of attacking the standard of living of ordinary Canadians and/or of trying to turn Canada into a northern "banana republic."

It is hard to comprehend the logic behind this kind of rhetoric. By far the greatest part of the foreign investment splurge was generated within Canada. Only one-quarter of the 1946-1960 expansion in foreign-controlled enterprises was funded from foreign sources.[3] During the last two decades, this portion has fallen under one-fifth. To a significant extent, the existing pre-war complement of branch plants, especially in the growth consumer industries of the manufacturing sector, simply expanded in step with the remarkably strong post-war domestic economy. Funding came mainly from retained earnings on operating profits made in Canada, loans from Canadian financial institutions and investors, and investment incentives built into the tax system. It is important to note, however, that the advantage of access to the relatively small share of imported foreign capital Canada utilized must be balanced against the inevitable return of dividends to foreign parents. During the 1970's, this repatriation had reached levels twice as great as the value of new foreign capital entering Canada.

The mistaken opinions of our political leaders in this instance would have been of little consequence for our inquiry if foreign investment had affected Canada's ability to export manufactures in a positive or even benign manner. As will become apparent, this was not to be. Rather, the branch plant economy was to reinforce and further institutionalize the inward-looking nature of the earlier import substitution model of Canadian industrialization. Although there were admittedly some exceptional firms, barriers to subsidiary exports generally were to come in two main forms: administrative and technological.

Most foreign parents imposed formal restrictions on the export of products from their Canadian factories. These limitations often were based in a conception of the Canadian market as part of the U.S. company's domestic operations. According to this view, the subsidiary had been allocated its territory within North America and exports were the province of the international division of head office. Yet, even if Canadian branch plants had been given complete export freedom, most were not in a position to make anything of it. C.P. Kindleburger reminds us that "a new good . . . is likely to expand exports to the extent that other countries are unable initially to produce it but want to consume it."[4] Unfortunately, Canadian subsidiaries lacked the technological punch to be able to generate internationally marketable innovations. Highly dependent on their parents for imports of machinery, processes, and patents, the technological capabilities of the typical branch plant were slight. They frequently extended no further than inconsequential modifications of the parent's line of products to meet the peculiarities of Canadian taste.

"Chronic" Technological Dependence

The tripwires of the import substitution for the Empire export strategy were discussed in the last chapter. One of the most important of these, it will be recalled, was the well-publicized desire of the other Dominions to initiate their own ISI process for the U.S. goods being shipped from Canadian factories during the 1920's and 1930's.

Nevertheless, those who understood the ultimate implications of this trend were less concerned than they might have been. L.D. Wilgress, then director of Canada's trade commissioner service, told the 1939 annual meeting of the CMA that the country would continue to have many advantages in exporting her manufactures to the "less-developed" agricultural countries now beginning their own secondary industries. The branch plants would save the day for Canadian trade. It was logical, Wilgress reasoned, for U.S. investors to assign "a share" of their export business to their Canadian subsidiaries because of the small size of our domestic market. "Although greatly assisted by preferential tariffs," he observed, "it is a natural tendency based on sound business practice."

Hence, in the course of time, "North American skill" and Canada's contiguous position to "the greatest and most progressive manufacturing country in the world" would allow us to move up the technological ladder. Rather than the consumer goods on which the modest export successes of the 1920's had been based, Canada's branch plants would now ship capital or producer goods such as machinery.

> . . . all the time these countries may be building up new manufacturing industries we shall not be standing still, but will be developing new export industries, the products of which will be shipped abroad in place of those no longer required in our principal markets because of the development of home industries. In other words, the process is one of constant change. Export opportunities for some products in certain markets may gradually be reduced but new openings will be created for other products.[5]

Wilgress's logic was actually very sound if applied to an industrial structure with a mature capital goods industry. As we already know, this was something Canada had never developed. Following their ISI pattern, Canadian manufacturers had for the most part left their technological base in the hands of others. We could hardly expect to export what we could not produce for ourselves. Worse, lacking a potent capital goods industry, from where was the stimulative impetus for the creation of new exportable products to come?

If there was ever any room for doubt in this matter, World War II dispelled it completely. Ironically, on the eve of the war, the president of the CMA had suggested that Canada was basically self-sufficient in machinery and "not depending too greatly on external sources for supplies which might be cut off by a war."[6] This was indeed a balloon begging to be popped. As a 1947 government report recorded, pre-war Canada lacked "an integrated heavy industry" and exhibited a "high degree of dependence upon American and British sources for heavy equipment, tools, and machinery, specialized materials and parts." Consequently, when the war came, "much of the machinery and equipment" for defence production "had to be imported" and a new Canadian machine tool industry "virtually created."[7]

In his authoritative history of the 1939-45 Canadian war effort, C.P. Stacey concluded that "Canadian industry generally was based upon American production methods, standards and techniques, and was dependent upon American imports of machinery, spare parts, subassemblies and components."[8] This observation was nowhere more true than in the capital goods industry. There, the situation was so desperate that it became the infant ward of the federal state. Through the Department of Munitions and Supply and various Crown corporations, the government centralized the purchasing, warehousing, and distribution of the nation's production machinery. Such matters as deciding on priorities for acquisition, reallocating machines between factories, and loaning equipment to manufacturers were all in the province of these agencies. So, too, were the design and engineering of new machinery and the supervision of production in new and existing machine tool factories in Canada.[9]

All of this unprecedented state control may have rendered the technological answers to Canada's wartime manufacturing headaches, but the changes it wrought were not sufficiently radical to provide for a long-term solution. No sooner did production fall back into private hands than the nation was in the midst of a capital investment splurge. While consumer goods industries were compensating for undermaintenance during the Depression and war years, new resource extraction projects were opening for business. Incredibly, two-thirds of the necessary machinery and equipment put in place for this investment in 1948 were imported, as were three-quarters of the machine tools. In that year as well, Canada was the world's largest importer of machinery, equipment, and parts, bringing in a total in excess of the combined value of American and British imports of these commodities.[10]

These massive imports of capital goods contributed in no small way to Canada's post-war foreign exchange crisis. In 1947, Alex Skelton, a principal adviser to C.D. Howe (who, as Minister of Munitions and Supply, Reconstruction, and then Trade and Commerce, dominated federal economic policy-making between 1940 and 1957), provided his boss with a strikingly clear exposition of Canada's quandary:

> Canadian manufacturing industry in general, and in particular Canadian branch plants modelled on the parent U.S. industry, consume a proportion of U.S. raw materials, semi-processed materials, tools, equipment and services in every unit they produce currently. If in addition, a capital expansion programme is being undertaken (as at present) this involves additional U.S. "content" (materials, services and capital charges).[11]

Skelton took care to distinguish between the "abnormal" causes of Canadian foreign exchange difficulties related to post-war dislocations and the "chronic" problems which stemmed from foreign direct investment. "Temporary expedients" would suffice for the "abnormal" predicament, but the "chronic" problems required "some fundamental adjustments." However, "the necessities of the moment may help in getting them started." In Skelton's mind, the needed "fundamental adjustments" would have weaned Canadian manufacturers from "simply accepting the convenient model of U.S. industry which is naturally based on U.S. raw materials." Pressure would have been placed on the branch plants to increase Canadian production content or to "develop specialized production in Canada for export to U.S. domestic or export markets as an offset to the Canadian industry's imports from the U.S.A."

Even though he averred agreement "in general" with Skelton's analysis, the policy solution of Howe and the Liberals leaned more in the direction of a "temporary expedient."[12] In November, 1947, the Emergency Exchange Conservation Act placed prohibitions and quotas on imports of consumer goods and demanded the licensing of imports of capital goods.[13] By this means, Howe supposed that the assembly character of Canadian industrial production could be rounded into a more complete process. The restrictions, Howe pronounced, "had the very decided effect of stimulating the manufacture of components which had previously been imported, not because they could not have been made just as well in Canada, but because it was easier to import them than it was to organize their production in this country." In this regard, the intent of the legislation was very similar to the 1920's attempt to upgrade the Canadian content of automobiles. Indeed, within the capital goods sector, automobiles and trucks were the primary targets for component replacement by domestic production. The other principal ingredient in the capital goods program appears to have been the deferral of investments for commercial, office, service, and amusement purposes.[14]

TABLE ELEVEN

Canadian Imports of Machinery and Imports Classified According to Purpose, 1946-1960 (per cent of total imports)

Year	*Machinery**	*Value ranked against other import groups***	*Consumer goods****	*Producer materials and equipment*****
1946	6	1	18	45
1947	7	1	24	47
1948	8	1	21	50
1949	7	1	25	48
1950	7	1	26	51
1951	8	1	23	49
1952	9	1	24	45
1953	9	1	26	43
1954	9	1	24	43
1955	9	1	25	44
1956	11	1	25	46
1957	11	1	24	46
1958	10	1	26	43
1959	10	1	29	44
1960	10	1	29	44

* excludes household and agriculture
** rank adjusted from 1946-1949 in concert with post-1950 DBS practice of separating refined and crude petroleum
*** includes farm and road transport equipment but excludes food
****excludes farm and construction equipment

SOURCES: Computed from Canada, Dominion Bureau of Statistics, *Trade of Canada*, vol. 1; *Canada Year Book*, various years.

In short, virtually nothing was being done about the "chronic" nature of the problem. As Table Eleven demonstrates, capital goods for the resource and manufacturing sectors flooded across the border before, during, and after the import control program was withdrawn in 1950. The most that might be suggested is that the domestic content of Canadian production was modestly augmented after 1951. But, unfortunately, that was all that seems to have been desired. Shortly after the Emergency Exchange Conservation Act was proclaimed, Howe signalled the manufacturers that he did not want them to rush into the production of capital goods that could not be "produced competitively in Canada under normal conditions."[15] He apparently felt that Canadian ISI manufacturing could be deepened by greater domestic production of components only if foreign machinery and technology continued to be used to equip our factories. To illustrate, he objected to a proposed 10 per cent excise tax on U.S. capital goods imports because Canadians could not supply such machinery. A tax would simply increase costs and discourage needed capital investment without checking imports.[16]

Without the necessary "fundamental adjustments" in the 1940's and 1950's, it should not be surprising that Canada remained dependent on foreign suppliers of capital goods through the 1960's and 1970's. In fact, we are still the world's largest machinery importer on a per capita basis.[17] Worse, as Canada has moved toward freer trade in recent years, our machinery and equipment manufacturers actually have been losing further ground because of the removal of a significant portion of their tariff protection. In 1965, they were able to supply 46 per cent of the domestic market but by 1978 this had fallen to 34 per cent. Our serious deficit position in this keystone sector for technological innovation is portrayed in Table Twelve. One bright spot in the otherwise bleak picture of recent years has been the growth of a moderately respectable export trade led by resource-based machinery. These same producers, however, have not been able to hold their traditionally solid share of the Canadian market.

Besides the long-standing import dependence of our capital goods sector, there are other ways of measuring Canada's inability to create exportable innovations. For example, a number of studies have shown that multinational firms generally prefer to concentrate their research activities in their home countries. Local patents are then taken out to protect this developed technology in host countries like Canada. Such patents have the dual functions of impeding local technological advance through imitation and adaptation and ensuring a monopoly position for the foreign firm in the local market. This monopoly

TABLE TWELVE

Machinery Trade by Major Machinery Producing Countries, 1973

Country	*Percentage of domestic requirements imported*	*Percentage of production exported*
United States	10	17
Japan	10	24
Federal Germany	34	63
Great Britain	34	50
France	50	45
Sweden	50	54
Canada	60	30
Canada (1978)	66	40

SOURCE: Canada, Employment and Immigration, Task Force on Labour Market Development, Technical Study 28, Peat Marwick and Partners, "The Medium-Term Employment Outlook: The Canadian Equipment and Machinery Industry," July, 1981, Exhibit II.

position allows the multinational to engage in a number of restrictive business practices, including limitation of export sales.[18]

Evidence of the link between the global marketing and product development policies of foreign firms in Canada has been mounting in the last two decades. It is now well-recognized that Canada is among the technologically weakest of the industrialized countries. A government report of the early 1970's found that approximately 95 per cent of patents issued in Canada are registered to foreign owners, mostly U.S. residents. Further, of twenty-five countries examined, Canada stood first in the percentage of foreign-owned patents and last in the percentage of domestically owned patents.[19] Other authors have pointed to the staggering expense of research and development activity in "high technology" manufactures as an incentive for the establishment of Canadian subsidiaries to help recoup some of this cost. As a consequence, Canada has been left with a "fragmented and inefficient" branch plant structure holding little "technological depth" and without "the size and sophistication needed to be competitive on world markets."[20]

Another study of fifty Canadian subsidiaries also discovered a strong relationship between the branch plant economy and the erection of technological barriers to manufactured exports. In general, it reported, the research facilities of the branch plants tend to be more directly related to product adaptation for the Canadian market than to innovation for export markets. In instances where the branch plants came up with innovations demonstrating export promise, parent head offices made decisions on whether production would remain in Canada, would be shared with another international division, or would be "pulled back" to the parent corporation. "In no case," it was affirmed, "did we find a Canadian subsidiary that felt it had the freedom to enter foreign markets at will with a product which it thought could be produced in Canada and competitively exported."[21]

The federal government response to branch plant reliance on technology transfers from their parents has been an attempt to fill Canada's innovative vacuum by giving financial support to a wide range of research and development (R & D) programs. In fact, the Canadian government carries out a larger proportion of national R & D activities, many with direct industrial applications, than is true for any other major industrial country. Yet, as Table Thirteen demonstrates, even massive government spending cannot offer a long-term solution to this structural problem. As one mid-1970's study put it, "broad brush" programs of state assistance for industrial R & D are not highly effective because "most of the high technology and manufacturing sectors of the Canadian economy are dominated by foreign ownership, but only certain types of subsidiaries have any real potential for innovation leading to greater exports and domestic employment."[22]

TABLE THIRTEEN

National Research and Development Performance, Selected Industrial Countries, 1977 or 1979

Country	*R & D expenditures as a percentage of gross domestic product*	*Average annual percentage change in the 1970's*
United States	2.39	1.5
Federal Germany	2.27	4.1
Great Britain	2.20	1.9
Japan	2.04	6.9
Netherlands	1.99	2.7
Sweden	1.87	6.5
France	1.81	3.1
Belgium	1.37	4.6
Canada	1.04	1.6

SOURCE: Statistics Canada, *Annual Review of Science Statistics*, 1981 (May, 1982), p. 9.

Administered Markets – ("Only in Canada, You Say?")

Reliance on borrowed foreign technology, as discussed in Chapter 2, does not by itself preclude the evolution of a more independent technological base capable of sustaining world competitive manufacturing. What is required is a commitment from industry to assimilate, adapt, and innovate on the base of the technology it initially borrowed. In our survey of the half century before World War II, we could discover no zeal for this endeavour on the part of the great majority of Canadian manufacturers. Observers of the time often concluded that our industrialists either were unenterprising or were mesmerized by the domestic market. We have intimated that more formal administrative barriers written into licensing agreements or genetically encoded in the subsidiary-parent relationship may have provided a better explanation for Canada's early silence in world markets. When we reach the post-war epoch, however, there is little room for further doubt. In keeping with the by then dominant presence of direct foreign investment in the economy, eyewitnesses after World War II began to record more clearly the restricted nature of Canadian production.

This era in Canadian trade was rung in with public alarms from the 1945 publication of *Canada and International Cartels*. Undertaken by the Combines Investigation Commission as the war was winding down, it was a remarkable study of export blocking. Three hundred manufacturing and trading companies had been surveyed to determine the effects of foreign ownership, patent and licence agreements, or other cartel arrangements on their international trade. The report distinguished three levels at which export restrictions had been placed on Canadian firms – licensee, branch plant, and international cartel. A number of instances were uncovered in which Canadian licensees were forbidden to export. The following company statement was cited as a typical example:

> We have confined our manufacturing and distribution of the various items of [deleted] equipment, produced under the patents and licences which we hold, to the Dominion of Canada because those patents and licences confer rights exercisable only within this country .... To the extent that any article we manufacture is patented our export of it to a foreign country would expose us to infringement proceedings at the instance of a patent-holder or licensee in that country.[23]

Not surprisingly, cases in which foreign branch plants had been left free to determine their own export policies were "relatively rare."[24] Generally, it was concluded, export policies were formulated to maximize the sales potential of the parent firms.

The most revealing data dealt with international cartels. These, according to the report, were formed through agreements between U.S. and European manufacturers to split world markets between themselves. Canada, for the purposes of such agreements, was considered as part of the U.S. market. If production was established in Canada it was on the condition that no attempt be made to export. One such cartel arrangement investigated by the Commission involved the chemical firm CIL (Canadian Industries Limited, jointly controlled by the U.S. DuPont and the British ICI, Imperial Chemical Industrial Limited). CIL, the evidence indicated, was viewed by its controlling partners as nothing more than their beast of burden in the Canadian market. Lammont DuPont, president of DuPont between 1926 and 1940, was quoted as stating that

> We regard CIL as the vehicle of industrial effort for ICI and DuPont in Canada . . . . The theory back of the CIL operation, so far as ICI and DuPont are concerned, is expressed in the old saying "Canada for Canadians" meaning–the industrial operations of the partners in Canada are intended to be conducted through CIL. CIL was not set up to do anything else and has, we believe, never been considered so. If the above is correct, it seems to us to follow directly and as a matter of course that CIL shall stay in Canada and not spread out into other countries, either by laying down plants, exporting their products or licensing under their processes, unless both ICI and DuPont believe it is advantageous to so spread out and then only to the extent and for the time and under the conditions that ICI and DuPont agree upon.

This policy, it was disclosed, meant that CIL had to resist "considerable pressure" from the Canadian government to develop its export trade and could not take advantage of tariff preferences in areas like the British West Indies and Australia.[25]

This report by the Combines Investigation Commission was the last published by the government to be so explicit on the subject of export blocking. And, naturally enough, the branch plants themselves were not about to proclaim from the rooftops their policies in an affair so potentially sensitive to Canadian national sensibilities. Yet, although unfortunately out of the reach of the general public, alarming evidence of the administrative barriers to Canada's manufactured exports has accumulated since 1945 in the files of Trade and Commerce.

Departmental awareness of the serious structural restraints on the trade of Canadian subsidiaries built steadily toward a crescendo in the first two decades following World War II. Directly after the German surrender, a meeting of the trade commissioner service was held to discuss the "absence" of an "overall" Canadian trade policy in respect to foreign enterprises. This division advised its deputy minister of its concern in this matter.

> Fear was expressed that some of the larger industrial organizations or agricultural groups are making their own export policies without consideration being given to the best interests of the country as a whole. A representative of an important Canadian company controlled from the U.S.A. manufacturing primary materials recently expressed the opinion that Canada should concentrate on the production of these raw materials and that his company was adopting the policy of in general discouraging the manufacture of finished goods from their raw material in Canada. Examples have come to the attention of the Department where parent companies abroad have restricted the freedom to export of their controlled branch industries in Canada.[26]

More and more such "examples" were to surface in subsequent years. Indeed, in the post-war period, Trade and Commerce correspondence became very matter-of-fact on the export blocking question. Take, for example, this reply to an overseas officer from a director of the Export Division on his department's failure to unearth a Canadian supplier for a potential foreign order. "I am not particularly surprised at the attitude of the manufacturers as most of the firms are branches of American houses and are not too interested in shipping from Canada," he said.[27] Or witness this response by a commodity officer in the Export Division to a complaint that a specific branch plant could not export. This firm, he noted,

> is controlled by its parent company in the United States as far as exports are concerned .... There are dozens of firms in the same category. They are established to manufacture for the Canadian market. There are also dozens of Canadian firms which are licensed to manufacture for the Canadian market only. The only way to solve this problem is for Canadian manufacturers to design and make competitive substitutes which can be exported. The above situation has existed in the industrial equipment industry since almost the time of Confederation and is a widely known fact in the engineering business.[28]

Trade and Commerce was frequently to find itself embarrassed and compromised by these circumstances. Many subsidiaries were in the habit of passing along foreign inquiries generated by the Canadian trade commissioners to their parent operations, who then pursued the order. The department appears to have responded by attempting to keep a record of the export policies of Canadian branch plants. But this system often broke down, much to the annoyance of the trade commissioners in the field.[29] In one particularly notable incident, the executive vice-president of a U.S. subsidiary explained to a trade commissioner who was soliciting orders on his behalf that his firm, after all, was not interested in exporting. Confusion had arisen from the unauthorized attendance of a company officer at a 1960 Trade and Commerce export trade promotion conference in Ottawa.

> I am sorry to admit that the whole situation is a complete surprise to me. Apparently when the invitation to attend the Conference was sent to [us] it was received by a junior member of our company and he took it upon himself to determine who should attend and what should be discussed. For this I apologize. So that you may set your records straight [this subsidiary] is a marketing group set up to sell all the products of the [U.S. parent] . . . . Any questions on policies regarding foreign export must be cleared with [our parent] at the following [New York] address.[30]

By 1957, departmental concern had grown to the point where Professor A.G. Huson from the Faculty of Business Administration at the University of Western Ontario was commissioned to do a special study on export blocking. Working with a survey sample of fifty foreign-owned subsidiaries, Huson determined that

> less than half have appointed Canadian export managers, less than one in four can be said to be developing Canadian export experience, only one in five have separate export organizations, and one in ten have their own independent foreign representative. Only one in three claim freedom to compete with their parent; only one in four, a voice in their company's export policy; and three-quarters declare that their exports are strictly controlled by the parent.[31]

It is reasonable to suppose that these figures roughly squared with the daily field experience of Trade and Commerce officers. Six years later, Huson's conclusions were cited in a background document prepared for a meeting of trade commissioners. As well, in their conference report, the trade commissioners repeated that "probably 75%

of the [subsidiary] companies have their exports strictly controlled by the parent."[32]

Unseen by the public, a miniature storm of activity gathered around this question through the late 1950's and early 1960's. In 1958, Trade and Commerce and External Affairs jointly agreed to approach U.S. parent companies in an effort to get them to relax export controls on their Canadian subsidiaries. "Few executives will deny," it was noted, "that U.S. control of secondary industry in Canada has a tendency to reduce prospects of export business for the subsidiary company, particularly of any exports to the U.S. market, unless a conscious effort is made in that direction." Still, these approaches should not be so aggressive as to leave any doubt "in the mind of U.S. executives about Canada's continuing interest in U.S. investment in Canada, and the continuing need for capital for future development."[33]

From this point, the topic of export barriers imposed by direct foreign investment in Canada emerged on a least five occasions in six years during formal, high-level departmental meetings – in 1958, twice in 1960, and again in 1962 and 1963. Until the last of these meetings, discussion always centred on how best to "exploit all opportunities for the education of the parent corporation in the Canadian point of view."[34] The education process, however, was slow, frustrating, and often checkmated. One trade commissioner, who called on a large number of parent companies in Chicago, listed the obstacles placed in his path:

> Some firms frankly designated the Canadian market as a domestic market in which they were not interested in export. Some had revised the organization of the Canadian company to fit in with their overall designs, reduced costs, and automatically cut out possibilities of export. Some stated that they were very desirous of expanding their Canadian operation through exports in order to make their Canadian firm pay, but felt that the high cost of parts and components which they had to bring into Canada, plus the smallness of the Canadian market, rendered Canadian products non-competitive. They pointed out that the very factor which encouraged them to enter Canada, i.e. the Canadian tariff, militated against the possibility of export. Some considered it advantageous to maintain the export offices in the United States, but it was evident quite often that the U.S. export office was not too conscious of the operation of the Canadian subsidiary.[35]

The account of another trade commissioner leaves us with a very clear sense of the curious mixture of humility, timidity, and missionary zeal with which the problem was tackled:

> . . . my own modest efforts during the time I have been in New York have revealed how tortuous and difficult it can be to influence parent company policies. At the outset, one normally requires an entree to the company for other reasons, in order to establish the contacts that eventually make it possible to allude to parent company policies without causing resentment. Some frustration results when, in many instances, one learns that Canadian subsidiaries are considered part of the parent company's domestic operations and *not* part of their international division. For example, about two years ago we established a contact with the head of the purchasing department of [a Canadian parent in New York state] . . . . This resulted in establishing a contact with the Senior Vice President in the International Division. Better than half a day was spent in the International Division, only to learn that the Canadian subsidiary is considered part of their domestic operation, and that only overseas plants reported to the International Division. Eventually, contact was established with a Senior Vice President in the domestic operations, who seemed to feel there was some merit in permitting their Canadian plants to seek markets in Commonwealth countries. However, he informed me that this would have to be a decision of the Financial Vice President and Treasurer, who would have to be convinced that the parent company's profits could be enhanced by diverting some exports from Canada. I lunched with the Treasurer, and while he seemed sympathetic, he advised me that this would be a matter of major policy requiring a decision of the Chairman of the Board and the Board of Directors itself. He promised to discuss it with the Chairman, and we are hopeful that, ultimately, some change in this large corporation's policies may be developed.[36]

Faced with responses like these, it is no wonder that doubts began to emerge on the adequacy of education alone. These doubts were to appear full blown in the subsidiary export session of the 1963 trade commissioners' conference in Ottawa. "It is becoming increasingly evident that contact between departmental officers in Ottawa and abroad with parents and subsidiaries alike could not possibly cover all the subsidiaries located in Canada, even after a long period of years," this group concluded in its final report. "A system of meaningful incentives and perhaps legislation, therefore, would seem necessary to orient the thinking of subsidiary companies toward the export field."

Additional and augmented tax breaks and government export services were among the incentives reviewed by the conference. The legislative mechanisms that received attention ranged from regulatory licensing to export quotas, all with a view to "provide a certain degree of export autonomy to existing as well as newly established Canadian subsidiaries." Not unmindful of the "immediate adverse reaction" such legislation might provoke, the trade commissioners nevertheless advised their political masters to proceed.

> Contact with subsidiaries and parents in the past and the experiences of other countries would suggest that foreign firms are not deterred by legislation which does not prevent a profitable return on investment. Undue anxiety and thus reluctance to consider any form of legislation dealing with foreign subsidiaries seems unwarranted.

Finally, the conference agreed that a new survey be conducted to further assess export autonomy among the branch plants. This was to be followed by "high priority" approaches to key firms.[37]

A thorough critique of foreign restraints on Canadian trade had become deeply imbued in important segments of Trade and Commerce by the mid-1960's. So much was this the case that when a prominent individual with a special interest in export promotion was preparing a speech on the topic "Canadian Businessmen – Are They Meeting the Challenge?" he approached the department for ideas and background information, and then as a response he was fired this missive by a clearly vexed division chief:

> The biggest problem facing the Department in its endeavours to expand Canada's exports rests in the fact that the major capital and industrial plant equipment manufacturers in Canada are controlled by foreign capital . . . . The foreign subsidiary companies . . . have the largest manufacturing complexes in Canada and, as a consequence, the financial resources to permit sales on an international basis . . . . Canadian companies in certain industries have been found to be less than keen when asked to consider doing further processing in Canada on certain raw materials . . . . This in turn leads to the question [of] foreign control of our larger industries and the effect on their Canadian subsidiaries' export policies. Many of these primary producers have plants abroad which fabricate goods for the world market from Canadian raw materials. The Canadian company in certain cases is limited to the Canadian market or, at most the Canadian and Commonwealth markets. In many cases the

Canadian company is unable to quote on export enquiries directly but must get the foreign parent companies permission which is not always granted.[38]

"Baying at the Moon"

When the trade commissioners advised against "undue anxiety" in confronting the branch plant barriers to Canadian export, they were to prove themselves far bolder than their political leaders. Virtually without exception, our elected officials ignored, misunderstood, or even deliberately obscured the issue. Wedded to the promotion of foreign investment as an instrument of economic growth, they were generally loath to rock the boat they hoped would keep them electorally afloat.

In some senses, C.D. Howe can be seen as the archetypal figure here. Understanding as he did the surface dimensions of the problem, he would have been delighted to enlist the voluntary co-operation of the branch plants in correcting it. Still, he simply did not consider the issue of sufficient importance to challenge their considerable economic and political power directly. Consider the previously discussed Emergency Exchange Conservation Act of 1947. Among Howe's principal objectives in bringing forward this legislation was to improve the nation's foreign exchange crisis not only by restricting imports but also by stimulating the export of Canadian resource *and* manufactured products. To this end, Howe's officials came up with a complex scheme to allow industries to import more if they increased their foreign sales in tandem. In an editorial entitled "Why we can't go on as 2nd class Americans," the *Financial Post* applauded Howe's initiative. "Both branch plants and a good many Canadian plants which have working agreements with U.S. firms have their activities regulated by assorted agreements on marketing, exports, pricing and so on," this business journal observed. "But if Canada is to go forward aggressively to full mature development, some way must be found of escaping our position of economic colonialism and of letting Canada have her full share of North American industry."[39]

In the longer run, Howe hoped a reciprocity treaty with the Americans would introduce more manufactured exports from Canada into the U.S. market. Prime Minister King scuttled the whole idea, although we will see in the next chapter it was in keeping with the free trade economic orthodoxy of the federal civil service elite in this era. Not only did King feel that such a program would be politically dangerous, but he viewed Howe's notion of selling manufactures to the U.S. as "absurd."[40]

King was right in this. Without a frontal attack on both the technological and administrative restraints outlined in this chapter, no general progress in exporting industrial goods could realistically be expected. More knowledgeable on this question than most of their successors were to prove themselves, Howe's opponents of the day taunted him with the feeble nature of his attempted reform. Concluding that branch plant behaviour could not be altered "merely by reasoning with them, or by any sort of inducement which has no teeth behind it," the CCF referred pointedly to the lessons on export blocking of *Canada and International Cartels*.[41] But it was J.M. Macdonald, president of the Dominion Progressive Conservative Association, who really belled the cat. He told Howe that "he might as well go bay at the moon" as get the subsidiaries to "change their whole way of doing things."

> I have talked to people in business who assure me that certain things are indeed possible. United States subsidiaries will be able to manufacture some things, some parts, and send them across the line, but I am assured that it cannot amount to much in a short time. It is reversing the trend; it is contrary to the policy that brought people here who set up industries in Canada, and the minister will have quite a time.[42]

As predicted, Howe's plan to persuade branch plants to export to the U.S. soon fizzled and died. Yet, in the boom conditions of the 1950's, the Liberals saw little point in pursuing the matter. Massive resource exports were filling the gap. As Howe mused in 1954 when he admitted that Canadian manufacturers were finding it "increasingly difficult" to compete on world markets, this "should provide no particular cause for alarm."

> Canada does not lack for export opportunities and it is not necessary or even desirable for Canadian producers to be able to compete in world markets in all lines of merchandise. In our principal staple export items, Canadian producers are highly competitive the world over. So long as this is the case there is little basically wrong with our foreign trade position.[43]

Yet, Howe had not dismissed the problem. Nor was he afraid to raise it again when it suited him. Perhaps prompted by evidence of export blocking presented at the hearings of the Royal Commission on Canada's Economic Prospects, Howe made a pitch for improved export performance from the branch plants in 1956 speeches in Milwaukee and Chicago. He complained:

> Too often our trade representatives abroad turn up export opportunities for a subsidiary operating in Canada only to find that the United States parent does not permit the export business to be done from the Canadian plant. Mind you we do not object to doing occasional export promotion for United States corporations but you will agree that it is rather difficult to justify the expense to the Canadian taxpayer. Once again I recognize that there are problems. But I do plead for a careful re-examination of export policies affecting branch plants . . . . I am not suggesting that U.S. corporations should act contrary to their interests. I am suggesting that they may be overlooking a good bet by not allowing their Canadian plants to take on more export business.[44]

His remarks were entirely consistent with his entire approach to the issue – co-operation, not coercion. In fact, it could well be argued that by speaking out Howe was attempting to forestall more drastic measures on the part of future Canadian governments. To illustrate, he drew the attention of his audience to the "rigid laws" restricting foreign investment in many countries. "There are no such laws in Canada. I hope there never will be," Howe affirmed. Nevertheless, he warned the U.S. businessmen that they must learn to "reckon" with the "pride" and "nationalism" of Canadians.

If Howe was reluctant to take the bit between his teeth here, at least he was straightforward about it. This is more than can be said for most who succeeded him at the locus of national economic policy-making. In general, politicians on both sides of the House of Commons maintained silence on the issue or minimized its importance. Their fire was saved for the far less meaningful problem of extraterritoriality. This is the application of U.S. law to American-owned subsidiaries in Canada to prevent them from accepting export orders from Communist countries like Cuba or China. Crying all the while that their rivals were surrendering Canadian sovereignty, the major parties used the issue of extraterritoriality as a convenient partisan club with which to hit each other when they were exiled to the Opposition benches. Meanwhile, it was (little or no) export business as usual for most Canadian factories.

The Conservatives had made some noises before being elected in 1957 that they were concerned about the more general problem.[45] Nevertheless, G. Churchill, their Trade and Commerce Minister, when asked about the matter in the House, lulled the members to sleep.

"This is a problem which is constantly under review," he assured everyone, "and by the process of education and persuasion we are finding that more and more companies are moving in the right direction."[46] Churchill's successor, George Hees, also found it expedient to duck direct questions on the issue.[47] Still, we have seen that, under the Conservatives, some Trade and Commerce bureaucrats refined a critique of foreign restraints on Canadian export trade.

When they returned to office in 1963, it would appear that the Liberals put a cap on these reform-minded civil servants. This was not what a casual observer of the Liberal re-entry might have initially expected. The Finance Minister, Walter Gordon, delivered a budget speech that U.S. investors found highly inflammatory. He called for a larger measure of Canadian ownership in the economy and greater controls over foreign direct investment. Export blocking was one area Gordon specifically singled out for corrective action: "Export markets should be sought actively wherever they may be found, and should not be limited out of regard for the interests of parent or associated companies abroad."[48]

But Gordon was not Minister of Trade and Commerce. That job belonged to Mitchell Sharp, a former deputy minister in the department under C.D. Howe and Gordon's nemesis in cabinet. Years later, Gordon was to refer with considerable understatement to Sharp's "lukewarm attitude on the independence issue."[49] Among Sharp's first business in his department was the scuttling of the trade commissioners' plans for a comprehensive survey of the export policies of U.S. parents.[50] It will be recalled that this had been by far the mildest of the recommendations on subsidiary exports to emerge from their 1963 conference. Sharp denied killing the survey, but went on record a year later with an intriguing definition of the national interest in this affair. He was opposed to asking the branch plant automakers if it was the "stated policy" of their parents to forbid exports outside of the Commonwealth. "I do not believe it would be in the public interest to give such general answers," he pronounced. "I feel they only confuse the issue."[51]

Gordon did not and could not survive the angry storm his budget attack on foreign investment whipped up both in the business community and in the Liberal Party. His promise of subsidiary export reform went with him. This, as well as other problems with branch plant performance, was now to be "addressed," and almost as speedily "resolved," by a set of guidelines for "good corporate behaviour" announced by the Liberals in 1966. Among the goals established was the "maximum development of market opportunities in other countries as well as Canada." Scarcely eight months later, the then Minister of Trade and Commerce, R. Winters, left the highly misleading impression that this thorny problem could be permanently resolved by such a superficial device. He paid tribute to the

> encouraging response as regards the development of export markets ... indicative of a growing participation by foreign-owned subsidiaries in markets abroad. I have been especially encouraged by the number of companies advising of their plans to give increased attention to foreign market opportunities, including those venturing into the export field for the first time.[52]

Buy Canadian

We will leave the last word to the manufacturers. How did they view their position in world markets as the modern era of branch plant dominance got under way? Remarkably, and risking some oversimplification, we find the same divisions around Canadian industrial strategy emerge here as we discovered in the earliest period of our industrialization. On the one side, led now by the foreign subsidiaries, stood the overwhelming majority oriented toward ISI and the domestic market; on the other, a small minority who lectured their compatriots on the virtues of developing internationally competitive specializations.

Chronicled in the last chapter was the withering away of Canada's Empire markets and with them the promise of a "permanent" basis for Canada's manufactured exports. During the 1940's and early 1950's, the demands of wartime production, combined with post-war dollar currency restrictions in Britain and the Dominions, destroyed most of what was still left of this trade. The majority of the branch plants had nowhere to turn but inward. With import replacement as their raison d'être, they carried with renewed vigour the turn-of-the-century banner "Canadian goods for Canadian people." Good, in this instance, was defined as those elements, like the tariff and immigration, which protected and extended the domestic market. Things which could threaten it, like freer trade and import competition, were opposed.

Exports, as they disposed of surplus production, were not in themselves bad. But home demand always came first. One CMA president, who apparently took exports more seriously than many, ventured so far as to say after the war that "Canada must produce first for Canada's needs but that in itself will not spell prosperity – a surplus must be produced for foreign markets before full employment can be reached."[53]

For a pesky minority, however, "surplus" export wasn't good enough. This group peppered the export sessions of CMA meetings with their quite different approach. To illustrate, one manufacturer summarized in a brief sentence the basis of an outward-oriented world specialization. "In our small Canadian population, the orders are comparatively small," he observed, "but in the export business there is no limit to the size of orders you may get, which would then cut down your costs and improve your export relations." In this regard, the presentation made by a Coleman Lamp and Stove official to the CMA was especially noteworthy. Pulling no punches, he lectured those "who feel satisfied with your smug little business at home, you who long years ago abandoned the pioneer spirit, who decry every little setback or depression which occurs here or across the line in the United States." During the Depression years of 1933 to 1938, he boasted, his company had tripled its overall sales. An export drive that increased the value of exports more than tenfold had made this possible. "Methods were improved and costs and selling prices were lowered as a direct result of the additional export volume," he related. This heightened efficiency allowed for even greater Canadian market penetration.[54]

Some of these outward-oriented industrialists were alive to the relationship between an independent technological base and the capacity to generate exportable innovations. T.L. Moffat, a household appliance manufacturer whose export objective was 40 to 50 per cent of turnover, wrote Trade and Commerce of the need for "vastly increased" government assistance for "research and engineering." In setting forth his case, Moffat paralleled many of the arguments presented in this book.

> It is important that Canadian manufacturers carry out a larger fraction of research and development work in this country rather than continue to import technical information. Of course it is realized that we cannot become leaders in all lines but there is no reason in the world why Canada, with the backing of an extensive research program, cannot attain a pre-eminent position in many products . . . . Two countries which have achieved outstanding success as a result of coordinated research are Sweden and Switzerland; notwithstanding many trade restrictions prevailing today, people everywhere specify and prefer Swedish electrical apparatus in many cases – chiefly because many of the products they turn out are superior . . . . Sweden has a comparatively small domestic market, yet Swedish competition in many items is felt in numerous foreign markets.[55]

The greater mass of manufacturers took offence at criticisms, direct or implied, of their export failings. "It is all very well," sniffed one

CMA president (who also happened to head a subsidiary), to advocate large-scale international trade, but

> our commercial relations should be guided always by the consideration of what is being made in Canada or what can be made in Canada. We should maintain such protective measures as will ensure the greatest possible volume of articles being made in Canada. We should extend our international trade by exchanging our products for articles which are not made in Canada or cannot be made in Canada.[56]

Yet another branch plant manager and CMA activist was to rail against the "illogical and misleading" opinion of many "experts" that export trade was to be the "provider of full employment, the fountainhead of prosperity and the panacea of all ills" in the post-war era.

> I am enunciating no new theory when I assert that export trade cannot possibly survive except by artificial aids (and in these I include letting the home trade subsidize it) without a flourishing home trade . . . . Therefore let us first enlarge our home trade by a larger population, by higher standards of living, made possible by lower production costs.[57]

Indeed, increasing the size of the home market through immigration was to prove a popular notion among the industrialists after the war. A 1947 survey of CMA members by *Industrial Canada* on "obstacles in the way of building up Canada as a strong industrial nation" returned Canada's lack of population as its most frequent response.[58]

The assumptions of this inward-oriented faction culminated in the period's one major campaign by the manufacturers to gain greater public acceptance for their brand of industrial strategy. Spurred by the economic downturn of the late 1950's, its "Buy Canadian" theme revived a crusade mounted periodically by the CMA since the early 1900's. Predictably, in none of its four points, on which "our very survival as a nation" was held to depend, was there any mention of exports. Import substitution was everything.

> The first is to invest in the development of our own industries. The second is to process more and more of our own raw materials. The third is to enforce a realistic tariff policy reflecting our hopes for our country's future. The fourth is to consume our own manufactured products.[59]

The target here, of course, was the consumer. Guilt was the major weapon as the manufacturers set out to establish the purchase of their products as an "economic commandment." The CMA president instructed his members that

> we've got to show that buying "Made-in-Canada" will bring prosperity to the family of the consumer to whom we are speaking .... We have got to satisfy the Canadian woman in particular that, unless she buys the goods made by Canadians, other Canadian wives will not have the money with which to buy the goods made by her husband or, for that matter, any Canadian worker. We have got to establish in the minds of all consumers that their individual well being ... is indivisible from that of manufacturing industry ....[60]

On the basis of our analysis, this approach seems absurd and even dishonest. As Table Eleven illustrated, imports of producer goods, notably machinery, equipment, and components, far outweighed imports of consumer goods in Canadian trade throughout this era. This, we have pointed out, reflects the relatively weak backward linkages inherent in subsidiary production. Not surprisingly, the branch plants were among the most enthusiastic promoters of "Buy Canadian": "It is vital to the future growth and independence of this nation that we reduce our imports of manufactured goods," declared the president of Canadian General Electric. At least one U.S. firm went so far as to cite the campaign as a factor in its decision to establish a new branch plant in Canada.[61]

Judging the "Buy Canadian" venture as a great success, the CMA was to keep it running for many years to come. In 1962, they received substantial support from the Ontario government, which launched its own $500,000 campaign to encourage citizens of the nation's industrial heartland to shop Canadian. The text of a saturation media blitz read "if each of us in Ontario diverted an additional $2 a week from imported to domestic goods ... [this] should create 60,000 new jobs." The Minister of Economics and Development told Ontarians that government and industry could do little, that it was up to the individual to do his best in reducing imports. "Government policies can only be translated into facts through the actions of individuals," he asserted. "We believe it is up to the individual to do everything in his power to work for a trade surplus."[62] He did not make it clear, however, how an individual Ontarian should act if he or she wished to create additional employment by prodding the manufacturers to create an export trade for Canada.

Conclusion

There are indeed great transformations to be witnessed in the more than quarter century surveyed here. Canadian industry, now dominated by foreign capital, entered its mature phase. Still, in many ways this maturity can withstand no more than a surface inspection. After nearly a century of steady growth, very little progress can be claimed by Canadian manufacturing in bringing a respectable portion of its products to a level where they would be able to stand on their own in world markets.

As well, the familiar elements of ISI appear in modern guise. Although we must acknowledge the existence of exceptional firms (for whom another study needs to be written), the mass of our manufacturers in this period proved themselves no less fascinated with "occupying" the home market than they did in the era of the National Policy. Technological dependence, whether measured through imports of capital goods or patents and R & D, has scarcely abated. And Canadian industry, bound by the administrative barriers to export trade imposed by its foreign owners, showed itself no more willing than ever to use this borrowed knowledge to assimilate, adapt, and innovate toward world competitiveness.

The state in this era is characterized by a divided outlook on these problems. Its Trade and Commerce bureaucratic arm, charged with the stimulation of Canadian exports, showed signs of becoming steadily more exasperated with the export blocking it identified as a structural feature of branch plant manufacturing. At the same time, the political arm of the state, which depends for its electoral health on a growing economy, appeared prepared to wink at these costs of foreign direct investment as long as the wider economic benefits promised by continental integration seemed secure. Uninformed and misinformed, the public lacked access to the information they would have needed to make their weight felt in this matter.

CHAPTER 7

One Crisis, Two Solutions

Choice has been a recurring theme throughout this book. We have witnessed, over nearly a century of time, Canada's political and economic elites arriving at policy and investment decisions which have together established an overall direction to our economic evolution. Contrary to those who posit various economic/environmental or political/social quasi-determinisms to explain Canadian industrial development, we have stressed the impact of choices made in the face of other options available to the policy-makers.

This approach especially informs our examination of the post-National Policy era in which modern Canadian manufacturing was founded. For that period, we chronicled the selection, both conscious and by accretion, of an industrial strategy with striking similarities to ISI. This path was neither imposed externally by British statesmen and capitalists nor delegated in any crude or direct fashion to some group of their Canadian proxies. That being said, the economic, political, and cultural constraints related to Canada's position within the British Empire seem to have proved extremely influential in the ultimate decision to place maximum emphasis on staples extraction, and the power brokers of Canadian economic policy remained satisfied with an industrialism whose horizons were bounded by the domestic market.

Once implanted, this ISI strategy itself conditioned future Canadian industrial expansion. Individual Canadian manufacturers who tried to deviate from the norm and establish a more independent, export-oriented direction for their firms risked both their capital and their sanity. How was the necessary back-up innovative support to be generated within an industrial sector that persistently exhibited extreme forms of technological dependence? Or, where was venture capital to be borrowed when the banks were accustomed to the safe returns guaranteed by the association of most Canadian manufacturers with already proven foreign firms and product lines?

Politicians, faced with the growing dominance of the branch plants, also found problematic the policy options which would have altered the rules of the ISI road. The cost of challenges on specific performance questions, like R & D or export blocking, would have to be weighed against the unknown value of possible gains in an overall economic situation which most judged already good. As they were now powerful citizens, the branch plants had the ability to punish or reward politicians. This could be done directly through campaign funding or by the provision of directorships and other favours on retirement. More significant, however, and far more subtle was the way in which the branch plants could now collectively manipulate the levers of economic expansion or contraction. Politicians were understandably loath to disturb the investment "climate" on which their electoral fortunes depended.

In listing these economic and political barriers to the reform of ISI, we must be careful not to slip into a static and deterministic explanation which precludes change. One way we can avoid this risk is by seriously considering the manner in which Canadian attitudes and beliefs about industrial strategy in general and export trade in particular have played a role in bringing us to where we find ourselves today. As R. Whitaker has wisely cautioned, the proper interpretation of broad national issues such as ours "resides not only in the particular economic structures thrown up by particular geographic factors, historical timing, technological levels, and world market conditions, but also in the peculiarity and uniqueness of particular cultural mixes – national experiences – which prestructure the perceptions by classes and individuals of the objective economic factors."[1] Accordingly, we will now shift our focus somewhat to probe Canadian "perceptions" of the "objective factors" surrounding them.

To a certain extent, of course, these attitudes have already been reflected in the previously recorded debates among both manufacturers and politicians. Still, in this chapter we will back off one step to review the intellectual origins of these popularly expressed ideas. By following this course, an important new dimension will be added to our inquiry. Not only will we benefit from a widened view of the context in which decisions were reached in the past, but a base will be prepared for subsequent discussion of the public policy controversies surrounding industrial strategy in the 1970's and 1980's.

Innis and Mackintosh

There is scarcely a richer intellectual tradition in Canada than that which surrounds the cult of foreign trade. Since the first years of

European conquest, Canada's ability to sell her products overseas has been viewed as the key to her material advancement. Consequently, for our political, economic, and intellectual elites, the interpretation of Canada's foreign trade statistics has often taken on the same oracular function that the examination of mystic omens provided for the elites of earlier societies. However, the first truly scientific approaches to the study of Canada's trading patterns did not begin to emerge until the 1920's and 1930's. From this point, we can trace the development of two divergent streams of analysis. Each of these became increasingly associated with a radically opposed public policy alternative on the question of manufactured exports.

The two camps began much closer than they find themselves at present. Both shared founding fathers in the elaboration of the staples approach to the study of political economy in Canada, H.A. Innis and W.A. Mackintosh. Practitioners of this approach have discovered relationships between Canada's heavy reliance on exports of raw and semi-manufactured materials and the development of our economy, politics, and culture.[2] A survey of the contributions of Innis and Mackintosh will help to clarify the more contemporary debates of their successors.

For Mackintosh, the pattern of economic development in the "pioneer" countries (i.e., the white British Dominions and the United States) depended on a linear progression through four stages. The first of these stages occurred in the earliest period of settlement, when the settlers realized that the "prime requisite of colonial prosperity is the colonial staple" and began a trade in available raw materials with the more mature European economies.[3] Exploitation of natural resources became the key to a rising living standard. Featuring an intensification of resource extraction, the second stage saw the construction of a transportation infrastructure and the adaptation of European technology to local conditions. Foreign investment played a vital role during this stage in financing the expansion of the staples economy. Mackintosh argued that it was the "life-blood" of a pioneer economy and the necessity for its repayment was a useful stimulus to productive activity.[4]

An "immature" industrialization behind protective tariff walls was the principal achievement of the third stage. In this era of industrial immaturity, however, the export of staples continued to be the focal point of economic development. Prosperity and industrial expansion were highly dependent on the level of demand for resource products from more mature economies. In the case of Canada, industrial expansion was "greatly helped" by the adoption of foreign techniques, methods, and management expertise.[5] The final stage was that of full economic maturity. Mackintosh said little about this stage. Still, it can be assumed that he was thinking of an economy like that of Germany or Great Britain, where economic expansion was in large degree self-sustaining and based on industrial rather than staples production.

For Mackintosh, therefore, the pattern of economic development in a country like Canada was rather uncomplicated. The staples economy transported a "pioneer" nation from stage to stage, finally metamorphizing itself into the butterfly of economic autocentricity. Mackintosh stated that "no large agricultural community has ever passed from primitive poverty to great prosperity except through the gateway of the one-crop system and the export staple."[6] Canada, according to Mackintosh, had passed through the "gateway" into the industrial immaturity of the third stage with the establishment of the wheat economy at the turn of this century. Further progress on the U.S. model was assured: ". . . as southern cotton started the wheels of American industry and commerce in the nineteenth century, western wheat has permitted the initial step of the Canadian advance in the twentieth . . . the world staple primed the pump of Canadian industry."[7]

Mackintosh did not come to any clear conclusion as to when or how the final stage of full economic maturity was to be reached by Canada. Indeed, he probably felt that Canada was to remain industrially immature for some time to come. A prediction of future trends in the Canadian economy prepared in 1939 by Mackintosh for the Royal Commission on Dominion-Provincial Relations seemed to locate the future of the country squarely in stage three. He forecast Canada's continued dependence on massive exports of raw and semi-processed materials, her continued vulnerability to "relatively great fluctuations" in economic growth because of variable demand for Canadian resources on world markets, and a slowed rate of growth in the economy unless new resources were discovered.[8]

In spite of the reluctance of the Canadian economy to progress beyond stage three, Mackintosh never completely abandoned his faith in the benefits of staples development. For example, he argued that staples-induced industrialization had, in the late 1920's, made Canada an important exporter of manufactured goods. Writing in 1933, he maintained:

> It must not be assumed that Canada is an exporter of merely raw materials; her exports of manufactured goods are important. In proportion to her population, her exports of manufactured goods are more important than those of the United States. Before the depression . . . per wage earner engaged in manufacturing, Canada

was exporting nearly five times as much in manufactured goods as was the United States. Hence, as a people, we are interested not only in international trade, but in international trade in all its branches.[9]

Innis's theory of Canadian economic development was at once more complex and more ambiguous than that of Mackintosh. Trade in staples between a colony and a more advanced economy depended, he observed, on the existence of a technological gap. The North American settlers, in order to provide for the continuation or betterment of their former standard of living, had to be able to purchase manufactured supplies from Europe. Resource products were returned to Europe to finance these purchases. The U.S., with a somewhat less difficult environment and a larger population, was able to close the gap and produce her own manufactures. The effect of the staples trade was dramatically different in Canada, Innis argued. Here, the trade in staples reinforced and widened the technological gap between Canada and the "centres of western civilization." Trading Canadian resources for the manufactured goods of the centre had the long-term effect of stimulating the further specialization of production in each society. Thus, it became increasingly difficult for Canada to catch up with the centre of the world economy, leaving her ever more dependent on resource exports. Innis described the process as "cumulative."[10]

Canada's role as a producer of staples, Innis argued, had generated a number of important distortions in her economic structure. These distortions in turn had posed policy problems for the political system. One such distortion Innis discussed was that of the "rigidity" of the staples economy. He used this term in relation to what he saw as overinvestment in the massive transportation infrastructure necessary to export resources. This overinvestment, he argued, led to "heavy fixed charges" on Canada's productive capacity with high capital costs and heavy interest payments to foreign lenders. A second and related distortion was held to be that of the extreme vulnerability of Canada's resource export economy to violent shifts in the world prices of her staple commodities. In combination, the effects of price vulnerability and cost rigidities were devastating, particularly in periods of economic downturn. Speaking of the Great Depression, Innis observed that "prices of raw materials for export, exposed to world competition, crush the primary producer between declining returns and relatively stable costs in terms of prices for manufactured products, of interest on debts, and of railway rates."[11]

Innis had relatively little to say on the process of Canadian industrialization. The themes that emerge from his scattered references to the topic indicate that he believed Canadian manufacturing had been distorted by the priorities of staples development. For one thing, industrialization had done little to close the technological gap between Canada and the more advanced centres of the world economy. In fact, the post-1879 tariff structure had simply acted to divert some U.S. productive capacity to Canadian soil by way of the construction of branch plants and the import of capital equipment. Consequently, Innis held out no hope of Canada becoming a significant exporter of manufactured goods, although he noted that some U.S. branch plants had been able to "take advantage" of preferential tariffs for Canadian goods in the British Empire. Still, the result of the unrestricted flow of U.S. investment into Canadian industry was to move Canada "from colony to nation to colony."[12]

Innis's failure to develop a more elaborate analysis of Canadian industry and manufactured exports is to a degree surprising. In the late 1920's, he had been one of two translators for an English-Canadian audience of the most systematic early study of the field. This was the work of H. Laureys, Dean of the Ecole des Hautes Etudes Commerciales of Montreal. At least in the Canadian milieu, it was remarkably ahead of its time. Contradicting completely Mackintosh's subsequent assertions that Canada was already an important exporter of manufactured goods, Laureys correctly observed that some 90 per cent of our exports were agricultural products and other raw materials. Manufacturers in the U.S. had more than doubled their exports since World War I. "Shall we remain inactive," he demanded, "letting others purchase these materials from us, or worse still, allowing them to come here and manufacture goods in Canada for their own profit?" Laureys did not believe that progress in industrial export would by any means follow staples development. Rather, entrepreneurship, organizational skills, and capital investment all had to be consciously stimulated if Canada were to succeed. He called for a "new mentality" on the part of Canadian manufacturers and traders who, "with some few exceptions," were unprepared to entertain the possibility of increasing industrial exports.[13]

It was difficult, Laureys acknowledged, for Canadian manufacturers to produce on a scale large enough to be efficient and, therefore, competitive on world markets. This was so, he observed, because of the small size of the Canadian domestic market and the impossibility of breaking through U.S. tariff barriers. These obstacles to expanded production were not, however, seen as insurmountable. Instead, Canadian attention should be diverted from its North American focus toward the expanding markets of less industrialized countries. Scientific product development and the promotion of specialized lines would allow Canadian industrialists to capture and hold a share of these foreign markets. Although Canadian manufacturers would be entering "the struggle" for international markets at a late date, "this fact enables us to profit, if we will, from the experience which other countries have so often dearly acquired."[14]

Innis, in his translator's foreword to the Laureys study, declared that a reorientation of Canadian production toward a higher proportion of manufactured exports was a "key" that promised "to some extent" to solve the twin problems of the staples economy – heavy overhead costs and price vulnerability. "Politically we have acquired our own autonomy," he mused, "but economically we are subject to, and dependent on, the fluctuations of highly industrialized countries consuming our basic raw materials, and to the competition of other countries producing the same raw materials."[15]

Why did Innis never write again at length on the issue of manufactured exports? We can only speculate that a distaste for social scientists who abandoned scholarship in favour of issuing prescriptions for public policies,[16] as well as a consuming fascination for the mechanics of resource export, diverted his attention from this important problem. Indeed, in his foreword to Laureys, Innis's only practical recommendation was the rather faint one of suggesting the appointment of a federal government commission to investigate the matter.

If Innis's analysis of the question of industrial exports could be said to have been underdeveloped, that of Mackintosh was fundamentally misleading. It will be recalled that he argued that Canada had already become an important exporter of manufactured goods in the 1920's. Again, in 1934, Mackintosh put himself on the record in this matter. Finding it necessary to decry a common assumption, the "considered opinion" of a number of Queen's University economists headed by Mackintosh held that Canada was not "an exporter merely of raw materials; her exports of manufactured goods are also important."[17]

As before, Canadian and U.S. progress in exporting their manufactures on a per capita basis was favourably compared. The role of U.S. technique, industrial knowledge, and even business personnel in generating manufactured exports like automobiles was applauded. Combined with Canada's "superior trade relations" inside the British Empire, U.S. branch plants, it was claimed, had allowed the nation "access to economies of production which the scale of her own industries could not maintain."

On the basis of the historical survey of Canadian industrial exporting that we have just completed, Mackintosh's conclusions here seem very thin. In fact, they were vulnerable to severe criticism even in the era they were written. On the one hand, Mackintosh did not understand the trade in manufactures rooted in imperial import substitution well enough to be able to identify it as both superficial and transitory. Indeed, he incorrectly suggested that the "major part" of the production of branch plant exports for the Empire was undertaken within Canada.[18]

On the other hand, he was working from an overly loose classification of manufactures. As a director of the trade commissioner service explained in the late 1930's when the Dominion Bureau of Statistics calculated that nearly three-fourths of Canada's exports were manufactured and partly manufactured goods, these were "not exactly the type of goods we have in mind when we speak of industrial exports." Most of them were simply "products which represent the worked-up form of the many resources Nature has supplied us in a bountiful fashion." If only goods which contained a "high degree of skill and labour content" were considered as "industrial exports," this completely altered the picture. Using that definition, only 16 per cent of Canada's total exports were highly manufactured.[19]

Mackintosh's opinions on these matters were never primarily confined, as those of Innis, to academic circles. Innis's distaste for academic involvement in Ottawa was not shared by his colleague, who wrote that "any social science must ultimately be justified by the basis which it affords for policy."[20] Accordingly, Mackintosh himself became a key civil servant advising both the Department of Finance and C.D. Howe from 1939-46. In his recent examination of the top bureaucratic "mandarins" during this era, J.L. Granatstein ranked Mackintosh close to being "a founder of the club" in spite of not becoming a permanent member of the civil service. His central standing was based in part on his recruitment, mainly from his own university, of other mandarins. As well, Mackintosh merited inclusion for his distinguished work on government advisory boards and royal commissions and in the civil service.[21] Another observer, in a 1949 study of the Canadian bureaucracy, identified Mackintosh as "the leading economic theorist" of the "inner spring of the governmental mechanism in Canada" during World War II.[22]

Readers who have been patient enough to follow our discussion of Innis and Mackintosh may wonder why they have been led so far in this direction. Writing many decades ago, these two scholars at one time may have figured largely in the academic world, but on what basis could they continue to merit our attention today? We have pursued their views simply because, as we will soon observe, the divisions between them were to become lines of demarcation in a war of ideas.

This battle has raged and continues to rage at present around Canada's industrial strategy options.

Accordingly, let us briefly reconsider their points of difference as they relate to macro-economic policy. While Mackintosh suggested that Canada eventually would achieve economic maturity through resource trade, Innis argued that the staples economy locked Canada into the position of a satellite of the industrial centres of the world economy. Mackintosh saw foreign investment as being both necessary and productive, while Innis pointed to the structural problems it created and remained profoundly suspicious of the U.S. investment in Canada's manufacturing sector. While Mackintosh contended, at first, that Canada was well on the way to becoming an important exporter of manufactured goods, and later, as we will witness, that our industrial export potential was being frustrated by tariff policies, Innis predicted that resource exports would continue to dominate our foreign trade, perhaps indefinitely.

From these two very distinct perspectives, we will now trace the emergence of two quite different schools of thought closely related to this book's inquiry into the failure of Canadian manufacturers to take advantage of their opportunities in world markets. A "nationalist" school, which extended from the work of Innis, took on the role of pessimistic critic of the overall direction of Canadian economic development policy. On the other side, a more optimistic "continentalist" school has often found itself defending both the resource export base of the Canadian economy and the place of foreign investment within it. These classifications, it is cautioned, are merely a shorthand. They symbolize the policy implications of the opinions and data of those who best typify the debate. Obviously, our sources are not self-consciously striving to fit our categories. Hence, not only may the totality of each author's work present a number of ambiguities and contradictions, but many might hotly deny membership in either camp. In this regard, Innis himself would be horrified. "Nationalism is still the last refuge of scoundrels," he once snorted.[23]

The Nationalist School

The mistaken opinion that Canada was already so industrially advanced that it had become an important exporter of manufactured goods could not have gone long unchallenged. During the last three decades, a nationalist school has been refining its critique of the optimism expressed in this and other points drawn from the Mackintosh position. Since this is not the place to examine the work of its individual contributors in detail, we would do well to begin our general review by setting out the three principal positions which have evolved within the school. First, we will witness a pervasive concern with the overdevelopment of the resource export sector of the economy at the expense of the industrial sector. Second, there has been a growing opinion that foreign direct investment in Canadian manufacturing has, among its many other negative effects, inhibited our capacity to develop an export trade in industrial products. Finally, some have warned that a failure to address and correct these trade problems will result in decreasing living standards or even a descent toward "economic underdevelopment."

Among the first after World War II to be troubled by Canada's inability to export her manufactures was D.H. Fullerton. Primary products, he noted, continued to dominate our export trade. While there had been a trend toward increased industrial content in Canadian exports, this "generally took the form of further processing of raw materials, rather than a gradual development of a separate and integrated manufacturing industry such as has occurrred in the United States."[24] Fullerton was jointly responsible, with H.A. Hampson, for preparing a study of Canadian secondary manufacturing for the 1957 Royal Commission on Canada's Economic Prospects. They concluded that the export sales of our manufacturers had never amounted to much when compared to their domestic sales. Further, at the time they were writing, industrialists were selling even less in foreign markets than they had during the 1920's economic boom. In 1929, they estimated, about 7.5 per cent of production was exported; by 1939 this had declined to under 7 per cent, and in 1955 the percentage had slipped to just under 6. Their "rather pessimistic general outlook" on Canada's manufactured export prospects led them to predict a further decline, to 5 per cent by 1980.[25]

In his 1959 analysis of the relationship between U.S. direct investment in Canada and the structure of our foreign trade, Hugh Aitkin confirmed many of Innis's earlier negative judgements on the subject. After 1945, he pointed out, U.S. investment in Canada flowed mainly into areas complementary to its own industrial economy, such as the production of primary metals, wood, and petroleum products. By this means, Canadian development in industrially competitive areas was discouraged. As a result of this bias of investment and production, Canada was cast in her structure of trade "in the role of a supplier of unmanufactured or semi-manufactured products," thereby "perpetuating Canada's traditional status as a staple-producing economy."[26]

The administrative barriers to subsidiary export also received some attention in this school during the 1950's and 1960's. However, because these scholars were denied access to the hard evidence we have surveyed, it is not surprising that there was relatively little comment on the topic which went much beyond assertion and speculation. For example, R. Dehem, in an aside to a wider examination of Canadian economic stagnation in the late 1950's, suggested that the "basic factor" in limiting the growth of secondary manufacturing in Canada was not our small national market but "the satellitic nature of most of our important firms." "They were established not as competitors in the world market," he claimed, "but as obedient subsidiaries expressly confined to the Canadian market, or, in some cases, to the Commonwealth area."[27] Similarly, a study for the Royal Commission on Canada's Economic Prospects concluded in a fairly general fashion that it was "not uncommon . . . [that] the Canadian subsidiary may be allocated the Canadian market alone, or the Canadian market plus certain export territories."[28] A.G. Huson, whose survey of the export policies of fifty branch plants for Trade and Commerce was given prominent place in our last chapter, later published a summary of these results as part of a wider critique of foreign investment in Canada. However, and perhaps understandably, he failed to cite his source. This lack of documentation may have caused his findings to be dismissed as conjecture. Huson, nevertheless, believed that they demonstrated that "in manufacturing, more often than not the Canadian subsidiary is precluded from exporting by its parent."[29]

By the mid-1960's, comments on the structure of Canada's export trade were becoming ever more alarmist. Industrial exports, for example, were examined in a 1965 report by M.G. Clark through a number of dimensions that unfavourably reflected Canada's relatively weak trading performance. Clark recorded, along similar lines to our analysis in Chapter 1, that "manufactured goods account for a smaller share of Canada's exports and a larger share of Canada's imports than any other industrialized country."[30] He also showed that Canada was not getting a respectable share of the post-1945 surge in manufactures as a component of world trade. Indeed, our increase in manufactured exports was "relatively small" even when compared to the achievements of other industrialized resource exporters such as Denmark, Norway, and Sweden.

The tendency for Canadian exports to have concentrated in products "enjoying less than average growth in world trade" was also taken to task in a 1968 study by B.W. Wilkinson. Nations exporting industrial goods, he indicated, had improved their terms of trade (relative cost of imports when charged against revenues for exports) since 1950. However, Canada, in common with the underdeveloped resource exporters, was faced with a deterioration. A striking comparison emerged from this data. Wilkinson became one of the first to point to the curious similarity between Canada's structure of trade and the structure of trade associated with economic underdevelopment. "Canada's position resembles more closely that of the less developed nations than that of the other developed countries," he suggested, with "a much larger proportion of primary products and crudely processed goods among Canadian exports, and of highly processed manufactures among imports than is true for other industrial nations."[31] Kari Levitt went much further along these lines in her popular and influential book, *Silent Surrender,* which first appeared in 1970. Basing her conclusions at least partly on the research of Clark and Wilkinson, she argued that the composition of Canada's trade was "suggestive of structural underdevelopment" and presented a "profile of a rich, industrialized, underdeveloped economy."[32]

The fear that something had gone radically awry in Canadian economic development escalated during the 1970's. Such concern was not merely confined to left nationalist groups like the NDP Waffle,[33] but, astonishingly, began to surface within the more legitimate precincts of the federal state apparatus. As a case in point, the Gray Report (1972), sponsored by a Liberal cabinet minister, observed that by comparison with other industrial countries, Canada's performance in exporting manufactures was "poor" and suggested that

> this is an important issue, since trade in manufactures is increasing more rapidly than trade in resources and the terms of trade are progressively turning against many resources. If Canada does not develop greater distinctive capacities or succeed in reducing costs as a basis for greater exports of manufactures, it may not maximize its potential for high living standards which ultimately depend on the most productive use of human and other resources. It could also lead to an economy more subject to cyclical fluctuations and result in a less stimulating social and economic environment.[34]

The Gray Report even presented one of the few empirical studies on export blocking ever to be published about Canada. Citing a 1969 Department of Industry, Trade and Commerce survey of nearly 1,000 subsidiaries, it reported that 58 per cent of U.S. branch plants and 43 per cent of other foreign subsidiaries were faced with export restrictions imposed by their parent companies. But these figures almost certainly greatly understated the actual situation. It must be emphasized that only subsidiaries with a declared export interest were included in this study. Consequently, a "significant number" of foreign-owned companies "serving only the domestic market" had no impact on the results.[35]

The Science Council of Canada, a federal government advisory body, became an intellectual leader in the parade of pessimism that characterized the nationalist school in both the 1970's and early 1980's. Although it released a score of reports which related to the export impotence of Canadian manufacturers, two were to receive special attention from both the Council's supporters and detractors.

The state of industrial research and development in Canada was the explosive in the first of these Science Council bombshells. Authored by Pierre Bourgault, it highlighted the "poor performance" of Canadian manufacturers in exporting their products. Finding on an historical basis "no apparent trend towards improvement," he recorded that between 1965 and 1969 Canada increased its traditional raw material exports at a level significantly greater than the expansion in world exports of these commodities. Bourgault concluded that it seemed clear "on a relative basis Canadians are increasingly becoming hewers of wood and drawers of water."[36]

Bourgault surveyed Canada's trade in certain key high technology sectors identified by the OECD as being of "particular importance to the industrial development of a nation. These included plastics, pharmaceuticals, scientific instruments, electronic components, machine tools, man-made fibres, iron and steel, and non-ferrous metals. In all of these sectors save two, Canada was faced with "substantial" negative trade balances and was "at or near the bottom of the list in a comparison of trade performances among Western industrialized countries." Although Canada maintained positive trade balances in both the iron and steel and non-ferrous metal sectors, Bourgault argued that this was "much more an accident of nature than evidence of technological capability" because we were unable to produce positive trade balances in the manufactured forms of these resources. Indeed, he pointed out that "while we are the world's leading exporter of nickel, aluminium and asbestos, and one of the leaders in platinum, we import more of the fabricated forms of these minerals than we export."[37]

Why was Canada in such a dismal trade position? In his answer to this question, Bourgault directly challenged a prevailing orthodoxy among our government, business, and academic leaders. Canada cannot export her manufacturers, according to this belief, because her domestic market is too small to permit efficient production in competition with more heavily populated nations. Bourgault responded that the alleged inadequacies in the size of Canada's domestic market were mainly visible from the perspective of the branch plant executives. They are usually "in the position of having to compare themselves with a parent who had access to the same technology and whose production level was greater than their own by a factor of ten."[38] Consequently, even if parents were to give such subsidiaries export freedom, these views on economies of scale and efficiency would make foreign trade seem unprofitable and therefore impossible. On an international basis, Bourgault observed, the Canadian domestic market must be seen as modest, not small. In 1970, according to his presentation, our gross national product was 25 per cent larger than that of Sweden and the Netherlands combined: two nations that do very well in exporting their high-technology manufactures.[39] The counterargument that such countries are not comparable to Canada because of their membership in larger trade communities like the EEC was minimized by Bourgault on the grounds that their export success predates their community memberships and even now is not confined to their bloc partners.

At the close of the 1970's, another Science Council investigation of "Canadian industrial underdevelopment" received widespread attention. Researched by J. Britton and J. Gilmour, this work was, if possible, more gloomy in assessing Canada's future trade prospects and more forthright in placing the responsibility for the situation on the shoulders of foreign direct investment than the earlier Bourgault study. Canada's "miserable performance as an industrial nation" was said to indicate "a nation retreating from industrialism" by "regression toward economies like that of Chile or Brazil."[40] In turn, our industrial export failure and general "economic underdevelopment" were directly linked to the high level of foreign control of our manufacturing sector. Import dependence on foreign technology, machinery, and components as well as inability to export were claimed to be characteristic of our branch plant producers, "whereas Canadian-controlled secondary manufacturing firms are the main ones penetrating foreign markets." Foreign subsidiaries operating in Canada were suggested to be free to develop foreign export markets "only in theory."[41]

The only corrective for these problems, according to Britton and Gilmour, is a "comprehensive industrial strategy" to overturn the ill-starred legacy of the past. Based on some level of tariff protection for most industries at least until the achievement of "an advanced technological capability," the strategy would attempt to promote "technological sovereignty" for Canada. This is defined somewhat grandiosely as "the development and control of the technological capability to support national sovereignty." The strategy would include a reorganization of existing industrial sectors to create newly rationalized and specialized firms with the production efficiencies necessary to achieve world competitiveness; the formation of "core" Canadian-controlled, technologically independent firms to take the leading role in their rationalized sectors; the selection of technological strategies appropriate to move core firms in promising industrial sectors into the twenty-first century; the promotion of small manufacturers to service the specialized production requirements of the core companies and world trading consortia to give them selling muscle abroad; and, finally, the rigorous regulation of foreign investment and technological imports into Canada.[42]

Because "by itself, the marketplace has proved unable to promote technological development and to ensure its correspondence with social and economic objectives," Britton and Gilmour contend that the state must intervene "at all levels" to pursue this strategy by promotion and regulation. Still, their concept of intervention does not appear to extend to government ownership of large blocs of the new industrial establishment. Rather, the state will beg, bribe, and threaten the private sector toward the achievement of technological sovereignty. Although certainly viewed as an obstacle to progress, foreign-owned firms will neither be dismantled nor nationalized. They will simply be squeezed out of their present dominant role by the growth of Canadian-controlled firms reaping the benefits of the comprehensive industrial strategy.[43]

The Continentalist School

In view of the overwhelming evidence of Canadian industrial failure in world markets, it became increasingly impossible, after mid-century, to suggest that our manufacturers were succeeding in world markets. Mackintosh, of course, did not create this belief; he merely gave it academic legitimacy. As we have witnessed in previous chapters, many influential Canadians had expressed their optimism on this question from the 1920's through the 1940's. Still, in testimony to the force of Mackintosh's inaccurate opinion here, standard Canadian economic history texts like that of A.W. Currie were repeating it to new generations of students as late as 1963. "Contrary to popular belief, Canada is an important exporter of manufactured goods," Currie wrote. "Even during the 1920s, the value of Canadian exports of manufactured goods was over three times that of the United States on a per capita basis."[44]

Generally speaking, however, by the end of the 1950's the comments of this school had become more temperate. Perhaps the best possible face on the situation was put forward by J.D. Gibson, general manager of the Bank of Nova Scotia. In 1958, he determined there was "no doubt" that the long-term trend was favourable to fuller industrial processing of Canadian exports. "But if past experience is any guide," he warned, "progress will be gradual and there may be considerable periods when no progress is made at all."[45] Although these acknowledgements of the very obvious structural weaknesses in Canadian trade began to surface, those who wrote in the continentalist tradition continued to deny energetically that the staples export economy and foreign direct investment were primarily responsible. This school minimized the negative "cumulative" effects of capital and trade dependency and sought alternative explanations in the more comfortable world of orthodox liberal economic theory: comparative advantage in resource trade, tariff barriers, and domestic market size.

At the twilight of his academic career, Mackintosh was well aware that Canada's economic development had been arrested in his third stage of industrial immaturity. He placed much of the blame for this situation on tariff barriers erected by our trading partners. In fact, both tariff and non-tariff restrictions on the free southward flow of Canada's products had denied our manufacturers a market size large enough to achieve the efficiencies necessary for world competitiveness. Dating from World War II, Canadian governments had adopted the correct policy, for Mackintosh, of pressing for freer trade, but they had been frustrated by the "almost theological" protective attitudes of various U.S. administrations.[46] It must be remembered here that Mackintosh's central role in the economic policy-making process during the war made him more than a simple observer of these matters.

As the 1960's got under way, Harry Johnson argued that the historic Canadian government policy of protective tariffs must also receive its share of blame for the inability of our manufacturers to export. The legacy of 1879 had fostered an "inefficient and backward" secondary industry. Free trade between Canada and the U.S., on the other hand, would lead it to become "efficient and progressive." "Canadian manufacturers, given free access to the large American market," he supposed, "would be able to specialize and obtain the advantage of large-scale mass production, and to exploit the advantages of a lower wage level and location close to some of the richest market areas in the United States." In the unlikely (for Johnson) event that the size of the Canadian manufacturing sector was reduced as the result of the introduction of free trade, this would simply indicate the beneficial operation of the invisible hand of comparative advantage and would signal an eventual rise in the Canadian standard of living. After all, the development of Canadian wealth had depended on the export of resource-based products. By promoting many inefficient secondary manufacturers, the tariff had "fostered the less dynamic sector of the economy at the expense of the more dynamic."[47]

Writing just one year later, H.E. English also stressed Canada's limited market size and the effect of tariff policy on the export performance of Canadian manufacturers. "The origins of such inadequacies of industrial structure are very often misinterpreted," English argued, "primarily because of the tendency to put too much stress upon foreign ownership of industry as a factor and too little appreciation of the implications of pricing by the Canadian tariff and the extent to which foreign tariffs prevent Canadian producers from realizing their potential."[48] Following English's line of reasoning, R.J. and P. Wonnacott suggested in 1967 that free trade between Canada and the U.S. would force a more efficient reorganization of Canadian industry and a net increase in the exports of manufactured goods.[49]

On the basis of another 1967 study, this time of sixteen manufacturing industries representing 22 per cent of Canadian production, H.C. Eastman and S. Stykolt concluded that our industrial structure was largely composed of inefficient units of "sub-optimal" size. These divided the domestic market into too many shares over too large a range of products. Small and inefficient, these firms would always find themselves at a disadvantage in world markets. Despite tracing the origins of our fragmented industrial sector to the pattern of branch plant investment, Eastman and Stykolt submitted that any attempt to make Canadian industry more efficient and internationally competitive by "imposing discriminatory disadvantages" on foreign firms would be misdirected. Rather, a reduction in the level of Canadian tariff protection would rationalize secondary industry. Mergers and the elimination of less efficient firms would increase the market size for our surviving firms. In turn, these rationalized firms would stand a better chance in international markets.[50]

As is now apparent, in its own particular way the continentalist school was troubled by certain characteristics of foreign direct investment in Canada. Still, their critique, unlike that of the nationalists, did not imply a set of restrictive government policies to regulate better performance. On the contrary, they preached economic salvation through the free movement of trade and investment across international frontiers. Mackintosh himself never lost his faith in the benefits to Canada of branch plant industrialization. He argued into the late 1950's that "we need United States markets. We need United States capital. We need United States industrial know-how."[51] This perspective made it extremely difficult for the continentalist school to appreciate the extent to which branch plant production was limited by institutional factors outside their purely economic model. Indeed, notable by its absence in the work we have reviewed to this point was any extensive consideration of the administrative barriers that we know to be so important in inhibiting Canada's industrial exports.

This brings us to A.E. Safarian. It was in unyielding defence of foreign direct investment that this member of the continentalist school established his academic reputation in the 1960's. Although his research covered many aspects of branch plant activities, in reference to our own discussion, Safarian took issue on three grounds with the argument that exports from Canadian branch plants are blocked by their parents in order to maximize home office export and profit potential. First, he suggested that the blocking argument was theoretically unsound as subsidiary exports were not, in principle, less profitable than parent exports. Next, on the basis of a survey questionnaire of Canadian branch plants, Safarian determined that only 7 per cent reported unfavourable export effects as a result of foreign ownership. If only firms with assets of $25 million or more were considered, 37 per cent reported favourable effects on their exports resulting from their affiliation. Lastly, again by survey, Safarian discovered no significant difference in the export performance of Canadian and foreign-owned firms. "The overall effects of affiliation on exports would appear to be either nonexistent or favourable except for a small minority of cases," he concluded.[52]

Readers who followed our discussion of administered markets in the last chapter may be tempted to pinch themselves at this point to see if they are still awake. Safarian does not appear to be describing the same country. How can we account for the discrepancy? A number of observers have commented on the validity of the survey techniques employed. For example, W.A. Dimma has pointed out that

> with questions to which there are "good" and "bad" answers in the Canadian context, there is a high likelihood of distortion in the form of either shading the facts a little or, for those of higher moral scruple, not replying at all. On this last possibility, Safarian mailed 1500 questionnaires and received back only 310, of which 280 could be used.[53]

As an indication of the reluctance of branch plants to answer Safarian's potentially embarrassing questions, we will recall that on his export query only 7 per cent of subsidiaries claimed unfavourable effects resulting from their affiliation. Yet, over one-half simply avoided answering this question and a further one-quarter settled for the somewhat indefinite "little or no effect."

Fraught with these problems of execution, Safarian's survey also demonstrates serious conceptual weaknesses in its comparison of the export performance of Canadian and foreign-owned firms. The pattern of foreign investment in Canadian manufacturing makes such comparisons highly suspect. As indicated by Table Ten, Canadian-owned firms tend to be concentrated in sectors which are declining or stable in world trade. They tend also to be smaller in size. Both of these factors make them less able to export. In contrast, branch plants tend to be concentrated in the most dynamic export sectors of world trade.

Although we have found it to be flawed in both design and execution, Safarian's work has been proclaimed gospel for the continentalist school since its publication in 1966. Constantly referenced by its adherents, it even found its way into the government-sponsored Watkins Report (1968) that was critical of foreign investment in Canadian industry.[54] An attempt to update Safarian's findings was made in a 1977 study for the Royal Commission on Corporate Concentration. On the basis of an investigation of a number of Canadian establishments, D.G. McFetridge and L.J. Weatherley claimed that "ownership exerts no effect on the export:sales ratio of firms operating in the manufacturing sector." Astonishingly, however, they admitted that their conclusion came from a survey sample which was neither random nor necessarily representative of the population of firms operating in Canada.[55]

During the 1970's, the free trade banner was carried to the public by the Economic Council of Canada. This federal government advisory body issued a series of academic studies celebrating the benefits of Canada-U.S. free trade and promising Canadians a 7 to 9 per cent rise in their gross national product after its introduction.[56] The campaign was climaxed with the Economic Council's 1975 publication of a simplified and popularized version of their creed, entitled *Looking Outward: A New Trade Strategy for Canada*. Warning that by 1980 Canada would be one of the only countries without open access to a market of at least 100 million people, this report contended that free trade would greatly stimulate the export of Canadian manufactures. Yet, atypical of this genre, *Looking Outward* also gave a frank rendering of the negative role of foreign investment in blocking industrial exports. It observed that foreign ownership of Canadian manufacturing had resulted in less specialized firms with a smaller capacity for product innovation and less incentive for management to develop a "genuinely autonomous industrial capacity" than might be expected from the norm in world production. Accordingly, export liabilities flowed from their position as "branch factories manufacturing derivative products at higher cost than the parent firm." Despite these structural problems of branch plant production, foreign investment, by itself, was not held to be to blame. Rather, these inefficient branch plants initially had been attracted to Canada by, and then simply evolved within, our tariff-coddled domestic market.[57]

This new, harder look at foreign investment through the eyes of the free traders has carried over into the analysis of the most recent prominent convert to the continentalist option. Toward the end of the 1970's, the Senate Standing Committee on Foreign Affairs came out stoutly in favour of the "strong medicine" of bilateral free trade with the U.S. This committee noted that under the tariff "the rule" was the establishment of "subsidiary companies designed to produce a similar range of products as the parent but often for the small Canadian market only." Thus, the critique has been widened here. It is not only the tariff but "the tariff combined with foreign ownership" which bears the responsibility for "a basically inefficient industrial structure with truncated branch plants producing too large a range of goods with too short production runs for too small a market."[58]

Conclusion

Our task in this chapter has been to probe the origins of Canadian attitudes about industrial strategy and industrial export failure by exploring the economic advice rendered by our nation's foremost social scientists. Our underlying purpose has been to determine how the viewpoints of Canadian decision-makers may have contributed to their failure over the last half century to address successfully these public policy areas critical to our national development.

We have learned that a key to our national confusion, ignorance, and inactivity in this field has been the dispute between the experts on the nature of the crisis, its solutions, and even its existence. To this day, no single model of analysis has been able to sweep its rivals from the field. Dating from the 1920's, we can trace the evolution of two positions on industrial strategy inspired by the work of the early Canadian political economists, H.A. Innis and W.A. Mackintosh. Unfortunately, neither of these scholars was able to provide the impetus needed for the necessary assault on the industrial export problem during his lifetime.

Innis, although he bequeathed his followers a pessimistic outlook on the overdevelopment of the staples export economy and a suspicion of foreign investment, simply never pursued an early interest in Canada's inability to export manufactures. Mackintosh, on the other hand, left a misleading model which supported an extension of the branch plant economy while denying that this held any fundamental incompatibility with Canada's long-term interest in developing industrial exports. Indeed, for the early Mackintosh, imperial import substitution had made Canada an important exporter of manufactured goods by the late 1920's.

In spite of their delay in recognizing the problem, during the last two decades the nationalist and continentalist schools have reached an uneasy consensus around the point that Canada markedly deviates from the typical trading pattern of an advanced, industrialized country. However, they continue to differ on the problem's causes, severity, and solutions. Export blocking within the branch plant sector tends to receive the blame from the nationalists who are genuinely alarmed that Canada is being deindustrialized and underdeveloped by foreign direct investment. The continentalists counter with criticism of the role of government tariff policies in sheltering inefficient Canadian manufacturers, foreign and domestic, from the harsh reality of world competition. While the former school directs greater state intervention through an industrial strategy, the latter pleads for free trade with the U.S., a policy solution that means a reduced role for government in the economy.

Secure in the bosom of economic prosperity and its defence of the dominant economic order, the continentalist school faced little real challenge to its position as the official purveyor of economic orthodoxy to Canada's state and business elites until the late 1960's. As the economic recessions of the 1970's and early 1980's worsened, however, the nationalists began to claim a larger following. Building on the groundwork set out by the government-sponsored Watkins, Wahn, and Gray Reports (1968, 1970, 1972) on foreign investment, the Science Council of Canada has taken on the role of an advocate of the nationalist school within the state apparatus. Meanwhile, the Economic Council of Canada and, most recently, the Senate Committee on Foreign Affairs are performing a similar function on behalf of the continentalist school.

The free traders' domination of intellectual debate in the 1950's and early 1960's was shaken by the emergence of the nationalist industrial strategy option. Consequently, the continentalists were forced both to defend their traditional maxims and to launch an academic jihad against the infidels in the 1970's. In this regard, R.J. Wonnacott has argued that "go-it-alone" industrial strategies "would be counterproductive, lowering Canadian efficiency and income rather than increasing it."[59] By way of illustration of his point, Wonnacott suggested that a whole new round of industrial inefficiencies would tag along behind an industrial strategy as the politicians directing it added "non-economic" goals such as the relief of regional disparities.

In reply, M.J. Gordon cautioned that Wonnacott's promotion of free trade with the U.S. is a "prescription for disaster."[60] As an alternative, Gordon recommended an industrial strategy based on the formation of "world scale national corporations" that would attempt to capture 50 to 75 per cent of the domestic market while developing export sales in specialized products. Wonnacott's contention about "non-economic" goals was flawed, he observed, by the mistaken assumption that private and social costs and benefits in an industrial strategy are identical. After all, the point of an industrial strategy is for the state to make choices which, although not profitable from the point of view of individual firms, are profitable for the country.

Recently, this debate has become increasingly visible, bitter, and personal. Within a prominent Science Council report, Safarian is attacked in these uncompromising terms: "repeated uncritical use of [his] work has delayed a general understanding of the real effect of foreign ownership."[61] Safarian has responded that the Science Council's work is badly written, dogmatic, selectively disregards previously published evidence, and is inadequately researched on its own account.[62] In separate assaults, K.S. Palda and S. Globerman have gone on to suggest that the Science Council's work is motivated by narrow self-interest. They are said to be "economic nationalists" (a terrible insult within the world of orthodox liberal economics), intent on pressuring the state to "underwrite remunerative employment to highly-trained research scientists."[63]

Who is likely to emerge the winner in this battle? Undoubtedly, the continentalist school has both the weight of its traditional dominance as well as the powerful social forces to which it is allied on its side. Nevertheless, if the economic dislocations of the 1970's and early 1980's continue, then, as we shall see in the next chapter, there are grounds to believe that the nationalist position could win some victories.

CHAPTER 8

Conclusion: The 1980's, Window on Industrial Transformation

Does import substitution still accurately characterize the path of Canada's industrial strategy? And, is it likely to continue to inhibit our export trade in manufactures for the remainder of the 1980's? For those who seek answers to these issues of national import, unhappily, the contemporary era supplies only further questions.

A number of difficulties confront the observer here. The first is the problem of perspective. Until now, our historical distance in this inquiry has allowed us to gather information widely enough to impose a general descriptive order on periods which, as we often noted, the actual participants themselves badly misinterpreted. We are similarly vulnerable. Caught in our own special relationship to present events, there is an understandable risk that we will fasten upon exceptional events, trends, and actors whose ultimate significance may be ephemeral.

Especially hazardous in this regard have been the last fifteen years. During this interval, exceptional changes in the world economic order have been under way. For one, the industrial countries have been moving toward freer trade through the General Agreement on Tariffs and Trade (GATT). Taken together, the GATT Kennedy Round (1968) and Tokyo Round (1979) have very significantly reduced tariff barriers to trade among its members. As well, there have been important shifts in production and investment. The worldwide growth in direct investment, particularly the wholly owned subsidiaries of the Canadian variety, has slowed considerably. While U.S. foreign direct investment still predominates the international scene, its proportion has fallen dramatically from a majority to a minority of new outward-bound foreign capital. Important, too, is the transfer of a growing share of production and investment to a small number of so-called newly industrialized countries such as South Korea, Brazil, Mexico, and Taiwan. These nations have consciously striven since the mid-1960's to reject their earlier experiences with ISI and now emphasize export-led growth.[1] Finally, in the last decade, grave and prolonged bouts of recession and inflation have done a great deal to obscure the long-term meaning of these modifications for the world economy.

Canadian Manufacturers Re-adjust

All of these trends have stamped their mark on recent Canadian economic development. While retaining its dominant position in secondary industry, foreign capital has slowed its growth to the point where it appears to be in slight retreat. Import penetration by the newly industrialized countries has taken its toll in bankruptcies, most notably in the labour-intensive clothing and textile sector. Energy costs have soared, but Canadian producers have enjoyed some advantages here over their competitors in other countries because of government policies which until now have held Canadian prices below world levels.

But it is in the theatre of tariff reduction that the most dramatic Canadian changes are taking place. A major victory in this field can be claimed by the continentalist school. Perceiving little advantage to protecting the Ontario and Quebec manufacturers making three-quarters of the nation's factory shipments, their cause was greatly assisted in this instance by the resource-exporting provinces. Under the influence of these domestic forces, as well as the various multinational interests who stand to gain from the greater production flexibility that free trade allows them, the federal government has been moving toward Canada-U.S. free trade, in fact if not in name, since the mid-1930's.

In 1970, nearly 55 per cent of Canada's imports of fully manufactured end products entered duty free.[2] By 1987, when the staged reductions of the Tokyo GATT are fully implemented, 80 per cent of current Canadian exports to the U.S. will enter duty free and up to 95 per cent will be subject to tariffs of 5 per cent or less. On the other hand, 65 per cent of U.S. industrial exports will enter Canada duty free and 91 per cent with rates of 5 per cent or less. As the Senate Committee on Foreign Affairs concluded, "a de facto free trade area" between the U.S. and Canada will then exist in respect to tariffs.[3]

Of course, we must be careful not to overstate the case. A number of important non-tariff barriers will still remain. These include government and business favouritism toward domestic industries in their procurement policies, government export incentives and subsidies, and discriminatory customs procedures. Most important here, however, is the exchange rate. With the Canadian dollar valued at 80 cents

U.S., domestic manufacturers continue to possess a very potent cost advantage over imports.

Between 1965 and 1978, the average rate of duty in Canada fell by nearly 40 per cent. This explains, in part at least, the shifting trade patterns portrayed in Table Fourteen. There are both positive and

TABLE FOURTEEN

Canadian Industrial Import and Export Trade in relation to Domestic Production and Demand, 1965-70 and 1979

	Exports (per cent of factory shipments)		*Imports (per cent of domestic market)*	
	1965-70	*1979*	*1965-70*	*1979*
Food and beverages	9	12	7	10
Tobacco	1	1	1	2
Rubber and plastics	4	8	16	23
Leather	5	8	18	34
Textiles	4	7	23	29
Knitting mills	2	2	16	31
Clothing	3	5	6	13
Wood products	40	57	9	14
Furniture and fixtures	3	9	5	13
Paper and allied	50	57	8	10
Printing and publishing	1	3	14	16
Primary metals	46	45	25	35
Metal fabricating	3	8	12	15
Machinery	33	53	65	75
Transport equipment	45	68	51	72
Electrical products	12	21	24	40
Non-metallic mineral products	6	13	15	19
Petroleum and coal products	2	11	11	3
Chemicals	15	29	11	35
Miscellaneous manufacturing	22	22	50	55

SOURCE: Senate Standing Committee on Foreign Affairs, *Proceedings*, December 9, 1980, pp. 14:26, 14:28.

negative aspects presented in this picture. On the one side, Canadian manufacturers are clearly enjoying some measure of success in allocating a larger proportion of their production to foreign customers. On the other side, imports have been increasingly effective in penetrating their home market.

The continentalist school proclaims that these developments substantiate their case: that as tariff barriers fall, Canadian production is being rationalized both by the elimination of inefficient firms and lines and the strengthening of internationally competitive producers. While there is an element of truth in this assertion, taken by itself it is almost certainly an oversimplification. We must be very careful to distinguish the meaning of rationality in this instance. From the point of view of the firm, national or multinational, rationality is most often growth and profit. The perspective of the national interest need not be the same. Indeed, although the continental rationalization of manufacturing may be well under way in the contemporary period, the industrial sector as a whole appears to be in decline. Employment has been steadily sinking and the cumulative trade deficit for the 1970's in fully manufactured end products totalled near a staggering $90 billion, with fully two-thirds of that amount suffered in the last five years of the decade. In the first two years of the 1980's, our end product deficit approached $40 billion.

Concealed within the aggregate losses and gains in Canadian trade displayed in Table Fourteen are the decisions of thousands of firms as to how they will cope within this new era of lower tariffs. In the public view, the most feared option is the shutdown. Whether this is through bankruptcy or simply the result of a judgement that Canadian demand could be filled more profitably from a parent plant, there have been enough spectacular closures to raise periodic charges that Canada is being "de-industrialized."[4] At the opposite end of the spectrum, some factories, particularly Canadian-owned establishments with some measure of control over their innovative capacity, have been gearing up to claim their place in the North American and world markets now opened to them through freer trade and favourable exchange rates. For example, L. Beaudoin, chairman of Bombardier of Montreal, has built his successful firm on an export strategy which reaches beyond the confines of the Canadian domestic market because "it is too narrow to allow planning for long term expansion and will not enable firms to build competitive power against foreign companies and their domestic subsidiaries."[5] Less spectacular than either of these alternatives has been the continuation of the traditional import substitution approach in a significant number of operations. With the sacrifice of one or two highly inefficient lines, the protection afforded against imports by the 80-cent dollar, and/or an institutional division of the North American market through administrative or licensing arrangements, these plants have been kept alive (at least for the present).

For a growing number of the branch plants, two new production and marketing strategies have come to the fore since the mid-1960's. These are known as continental rationalization and world product mandating. The former involves the selection of a limited number of products the Canadian branch will manufacture or assemble for both the United States and domestic markets. The latter is similar in its attempt to take advantage of specialized efficiencies. However, in its full form, the mandate allows access to the world market, cuts the requirement of buying components from or through the parent, and develops independent Canadian research and development and international marketing capacities. Neither of these approaches is as novel to the contemporary era as is generally believed. By the end of the 1940's, senior Trade and Commerce officials were, as we previously noted, painfully aware that the parent-subsidiary link of Canadian branch plants effectively barred them from entry into the U.S. market. Accordingly, they expressed interest in arrangements for the continental production by Canadian plants of lines discarded by their parents, as well as "world export rights [in] models or types of products having a high labour content . . . which might be manufactured at lower cost" in relatively low-wage Canada.[6]

As far as these mechanisms shake up the traditional domestic orientation of Canadian branch plant manufacturing, they demonstrate positive aspects. In this regard, given the increased autonomy a subsidiary will enjoy, the world product mandate shows particular promise.[7] Still, a recent Science Council study indicated that it has not yet proved to be a very popular option as "very few subsidiaries have world mandates in products accounting for more than a minor proportion of the subsidiary's total output."[8] The Canadian benefits of schemes of continental rationalization are far more dubious. As they do nothing to alter the administrative and technological impediments to Canadian export that we documented in Chapter 6, at their worst they cede the North American market for certain unpopular and obsolete products to Canadian subsidiaries in order to keep the parent's foot in the door for the import of its other commodities.[9] The Auto Pact stands out here. While the continental market shifted from large vehicles to smaller fuel-efficient vehicles as a result of the fuel price hikes of the 1970's, the U.S. parent companies, under U.S. investor, government, and labour union pressure, made only token efforts to re-equip their Canadian plants to produce the new subcompact cars. The result has been Canada's cumulative deficit in Auto Pact trade of $14 billion, nearly half of which was suffered in the last three years alone.[10]

To recapitulate, the last decade's upheavals in world trade and investment by no means have passed over Canadian manufacturing. Noticeable readjustments have been under way since the mid-1960's and are likely to continue into the late 1980's as the effects of the GATT Tokyo Round become manifest. Emerging from altered company policies on production and marketing, a variety of new paths and directions for Canadian industry now seem possible.

As to which mix of decisions is likely to emerge as our era's industrial strategy, we can only speculate. It is certain, however, that a window has appeared for the transformation of Canadian manufacturing into a more autonomous and export-oriented form. But will it be opened? That, unfortunately, is not so clear. Although the process of change has been gaining momentum for some years, Canada's industrial future seems ominous if judged from the perspective of the national interest in increasing employment and balancing our international payments. It could well be that the administrative and technological barriers to Canadian export, which provided our focus in Chapter 6, are simply being replicated in new configurations.

Many authorities have pointed to the role of government as a crucial determinant in the shift from ISI to an export-led model in the newly industrialized countries. Among state policies which have been crucial are attempts to negotiate and regulate a better export deal from foreign branch plants.[11] In Canada's present condition, this would also appear to be vital here. With so many key industrial sectors that should be export leaders remaining in foreign hands, lowered tariff barriers can prove to be only one aspect in an overall solution.

Nevertheless, the prospect for interventionist leadership from Ottawa must be judged as poor. One recent study of policy-making in the federal arena concluded that "Ottawa's true religion is drift: a lack of innovation; a failure of comprehensive planning; an unwillingness to define the national interest."[12] Yet, there are always exceptions to every rule. Taking nearly everyone by surprise, the power of foreign capital in the Canadian petroleum industry was not long ago directly challenged by the National Energy Program.[13] Have we reason to anticipate that before the 1980's are over we may witness another such confrontation, this time over industrial strategy? Before we can address this question directly, it will be necessary to draw together some of the lessons we have learned about the development of state export policies in Canada.

Export Promotion in the Growth of the Canadian State

The federal Department of Trade and Commerce has never been far from the centre of our account of the twentieth-century failures of Canadian manufacturers. From its birth in 1892, Trade and Commerce was provided with an external trade orientation as it inherited a patchwork quilt of overseas part-time trade agents and subsidized shipping lines previously administered by the Department of Finance. At first, neither the new department's purpose nor its clientele seemed clear. Manufacturing interests had petitioned the government, from at least the mid-1880's, to furnish them with a foreign network of state export agencies such as those available to industrial capitalists in Great Britain and the United States.

By the turn of the century, demands for these services became more intense. The newly reorganized and expanded Canadian Manufacturers' Association denounced Trade and Commerce export efforts as "notorious . . . inadequate and disappointing."[14] As a result, the department's capacities were significantly upgraded in the period before World War I. The number of overseas postings was gradually built up and the trade commissioners' reports began to be published on a weekly basis.

Although some transport and merchant interests were alive to an expanded role for Trade and Commerce in overseas markets, the department was drawn mainly into the orbit of industrial capital. A close relationship with Trade and Commerce in its formative years before the Depression of the 1930's was earnestly cultivated by the small minority of Canadian manufacturers who seriously pursued export trade. This level of involvement was not matched by the exporters of Canada's staple resources. Long pre-dating the establishment of the department, the trade in staple commodities such as wheat, flour, cheese, and timber had developed its own export channels and found little use for Trade and Commerce services in ordinary circumstances. As late as 1929, a Minister of Trade and Commerce spoke of the essentially private organization of the staples trade and of how the department could not be "of very much assistance" to it.[15]

Yet the affinity between Canada's manufacturers and the department was only apparently close. Indeed, the relationship was frequently an uncomfortable one for both parties. The trade commissioners found that most of their clientele, caught in the dual dependencies of ISI – foreign technology and the domestic market – were unwilling or unable to develop the specialized world competitive products necessary to enter export markets. If export was attempted, it was often half-hearted, amateurish, and related to a temporary glut on the domestic market. In this context, the trade commissioners were frequently discouraged or disgusted – sentiments often reflected in their published reports. The manufacturers found it necessary to plead for more discretion. As a result, in the mid-1920's, the director of the trade commissioner service ordered his officers to stop "unfavourable appraisals" in their reports and to emphasize the "good features" of Canadian export practice. This was often a difficult assignment. As one trade commissioner wryly remarked in reply, "in nearly every report written with the purpose of pointing out how trade may be increased, it is very difficult to avoid mentioning methods employed by Canadian exporters which are the cause of their losing part of the business."[16]

As the twentieth century progressed, Trade and Commerce shared in the spoils of the general growth of government activities. It began to take on the characteristics of an omnibus department with many diverse responsibilities, some of which, like the Dominion Bureau of Statistics (1918), bore little or no relation to the promotion of export trade. Nevertheless, the core of the department, its raison d'être, remained its overseas activities. The trade commissioner service grew from twenty offices in fifteen countries in 1911 to thirty-four offices in twenty-seven countries in 1939, to fifty-three offices in forty-three countries in 1955.

Although this expansion was initially propelled by the export needs of a select minority of Canadian manufacturers, the special circumstances of the 1930's, 1940's, and 1950's permanently widened the mandate of Trade and Commerce to include resource exporters. The desperate cry of staples producers for government assistance in resuscitating their international sales after the collapse of world demand in the early 1930's started this process. As well, the growing complexity of the post-Depression economy, with its increasing need for state intervention to grease, fuel, and repair the capitalist accumulation process, drew Trade and Commerce and other related departments into new involvements in resource production and trade. These activities included the encouragement of orderly marketing and price stabilization through cartelization and supply management to reduce surplus capacity. The strategic demands of World War II production and Cold War stockpiling of resources such as nickel and aluminum reinforced these trends.[17]

The emergence of resource exporters as major users of Trade and Commerce services led to a personality crisis within the department, which brought it to a state of near-schizophrenia. On the one hand, its traditional experience taught it that there was something radically wrong with the ISI pattern of Canadian industrialization that prevented it from reaching maturity as an actor in world markets by transforming more of our raw materials into fully manufactured exports. It was also becoming apparent that the advancing importance of foreign branch plant industries had only supplemented and consolidated the earlier problems of the inward-looking, technologically dependent ISI model. As we recorded in Chapter 6, within this perspective a potential challenge to foreign investment and staples export was gathering force.

On the other hand, Trade and Commerce had now developed new allegiances. By submitting itself to the power of continental market forces and facilitating our role as a resource hinterland of U.S. capital, it was accepting a significantly more limited future for Canadian industry. Not only did the department co-operate fully with U.S. investors in the creation of the "new staples" (minerals, petroleum, pulp and paper) export economy,[18] it also furthered the cause of foreign investment in the industrial sector. From the 1920's, the attraction of branch plants to Canada became an important departmental objective, particularly on the part of posts located in the United States. During the first fifteen years after World War II, the main work of the department's Industrial Development Branch, presumably reflecting its notion of what "industrial development" entailed, was the recruitment of branch plants.[19] Its campaigns for foreign investors featured the hard sell:

> Here is a young and vigorous nation, growing at a rate unsurpassed anywhere in the world. Here is a rising star in a world of far too many limited horizons. Here is an opportunity – *your opportunity* – to expand with Canada.[20]

In the early 1960's, the Industrial Development Branch, perhaps reflecting some of the department's internal divisions on this issue, changed its emphasis from enticing new branch plants to promoting licensing arrangements between foreign firms and Canadian manufacturers. While apparently more nationalist, this new policy simply reinforced the dual ISI dependencies – foreign technology and the domestic market. "Imports of manufactured goods into Canada are substantial, both in absolute and per capita terms. Licensing arrangements provide a logical means for Canadian industries to produce many of these goods," the Industrial Development Branch reasoned.[21]

In some senses, this submerged conflict over the meaning of economic development in Canada was institutionalized by administrative means in 1963 when the industry program of Trade and Commerce was severed from the department. At that time, a new Department of Industry was created with a mandate to promote the development of manufacturing. It appears, in retrospect, that this move was both an expression of concern that Canadians were missing the industrial boat[22] and a tacit admission that the issue of industrial development tended to be downplayed in a Trade and Commerce schooled, in the post-1945 period, in the continentalist logic of Ministers like C.D. Howe.

The split, however, was not lengthy; the departments were reunited in 1969 under the title of Industry, Trade and Commerce (ITC). Strikingly, the government justified this reversal by explicitly recognizing that Trade and Commerce had been, to some extent, riding the wrong horse, that the historic trend in world trade was more favourable to industrial, not resource, exporters. The new Minister, Jean-Luc Pepin, made the key connection between industrial development and trade expansion which fundamentally contradicted the traditional inward-oriented ISI model. From this point, he suggested, the department would promote the establishment of world competitive manufacturing sectors: "To produce . . . goods competitively, we must win as many domestic and foreign markets as possible, so as to make economies of scale and specialization. In other words, to sell mining, logging, school and medical equipment on the Canadian market, we must also be able to sell it on the foreign market, so as to achieve competitive prices."[23]

It would seem that the merger considerably reduced tensions between the two departments over economic development strategy. As one senior civil servant noted, "in the early 1960s . . . they each come up with opposite solutions to problems. Bringing those two together produced a unit that came up with reasonably balanced policy."[24] This balance, however, did not fulfil the high expectations raised at the time of the merger. No new policy instruments were devised during the 1970's to confront directly and meaningfully the administrative and technological barriers to ISI export. Rather, the department simply refurbished and expanded its established attempts to buy performance improvements from Canadian industry by offering it all types of export and product innovation subsidies.

Currently, the overseas trade commissioner service of the department has ninety-two offices in sixty-seven countries which processed close to 120,000 inquiries for export assistance in 1979-80. Other export services include a Promotional Project Program, which organized and subsidized Canadian business participation in foreign trade fairs and sales missions, as well as Canadian tours by foreign buyers. In 1979-80, sixty-two trade exhibits, twenty-nine trade missions, and nearly 900 tours cost $6.5 million. The department's Enterprise Development and Export Market Development Programs together granted over $93 million and loaned a further $150 million in 1979-80 to assist small and medium-sized firms to become internationally competitive. Exporters of military hardware were funnelled $58 million in aid through the Defence Industry Productivity Program.[25]

Industrial Strategy and Manufactured Exports

Having set out some of the principal features in the topography of state involvement in the field of export promotion, we will now examine some of the major considerations in its evolution during the exceptional economic dislocations of the last fifteen years. As was made plain in Chapter 1, we are in the midst of a serious export crisis in manufactured products which is hemorrhaging our balance of payments and seriously aggravating our unemployment difficulties. Even the large banks are worried. The president of the Royal Bank of Canada was recently moved to warn that, "in the scramble for world markets, Canadians are being left behind. The problem is serious enough to justify a full-scale national campaign to promote exports."[26]

When the banks speak in tones like these, the government of Canada is very likely to pay attention. But what to do? On the level of grand theory, two opposing positions have traditionally been available to policy-makers who wished to address the failure of Canadian industry to export. The roots of these positions can be traced back to the National Policy debates of the late nineteenth century. On the one side, the continentalist champions a free flow of trade and investment in North America. On the other, the nationalist pumps for state intervention to produce a domestically controlled pattern of economic development.

In more specific terms, the continentalist approach has minimized the industrial trade predicament, proposing that we break down the tariff barriers sheltering our weak, inefficient manufacturers. Canada then could concentrate on exporting the resource products in which we have a comparative advantage. In time, the discipline of the market would leave us with a smaller, but healthier and more internationally competitive, industrial sector. The nationalist approach argues that foreign investment has prevented us from going beyond being "hewers of wood and drawers of water" by transforming our abundant raw materials into fully manufactured products for sale in world markets. An industrial strategy, organized by the state with the purpose of reorienting and reconstructing the branch plant economy, is mandatory if the mistakes of the past are to be corrected. During the 1970's, advocates of these apparently antithetical points of view became institutionalized in two state advisory agencies – the Economic Council of Canada for the former and the Science Council of Canada for the latter.

Federal government policy-makers unquestionably have fallen much further under the influence of the continentalist school during the last half century than that of its rival. A number of factors account for its sway. First, in advocating for Canada a basically unrestricted movement of trade and investment, the continentalist appoach echoed the lessons of the comfortable world of orthodox liberal economic theory taught to civil service managers in most universities. Second, we must consider the central role of one of the most important theorists and popularizers in this school, W.A. Mackintosh. The attractiveness of Mackintosh's optimism, when compared to the pessimism of Innis and his followers, was enhanced by the fact that his theory coincided with a virtually uninterrupted economic boom from the 1940's to the 1970's. Further, Mackintosh himself became a key civil servant, recruiting other mandarins as well as advising both the Department of Finance and C.D. Howe. Finally, and perhaps decisively, by applauding the role of foreign investment in Canadian development, continentalism could attach itself very compatibly to the ever-growing political and economic power of the branch plants.

In spite of the long-standing force of the continentalist position within the senior civil service in Canada, one might have suspected their growing disillusionment during the last two decades. As noted before, considerable movement toward free trade with the U.S. throughout this period has not solved our economic problems. In fact, Canada has faced ever worsening industrial employment and balance of payments difficulties. In addition, it is hardly alarmist to conclude that Canadian manufacturers may have failed once again to take their full place in world markets. Of any Canadians, Ottawa's senior bureaucrats are in the best position to understand the technological and administrative barriers accompanying branch plant production that are intimately linked to this failure. For example, Trade and Commerce records confirm that where patents and licences had first prevented the exports of Canadian-owned firms, after the Great Depression, directives from head offices in New York and Chicago intent on rationalizing their international marketing strategies became the most formidable obstacle to our manufactured exports.

If there was any doubt in this matter, the 1963 trade commissioners' conference could have left none in the minds of the superiors of these middle-rank officers well seasoned by service in the export trenches. Here, the trade commissioners' many frustrations with the branch plant modus operandi were fully ventilated and recorded. "It was generally accepted that if any worthwhile improvement in Canada's export trade is to be achieved, subsidiaries of foreign organizations must play a more active role," these officials bluntly concluded.[27] Their critique of foreign direct investment in Canadian industry was thorough and sophisticated; their recommended policy instruments were interventionist to the point of legislative regulation.

> In too many instances the subsidiary is established as a branch office to supply merely another sector of the North American market and to take advantage of the abundance of natural resources in Canada – thus to become an obedient satellite and not a competitor in world markets. Such an attitude has interfered with product development and research, with diversification of products and markets, with growth and operation of plants at a higher rate of capacity, and with the development of a more flexible and self-sufficient industry . . . . Experiences of the past reveal that the piecemeal, uncoordinated approach, particularly in the absence of legislation or specific policy aimed at the root of the problem, can have at best only limited success in achieving the (subsidiary export participation) objective.[28]

To repeat, as the trade and investment disappointments of the continentalist program unfolded during the last decades, it would have seemed reasonable to suppose that the senior bureaucrats and politicians who guide ITC and the Department of Finance might have begun to look again at some policy option, such as an industrial strategy, which would have attempted meaningfully to obtain a better performance from the branch plants. For the most part, they did not. The pressure of traditional department thinking as well as the prevailing academic orthodoxy of the continentalist school made it difficult for them to weigh the industrial strategy approach on its merits. When the power of foreign firms and their governments was considered, an industrial strategy was also rated to be extremely hazardous. Others were opposed ideologically to state intervention on the massive scale required to administer an industrial strategy. For example, as early as 1946, a Trade and Commerce official had summed up the subsidiary export blocking situation by observing that "apart from an educational programme which the government is now carrying out, nothing can be done short of taking plants over from private industry, a move which is out of the question."[29]

Finally, many still viewed the issue from the simplistic perspective of the 1950's, which held that foreign investment had caused the postwar economic boom rather than simply being the main beneficiary of it. Warts of the industrial branch plants, such as their failure to export, were to be passed over in a larger vision of the supposed advantages of economic expansion as directed by foreign investors. Accordingly, less than three years after a senior officer in Trade and Commerce had concluded that "foreign capital" was the "biggest problem facing the department in its endeavours to expand Canada's exports,"[30] departmental Minister Robert Winters, either misled or deliberately misleading, put himself on the public record in 1967 by asserting that

> . . . nothing uncovered so far by the Department or any independent researchers would indicate that there is any validity to the charge that foreign ownership per se acts against our national interests . . . . For example, some have argued that foreign subsidiaries do less than their share of exporting – a claim which, if widely proven, would be of very serious concern to me, as Minister of Trade and Commerce. Some companies do have their sales policies determined at head office and do not export from Canada. But the majority of subsidiaries do export now and some of the remainder indicate that they intend to do so. The statistics we now have are the best proof of their performance. We will continue to encourage the few stragglers as indeed we do for Canadian-owned companies.[31]

For all these reasons, the bureaucratic elites of Finance and ITC systematically thwarted the first tentative initiatives in the industrial strategy direction taken by the Priorities and Planning Committee of the Trudeau cabinet in the early 1970's. Industry, Trade and Commerce, according to one insider, responded "to the form of the [industrial strategy] demands while ignoring their content" by launching an elaborate consultation process where various manufacturing sectors could inform the department of the areas in which they felt public sector activities could assist industrial development.[32] In this manner, the department deflected a menacing policy direction into its own familiar turf – export and product innovation subsidies. Predictably, when asked, the manufacturers told ITC that their ideal industrial strategy would feature more lavish and better co-ordinated spending and tax incentive programs and fewer public restraints on their activities.

The climax of the consultation process launched in the 1970's was the publication of *Strengthening Canada Abroad,* the Hatch Report, prepared for ITC by a task force of businessmen. Established in the midst of what the Hatch Committee admitted was a "pressing and urgent" trade and balance of payments crisis directly related to Canada's industrial export failure, its recommendations were meant to help "resolve an increasingly intractable problem." Eight in all, these recommendations showed little vision beyond the horizon of a more vigorous shake of the expenditure tree. They wanted a system of tax incentives for exporters, subsidized and expanded export insurance, a reorientation of Canadian foreign aid toward their needs and away from its "overly philanthropic giveaway approach," and an upgrading of the trade commissioner service. Curiously, after outlining the negative relationship between branch plant technological dependence and export potential, the Hatch Committee recommended "a more liberal policy" toward foreign direct investment, which "needs to feel welcome in this country." However, free traders would not have found all that much comfort either among these businessmen. "It is a beguiling point of view," they said. "It may be right in the long term. But if the short term isn't played right there may not be a long term."[33]

While the business community and Industry, Trade and Commerce clearly have wished to avoid greatly disturbing the industrial status quo, the public appears more aggressive than it has ever been on the question of controlling foreign investment. Whereas in 1956, 68 per cent of Canadians believed U.S. investment had been good for Canada, in 1978 only 30 per cent held this opinion. In addition, nearly one-half of Canadians currently support the idea of buying back majority control of U.S. companies operating in Canada even when loaded with the intimidating qualification that "it might mean a big reduction in our standard of living."[34] The continuing economic downturn in recent years, with layoffs and plant shutdowns by many branch plants, has almost certainly hardened these opinions. One indicator of this can be found in the results of the 1980 federal election. Desperate for Ontario seats, the Liberals promised an industrial strategy for Canada and implied a tougher line on foreign investment.

For the shot in the arm his industrial strategy plank gave the Liberal campaign in Ontario, Herb Gray was rewarded with the Industry, Trade and Commerce portfolio. He promptly signalled the manufacturers that it would be unrealistic to expect the continuation of a "hands-off" industrial development policy. "The time has come," he said, "for Canada to learn from the examples of others' successes."[35] In July of 1980, Gray presented a remarkable document to cabinet, especially notable for three radical departures from the traditional public face on industrial expansion which has dominated ITC in the past. First, it was contended that the branch plant economy presents serious structural barriers, both administrative and technological, to the realization of Canadian industrial potential. Second, these structural barriers cannot be corrected simply with expenditure programs. Finally, it was suggested that the government must begin to monitor the branch plants with an eye to framing "regulatory mechanisms" to "ensure that MNEs (multinational enterprises) perform to world standards in terms of innovation and export freedom." As for the current federal policy instrument in this field, the Foreign Investment Review Act, since it did "not pertain to most of the activities of MNEs now operating in this country," it was seen as an "inadequate tool to fully address" the problem.[36]

It is clear that Gray's analysis caused a sensation in upper-level Ottawa. Certainly, it was not very long before word began to leak out that he was having difficulty in selling his ideas to cabinet. The efforts of Economic Development Minister H.A. Olson to "moderate" Gray's impact by introducing a rival document for cabinet discussion were an open secret.[37] It took nearly eighteen months after Gray's initial presentation to cabinet for a much briefer statement entitled *Economic Development for Canada in the 1980s* to be introduced as a supplement to the November, 1981, budget.

By reaffirming the tenets of the non-interventionist approach which we have seen to be characteristic of the political and bureaucratic elite in the federal government, *Economic Development for Canada* stands almost any sort of industrial strategy, however meek, on its head. Extremely short, it nevertheless successfully communicated three simple messages to Canadian capital. First, in the coming decade, its leading investment opportunities would be in resource exploitation, not industrialism. Second, as economic development would be resource-led by $440 billion in potential mega-projects, Canadian industry could discover its niche through orienting itself to the domestic market to fill the need for manufactured inputs generated by all this activity. Finally, the government had no intention of monitoring or controlling foreign investment, outside of the energy sector, in a more rigorous manner.[38]

A number of considerations appear to have influenced this return to the womb of the nineteenth-century National Policy. As we know from Chapter 2, this also featured a resource-led economic development strategy, massive state involvement in the construction of infrastructure, and a healthy dose of import substitution industrialization. Desperate to show direction in a period of intense economic dislocation, desirous of breaking partisan ground in the western provinces which have the lion's share of the mega-projects, exhausted by its labours in the constitutional and energy fields, and afraid of a certain confrontation with U.S. business interests and the Reagan administration, the federal government simply lacked the political will to bite the industrial strategy bullet and move beyond the traditional economic policies that have largely shaped the present chronic export, balance of payments, and employment crises.

In the rush to promised resource riches – "in a world of potential shortage, our opportunities are greater than ever before" – some symbolic sacred cows were slaughtered. Take, for example, the policy direction behind the 1969 merger of Industry, Trade and Commerce. No longer was the illusion maintained that the government, by bribery and cajolery, can lead Canadian manufacturers out of the ISI wilderness toward the goal of creating specialized, internationally competitive products and firms. Advised by Gray that a serious commitment to this goal required the development of a more interventionist stance with regulatory weapons, Senator Olson preferred to abandon the project for a return to a simpler age. Putting this retreat in as positive a light as possible, he assured Canadians that they were no longer worried about supplying the world with their raw resources. Indeed, our preoccupation with "moving away from being hewers of wood and drawers of water is all behind us. We're not going to process every one of our natural resources into the final product."[39]

In this eagerness to renounce a policy direction that was never systematically pursued, it is not very surprising that Industry, Trade and Commerce has been split apart in the wake of *Economic Development for Canada*. A new Department of Regional Industrial Expansion, charged with the special role of supervising government involvement in the mega-projects, has been formed from an amalgamation of the department's industry, small business, and tourism programs with DREE. The international trade development program moved to become a division of External Affairs with its own Minister of International Trade. Gray was left with the Regional Industrial Expansion portfolio from his old department. More recently, at the end of September, 1982, Gray was further exiled to the post of Treasury Board President, where he was unlikely to pose any further immediate threat to the branch plant status quo.

Conclusion – Out of the Question?

Must an industrial strategy now be considered an extinct species in Canada? Is the lesson we might learn from November, 1981, to be that any attempt to control the branch plant manufacturing sector is as "out of the question" in the contemporary era as it was after World War II? Let us indulge in some informed speculation on these matters.

To begin, although the regulatory route to an industrial strategy and the export benefits it might be expected to deliver have been discarded for the present, this does not signify that the government is likely to turn its back completely on Canadian manufacturing. The message of *Economic Development for Canada* was not that industrial development lacks consequence or relevance, but rather that the engine of economic recovery must be resource exploitation. In fact, the importance of a "progressive reorientation and restructuring of the manufacturing sector" was noted as well as "the revitalization of industrial capacity towards specialized international competitiveness."[40] Still, government will continue to use money, not muscle, to induce reform.

Unquestionably, new funds for ITC's trade and industrial development programs have recently been injected into the department. This has lifted these activities from the expenditure doldrums where they were becalmed in the 1970's. During the last two years, funding has grown at a rate approximately two-and-a-half times greater than that of the federal government as a whole and moderately faster than even the much favoured Economic Development expenditure envelope in which they are contained.[41] One suspects that these programs will continue to be generously endowed. Our analysis suggests that the trade, balance of payments, and employment crises are likely to persist. Lacking the will to regulate, ever higher expenditures to buy a few improvements from the branch plants will seem the only way to go. Nevertheless, this route holds little more hope for the 1980's than it did for past decades.

It matters little to what extent trade promotion programs are refined or expanded. They exist on the premise that large numbers of Canadian manufacturers are potentially interested in increasing their penetration of world markets or have the technology to generate exportable innovations. Such an assumption is likely to continue to be fanciful when the most export-oriented industrial sectors are foreign-controlled. Without regulatory supplements, these trade promotion programs are, at best, inefficient since they provide a full range of export services to a small minority of firms. According to Michael Wilson, former Conservative Minister of State for Foreign Trade, two-thirds of all Canadian exports are handled by only 178 firms.[42] At worst, by providing the same kinds of export services offered in other liberal democracies not faced with the structural barriers of the branch plant economy, they create the illusion that nothing more need be done by the state to correct the problem.

Are further subsidy programs all that we can expect in this area? Some observers suggest that the very structure of our political system may be incompatible with the major economic reforms, and direct challenge to the power of foreign capital, which would be the necessary basis of any industrial strategy designed to break down the administrative and technological restraints arresting the full development of Canadian manufacturing. This, for example, is the position taken by R. French in his insightful review of federal industrial policy-making during the 1970's. On the one side, he noted the formidable barriers to meaningful change erected both by powerful vested political and economic interests as well as conventional bureaucratic wisdom and practices. On the other, he pointed out that a government would have to be prepared to wait for ten to twenty years to realize the fruits of any industrial strategy initiatives. Accordingly, with the benefits vague and distant, and the opposition immediate and well-organized, the political system itself has militated against radical solutions to our industrial difficulties. As French concludes, "democratic governments are nothing if not risk averse."[43]

At this point, our conclusion teeters on a fine edge. Although I have consciously striven throughout the book to be more descriptive than prescriptive, the reader by this point can have little doubt as to the author's own preference for a fundamental reorientation and restructuring of Canadian manufacturing. After leading you through a hundred years of the Canadian industrial wilderness, I confess to being sorely tempted, like others who have preceded me, to now stand on a mountain with the outspread hands and raised voice of a biblical prophet to predict either forty years of feast, if the wicked are vanquished, or forty years of famine, if they are not. Yet, I cannot help but feel that there is much in the contemporary era which makes the use of such a conventional literary formula out of place. We may be at a very unique juncture in Canadian economic development in which it is possible, without wistful prescription, to foresee the fracture and even eventual dismemberment of the until now apparently unassailable continentalist fortress.

I will attempt to support this somewhat daring assertion with the assistance of a policy-making framework currently in vogue among political scientists. C. Offe has pointed to the community of interest shared in all liberal democracies by politicians, bureaucrats, and business people in expediting their country's ongoing process of economic expansion and renewal. Business seeks the profitable fruits of capital accumulation while government seeks the tax revenues and political advantage of appearing to be efficient and progressive economic stewards. This community of interest, Offe submits, prompts two distinct policy constellations.[44] In the first of these, the state allocates or distributes its fiscal resources toward those objectives (as, for example, funds for export subsidy programs) identified through the representations of interested firms and individuals.

But this is not the only or even most important way in which the state has intervened in capitalist economies in the twentieth century. Policies in areas such as education, industrial research and development, energy, and transportation can often be classified as "productive" in the sense that they seek to create new economic resources rather than simply redistribute what is already available. Significantly, the productive policy process does not proceed by the normal rules of pluralist interest group lobbying. Rather, productive policies must be generated within the state apparatus itself, as the perspective of the individual competitive economic enterprises is usually too narrow to formulate specific demands and inputs in these broad areas. Yet, the viability of the modern economy depends on the successful planning and execution of productive policies.

The historical record presented in this volume makes it clear that until now the industrial export policies of the Canadian government have been mainly of the allocative or distributive variety. Yet, the administrative and technological barriers of Canada's branch plant production seem impervious to these policy instruments. A more comprehensive and interventionist set of policies in the "productive" mode appears to be required. These would likely be based on the establishment of minimum export and research and development standards or quotas for large foreign-owned manufacturers backed with regulatory and tax incentive/penalty teeth. An industrial strategy of this type would be, of course, so far at variance from the wishes of the firms themselves that it would of necessity, as with all productive policies, be generated with the state apparatus itself. Indeed, such an industrial strategy would have to be conceived in the certain knowledge that it would be bitterly opposed both by the most powerful economic actors in the country and by the U.S. government.

Given the furies that such a policy direction would inevitably call up, is it really reasonable to suppose that the Canadian state might be driven to attempt a renegotiation of the terms of entry for foreign capital into the country to promote the rather abstract objective of maintaining the long-term health of the Canadian economy? After all, in the past the costs of proceeding in such a manner have obviously been perceived as being too high. Given a progressive deterioration in Canada's already dismal industrial prospects in the coming years, two factors highlighted in this chapter's analysis may serve to alter these former calculations. First, we have discovered that the 1970's and 1980's present a unique economic window on industrial transformation in Canada. Second, the state, although it has *learned* the extent of the hidden costs of foreign investment in the industrial sector, has failed for reasons already specified to *act* on this knowledge by prying open the window.

It is unreasonable to expect that this must always be the case. The partnership between the Canadian state elite and foreign capital has always been predicated upon the continuance of economic growth.

Without economic growth, the social harmony on which in the past the electoral fortunes of the Liberal and Conservative Parties have depended becomes threatened. The balance of regional electoral forces resulting from the Liberal stranglehold on Quebec and the corresponding Conservative strength in the western provinces means that for either party to assemble a governing majority they must court the support of the relatively volatile electors of the Windsor to Oshawa industrial corridor. If the trade, employment, and balance of payments problems were to continue to be extremely grave, or worsen, *and* the responsible policy-makers become convinced that their traditional options – increased industrial subsidies, intensified resource exploitation, and freer Canada-U.S. trade – can no longer produce the required improvements, the unthinkable then may become thinkable. On this basis, then, we might anticipate the adoption of new, more aggressive attitudes toward the foreign firms that dominate Canadian industry.

While the theoretical underpinnings of a new "productive" state initiative in this field seem currently to be in place, can we really expect to see it emerge? From the outset, it must be recognized that the Liberals are more likely to take such a leap into the unknown than are the Conservatives. As the party of near permanent opposition, the Tories do not have to move at present beyond denunciations of Canada's dismal economic record in order to attract the votes of the discontented. In addition, the Conservatives in recent years have come to ally themselves very closely with the ultra-conservative forces of U.S. Reaganomics. In fact, Tories have gone so far as to argue that Canada's economic woes are largely attributable to alleged Liberal government interference with foreign investment through such relatively ineffective policy instruments as the Foreign Investment Review Agency. Once in power, however, the Conservatives would soon find themselves confronted with the same economic and political realities which have backed the Liberals into a more nationalistic posture in recent years.

As the party of near permanent government, the Liberals have been more directly accountable to the voters of central Canada for our manufacturing woes. As a consequence, they have found themselves flirting with attempts to negotiate a better deal for Canada from foreign investors at various times since the 1960's. Admittedly, little of substance has come from their gyrations on this question, except for various policy studies and the creation of the Foreign Investment Review Agency (which, it must be remembered, monitors only new foreign investment in Canada, not what is already here). Still, economic nationalism proved its value as a vote-getter in southern Ontario in the 1980 election. As well, the National Energy Program of that same year, which tackled the multinationals through an integrated package of incentives, regulations, and nationalizations, also received widespread popular support over the hysterical protests of the business community. After the rapid collapse of their 1981 megaprojects strategy, the Liberals now seem poised to announce a series of industrial strategies for sectors such as machinery and automobiles.[45] Past practice would lead us to conclude that these would again be allocative in nature and thus would do little to alter the administrative and technological barriers which have arrested the full development of Canadian manufacturing. Present economic realities would lead us to hope for a great deal more.

CHAPTER 9

Afterword: The March to Continental Free Trade

Written in the summer of 1982, the previous chapter directed the reader's attention to a number of significant factors then calling the old ISI regime of Canadian manufacturing into serious question. While their precise impact was at that point far from clear, these factors centred on the worldwide upheavals in trade and investment of the 1970's and early 1980's associated with the retreat of U.S. foreign direct investment, the competitive rise of the newly industrialized countries, and, most especially, the incremental dismemberment of continental tariff barriers under the GATT. In this unstable environment, any prediction of the precise future direction of Canadian manufacturing was judged to be "hazardous."

Only three years later, in late 1985, much that was obscure in 1982 about the mix of state and business decisions, which will together shape our era's industrial strategy, is now coming into fuller view.[1] Quite suddenly, it seems, manufacturers have abandoned their traditional home market obsession and, instead, demand that the Canadian state negotiate guaranteed treaty access to the U.S. for their products. After existing for a century, ISI is plainly and rapidly being superseded by a new system of continental production. Nevertheless, examination of the most recent free trade turn in Canadian economic policy will make it apparent that the new continental scheme fails to break completely the old administrative and technological shackles imprisoning our manufacturing. Free trade, no less than ISI, equally has the potential to arrest the development of Canadian industrialization.

Still Not For Export

One of the primary reasons that the current business and government free trade initiative seems so dramatically innovative is that until very recently the old ISI production forms seemed extremely entrenched. Most foreign parents administratively blocked exports from their Canadian branch plants during the 1950's and 1960's according to our review in Chapter 6 of documents gathered mainly from the files of the federal trade commissioner service. This material brought us to the conclusion that export blocking was an important contributor to the failure of Canadian manufacturing to become internationally competitive in the modern era.

New evidence that emerged just after the publication of Chapter 6 allows us to extend this analysis with considerable confidence right into the contemporary era. A leaked 1977 memorandum on export blocking from an assistant deputy minister in the then Department of Industry, Trade and Commerce (ITC) confirms suspicions that this issue was as salient in the 1970's as it had been in the previous two decades.[2] Citing evidence from "a multitude of sources" including interviews with senior executives, departmental contacts, Statistics Canada data, and private studies, this memorandum pointed to "considerable evidence" that Canadian branch plants were "not aggressively seeking export opportunities abroad. Because of corporate policy, many firms are either unwilling or unable to pursue projects abroad. . . ." In so saying, this high official dismissed the "good corporate behaviour" export and procurement guidelines for subsidiaries established in 1966 by Robert Winters and described in Chapter 6. In contrast to the glowingly optimistic reports that Winters himself had given on the success of these guidelines, the assistant deputy minister judged that "although eleven years of records exist, there is little evidence that [they have] had the desired effect in altering company policies."

Appended to the report is a joint ITC-Export Development Corporation (EDC) study of the export practices of five branch-plant capital equipment manufacturers. This industry group is of critical importance in international trade because it can provide the technological leadership for the creation of new exportable innovations in other sectors. The authors of this appendix took care to point out that although their findings applied specifically to the five surveyed companies, they were "general enough in nature to apply to a broad range of foreign-owned subsidiaries in Canada."

Established to "penetrate and secure the Canadian domestic market," most of the surveyed firms had "significant limitations on freedom to initiate exports." The study submitted that they had "little or no export marketing strategy, per se, but export on an opportunity basis usually as an extension to the market of their domestic lines." Basic decision-making on international marketing "is almost always centred outside of Canada and rationalization of the parent firm's objectives takes precedence over those of any branch plant or host country." The formation of Canadian export consortia had been frustrated because even if one firm "had freedom to export, usually one or more of the partners would have limitations put on them by their parents and the bidding attempt on any tender would eventually abort." Still, one factor that could sometimes persuade these subsidiaries to export was access to EDC or Canadian International Development Agency (CIDA) financing. On the other hand:

> We have evidence that four of these firms (all with capacity in their plants) recently referred export business obtained by Canadian engineers to their parents or related foreign companies because EDC or CIDA financing was not required. The Export Manager of the fifth firm pleaded with us to put pressure on his company so that he in turn could press his parent for export freedom because without EDC or CIDA financing he had none.

Chapter 8 observed that the allocative policies designed to buy or subsidize performance improvements from our manufacturers are for the most part ineffective in the face of the administrative barriers to Canadian industrial export trade encoded in the structure of branch plant production. This same conclusion had also been reached by the ITC bureaucrats of its International Financing Branch.

> They are now convinced that the answer lies not in increasing ITC resources devoted to this activity, but in the readiness of the Canadian export community to pursue the business. In discussions with the companies, many reasons are given for the absence of Canadian interest in multilaterally financed projects but most excuses are related to our alleged uncompetitiveness in world markets. Yet these same companies, when pursuing EDC financed business, are very vocal about their international competitiveness and only emphasize the need for competitive government financing.

Accordingly, this assistant deputy minister recommended, as had his predecessors in the 1960's, that direct action should be taken against offending foreign firms. Subsidiaries, he proposed, should be cut out of CIDA projects and ITC and EDC support programs unless they could demonstrate that they had export freedom. As we have seen to be the case in all the previous instances where pressure for remedial action against export blocking was generated within the bureaucratic apparatus of the state, nothing concrete was ever to materialize at the political level.

Reshuffling Continental Production

Until the later 1970's, then, it seems reasonable to suppose that the old ISI production system, as institutionalized by the branch plants, survived virtually intact. As we observed in Chapter 8, however, the worldwide upheavals in trade and investment of that period forced U.S. parents to do some rethinking of the traditional formula under which their Canadian miniature-replica satellite plants were engaged primarily in import substitution. We noted as well that some innovative Canadian-owned firms have experienced spectacular recent success in breaking the ISI mould. Of particular significance in this process was the tariff liberalization that was taking place as a result of the Kennedy and Tokyo rounds of the GATT and the 1965 Auto Pact which will bring us toward "de facto free trade" with the U.S. by 1987 according to the Senate Committee on Foreign Affairs. Perhaps a more important stimulus for reconsideration of the ISI framework has been the highly unstable international trade arena of recent years where manufacturers from the European Economic Community, Japan, and even the newly industrialized countries such as South Korea, Brazil, and Mexico have experienced considerable success in the hitherto almost unassailable fortress of the North American market.[3]

Some firms have already shut their doors and now supply their Canadian customers from elsewhere. Others, likely the majority, find inspiration in the model provided since the mid-1960's by the U.S. automakers who rationalized their continental production under the Auto Pact by selecting a limited number of lines that can be manufactured or assembled in Canada for the entire North American market.[4] As we will soon determine, the rationalization process has been rapidly accelerating in Canadian factories during the last ten years. From the multinational's point of view, there are definite advantages to continental rationalization because improvements to efficiency and productivity can be translated into improved competitiveness. Who can say, for example, how much greater the import penetration of Japanese and European automakers might have been in the last fifteen years without a rationalized North American industry to engage them?

For Canada, the benefits of continental rationalization schemes are less obvious. In the branch plant sector, at least, the production system has simply been *reshuffled* rather than *transmuted* insofar as our factories continue to be organized in accordance with continental marketing strategies established in U.S. head offices rather than becoming highly efficient and technologically advanced plants capable of autonomously generating world-competitive products. Under the Auto Pact model, for example, managerial authority, research and development, and export marketing all remain the prerogatives of the U.S. parent firms. Progress toward world product mandates, discussed in Chapter 8 as a more radically beneficial form of industrial reorganization that cedes such activities to Canadian subsidiaries, has been disappointingly slow. According to a 1981 Ontario government survey of nearly 400 of its largest multinationals, only one-quarter claimed such mandates.[5] A sizeable proportion of these arrangements may merely be continental rationalizations in a more politically acceptable guise. One 1983 study of twelve computer subsidiaries observed that while eleven claimed world product mandates:

> after in-depth questioning, it was apparent that the majority of these so-called WPMs (or missions) were neither unique nor broad. Furthermore, almost all of the WPMs appeared to be for products that were nearing the end of their life cycle. Based on the interviews, the two researchers have concluded that it has become common to label regular corporate activities as being "WPMs." This is probably due to pronouncements by the Government of Canada and the Science Council that WPMs are desirable for the development of Canadian manufacturing.[6]

A more recent study also points to the key role of the state in assisting Canadian subsidiaries through grants and preferential purchases to "persuade" foreign parents to cede world product mandates and to "defend" these mandates once acquired. In so doing, the Canadian government "does not acquire a vehicle for the pursuit of national policy goals, since the future of mandating remains, at bottom, the prerogative of parent companies."[7]

Hand in hand with the movement toward continental rationalization has come a fundamental change in the traditionally fanatical obsession of Canadian manufacturers with "fully occupying our home market." As we observed in Chapter 6, through the 1940's, 1950's, and early 1960's, industrialists publicly promoted those elements, like the tariff and immigration, which protected and extended the domestic market, and opposed freer trade and import competition. Nevertheless, recognizing that the global trend was away from protectionism, they gave grudging support to the 1967 Kennedy GATT as long as the federal government would provide "adjustment assistance" to firms that suffered from the new trade regime. At the same time, they held to their customary position that "existing custom duty rates in the country are barely adequate to provide the necessary climate in which Canadian industry can flourish and grow."[8]

After the staged process of gradually lowering tariffs in the Kennedy GATT had got under way without bringing devastating consequences, and when manufacturers began to assess favourably the Auto Pact as a possible model for the organization of production in their own industries, there was less ambiquity about and more real enthusiasm for further Canada-U.S. tariff reductions. For example, a 1972 mail poll by *Industrial Canada*, the organ of the Canadian Manufacturers' Association, found that two of its responding readers answered "yes" to the question "Should Canada be working toward a North American Common Market?" for every one who answered "no."[9] By the end of the 1970's, the manufacturers had absorbed further staged tariff reductions, experienced the full force of the international trade dislocations noted earlier, and still had the Tokyo GATT reductions to look forward to in the 1980's. Accordingly, the CMA felt it was an appropriate moment to canvass its members more completely on Canada-U.S. free trade. When asked in 1980 to assess the net impact on their firms from such an arrangement, approximately two-thirds estimated that it would either have no effect on business or would lead to expansion while only one-third felt it would result in contraction.[10] Just five years later, the 1985 Macdonald Royal Commission suggested that the percentage who foresee contraction may now be as low as twenty.[11]

In this context, it is not especially surprising that the Canadian Manufacturers' Association has come out strongly in the mid-1980's in favour of Canada-U.S. free trade. Insight into the logic that has propelled this attitudinal revolution can be found in the testimony of R. Phillips, president of IPSCO, a Regina steel producer, before the special House of Commons-Senate Joint Committee examining the issue of Canada-U.S. free trade in the summer of 1985. "I do not think there is an entrepreneur in Canada," he argued, "that cannot adust [to free trade] over a period of ten years, because we are used to making all sorts of changes in our markets more often than every ten years."[12]

The 1985 Free Trade Initiative

With the 1987 approach of "de facto" Canada-U.S. free trade with respect to tariffs, readers might legitimately question what induced the Mulroney government to repoliticize what has historically been an explosive issue in Canadian politics by announcing in the fall of 1985 that it was seeking bilateral trade negotiations with the Americans. As we shall see, a unique conjuncture of three circumstances prompted this initiative.

At the heart of the first factor lies an attempt to find a solution to the underlying and continuing crisis chronicled by this book of Canadian economic development in general and Canadian manufacturing in particular. In Chapters 7 and 8, we observed how, in the last decade and a half, politicians, civil servants, and business and labour leaders have embraced with optimistic enthusiasm a succession of economic slogans they hoped would orient the way toward industrial prosperity and greater employment. In the 1970's it was industrial strategy, and in the early 1980's, megaproject resource development.

The industrial strategy option with its interventionist overtones and its attack on foreign capital was never particularly well received in business circles. The early capsize of the megaproject strategy in the wake of falling oil prices opened the door for a new look at an old policy through an intense round of evangelizing through the ranks of the business community by the continentalist school on behalf of free trade. Much has been promised, little has been made specific. As a result, confusion over the meaning and impact of freer trade with the U.S. is as commonly expressed among some business groups as is the certainty that it will offer solutions to high unemployment and rising prices as well as low productivity and weak markets. Take, for example, this response by J. Geldart, president of the Atlantic Provinces Chamber of Commerce, to a question from the previously mentioned 1985 Commons-Senate Committee as to whether her organization had enough information to support its "general feeling in favour" of freer trade.

> Can we afford to wait? I think that is another thing we have to look at. I believe we have to do something. Is it going to take 50 years? Someone told me today that it might take 50 years to figure out what the ramifications of this are going to be to Atlantic Canada and for it to get ready. We have to do something . . . I think that is what our resolution [favouring free trade] reflects – the general desire and will to get on with the business of selling more to bigger markets. And we see New England as the big market.[13]

This search for a simple, practical, and ideologically acceptable formula to address Canada's complex economic difficulties brings us nicely to the second factor that has convinced the Conservative government to give continental free trade priority within their policy agenda. They believe it will offer them partisan advantage. To begin, it is an issue with appeal for two important strands within the party[14] – the traditional western free trade electorate and the neo-conservatives who favour it both because free trade smacks of free enterprise and because an agreement would bring Canada closer to Reagan's America. As well, as we shall soon see, business interests important to the party have impressed upon the Tories their need for such an agreement. But it is also an issue the Tories feel can be sold to the public as a demonstration of their "decisiveness and consistency" in formulating an "economic renewal program." Conservative Party polling has indicated, according to a document leaked from the Prime Minister's Office, that:

> The majority of Canadians do not understand fully what is meant by the terms free trade, freer trade or enhanced trade. The popular

> interpretation of free trade appears to be keyed to the word "free." It is something for nothing – a short cut – to economic prosperity. It is bigger markets for Canadian products, more jobs, more of everything. It is, as Terrence Wills of the Gazette puts it, having your cake and eating it too . . . . But are respondents really thinking when they express their opinions on free trade? Gregg suggests not, calling the free trade issue a "non-brainer" . . . .[15]

As long as the issue remains a "non-brainer," the Tories will be able to claim credit for their sound management of the Canadian economy, the document suggests. However, the generalized public support for freer Canada-U.S. trade is "extremely soft" and "significant risks" attend a failure to manage the issue in such a way that the public begins to pay attention to the specifics of the question. "The strategy should rely less on educating the general public than on getting across the message that the trade initiative is a good idea," the document concludes. "Benign neglect" should be the goal because "it is likely that the higher the profile the issue attains, the lower the degree of public approval will be." In spite of the risks, the Conservatives have determined that from a partisan perspective, after an undistinguished first year in office and an extremely rocky path littered with bank failures and rancid tuna to cross at the beginning of their second, the policy leadership and initiative shown to the public by being seen to seize the moment to enter free trade negotiations with the U.S. make it worth the gamble.

To this point, we have examined two factors that have propelled Canada-U.S. free trade to the head of the political agenda. Both of these invoke free trade as a symbol: for business as a symbol of its hopes for a quick and painless solution to Canada's industrial ills; for the Tories as a symbol that can be turned to partisan advantage by demonstrating their economic management skills. Our third factor is grounded far more in the concrete realm of commerce. In the context of the extensive trade liberalization that we have seen has already taken place between the two countries, Canada's economic elites have both short- and long-term concerns with the security and stability of the new continental trading environment that they would like to see addressed through a trade treaty.

Witness after witness from the Canadian business establishment appearing in the summer of 1985 before the special Commons-Senate Committee targeted non-tariff barriers as the real subject of any future Canada-U.S. trade negotiations. "Tariffs are already very low on Canadian steel products entering the U.S.A.," observed J.D. Allen, president and chief executive officer of Stelco, "in fact, it is not the tariff but rather the increase in non-tariff measures that affects the flow of steel."[16] R. Booth, chairman of the CMA Trade Policy Committee, submitted:

> Whether one is talking about trade enhancement, free trade, and so on is not irrelevant, but is a side issue. Essentially, what we are urging is an effort to remove the non-tariff barriers. We acknowledge your point that indeed tariffs are coming down and, by 1988, will be virtually eliminated on the majority of goods. So it is essentially the non-tariff barriers which are the issue.[17]

F. Petrie, president of the Canadian Export Association, made much the same point in observing that "trade between Canada and the United States is not regulated as much as it has been in the past by the tariff. It is really the non-tariff barriers that are the main villains, so to speak, in our access to the United States."[18] Finally, J. Hale, vice-president of the Canadian Organization of Small Business, related that "COSB's experience in assisting members with trade-related issues has underlined the fact that non-tariff barriers are often a far more significant obstacle to smaller companies entering the U.S. market than are formal tariffs or import quotas."[19]

The concern here with non-tariff barriers is not simply an abstract one relating to a relatively small amount of lost potential business. Rather, the Canadian economic establishment fears that the weighty investments, actual and anticipated, that they have made in continentalizing production may be rendered unprofitable by the vagaries of the U.S. political process. A. Powis, chairman of the Task Force on International Trade of the Business Council on National Issues, pointed to the massive current U.S. trade deficit as the most significant factor in promoting the recent American use and threatened use of non-tariff barriers and suggested that "just in our own self-defence, we had better get in behind those things." He went on to declare that:

> . . . most of their anger, in fact, almost all of their anger, is directed toward the Japanese, Brazilians, or Europeans. Nobody seems to be particularly mad at Canada, in spite of the fact that we are the second largest contributor to their trade deficit. But the dangers, I think, are very real. All you have to do is spend a few days down in Washington to realize how real they are. We are facing a threat right now of legislated lumber quotas, tariffs and whatever, which could absolutely devastate whole sectors of this country.[20]

J.D. Allen of Stelco related how his company was caught unprepared for this "threat" and how surprised and disappointed they were to discover themselves considered a "foreign" firm when they had previously thought of themselves as partners with U.S. manufacturers in a struggle to keep "the North American product competitive."

> Our shipments travel daily by truck and rail across our joint border, whereas imports from the rest of the world tend to be boatloads being brought in by trading companies. . . . In essence we are just like U.S. steel suppliers. It was quite a surprise, then, to find ourselves in early 1984 being painted with the same brush as offshore suppliers, and potentially headed for quotas that were directed at the rise of unfairly traded imports from offshore into the U.S. We had never really planned for such a dilemma.[21]

At the mid-point of the 1980's, then, in pressing for free trade negotiations with the U.S. as its immediate and urgent objective, Canada's economic elite seeks relief from the nightmare of having the southward flow of its products halted by a soon-to-be-erected wall of non-tariff barriers. H.E. Demone, vice-president of National Sea Products, argued that the impending 1986 U.S. Congressional elections dictated a promptly organized Canadian trade initiative.

> A year from now the mid-term U.S. elections will certainly be under way, at least the campaign. The American legislators will come under pressure from their constituents for increased protectionism. With the current structure of the Canadian fishing industry, the threat of countervail action by American interests will be of ever increasing concern. If such an action against fresh or frozen fish were ever to be successful, it would put the long-term viability of the entire industry in jeopardy.[22]

Some business leaders are convinced that if Canada simply declared its intent to begin negotiations now, they will gain safe harbour for their exports for some years to come. D. Morton, president and chief executive officer of Alcan, takes this view.

> We believe that a clear commitment by Canada to enter into negotiations with the U.S. to explore the issues for freer trade would have the effect of delaying or maybe even exempting Canada from the effects of actions that by many people's standards now appear to be inevitable in the U.S. in the coming period. And even though the negotiations may take months and the implementation may take years, the fact that they are started and the intent would be an immense barrier against such action against us.[23]

While some business leaders point to the tactical use of free trade negotiations as a short-term defensive measure, others are more concerned with stabilizing and extending their existing investment in continental integration. For example, R. Varah, director of commercial development for Dofasco, decried the "air of uncertainty" that had resulted from the U.S. use of non-tariff barriers:

> . . . one does not go ahead and make any long-term investments, or even short-term investments when that kind of cloud is hanging over one's industry and its access to the U.S. market. So one might say that it [free trade] would be more appropriate for secure access rather than more access.[24]

R. Cyr, chairman of the Canada-United States Advisory Committee of the Canadian Chamber of Commerce, put the same argument rhetorically. "What companies will be willing to invest in Canada if this atmosphere of uncertainty and constant harassment of our exports continues?" he asked. "What jobs will be created without investment?"[25] The submission of the Canadian Export Association also underlined the importance of a Canada-U.S. trade treaty in creating an attractive investment climate. "To plan effectively and to invest with confidence, many Canadian industries need assurance of access to the United States market," it noted. "Stability is the key consideration here."[26]

Grafting an Industrial Strategy to Free Trade?

We are witnesses to an apparently irresistible march toward Canada-U.S. free trade. The future possibility of the state formulating a nationalist industrial strategy designed to break down the administrative and technological restraints arresting the full development of Canadian manufacturing might now seem to be finally precluded. After all, Chapter 7 detailed the manner in which free trade and industrial strategy have evolved as radically opposed public policy alternatives. Will not ascendancy for the former mean oblivion for the latter? During the last three years the nationalists would appear to be in retreat and even public opinion is deserting their cause.[27] However intellectually tidy it might now be to proclaim the end of the debate, here, as at earlier points in this book, we must take care not to slip into a static and deterministic analysis that depreciates economic and political choice and therefore precludes change.

Written long before free trade was placed formally on the policy agenda and at a time when nationalist sentiment still seemed strong, Chapter 8 nevertheless reasoned that there was only a poor prospect for interventionist leadership from Ottawa for "productive" rather than "allocative" industrial policies given the weight of bureaucratic inertia, the power of foreign capital, and the traditional dominance of the continental approach. A poor prospect but *not a non-existent one,* because it was argued that if our industrial trade, balance of payments, and employment crises persisted, then for Canada's political elites the unthinkable could of necessity become thinkable. The *potential* for the creation of "productive" policies to wring a better deal from foreign capital was there in the early 1980's, and that potential is still here.[28]

This is not to suggest that Canada's state and economic elites enjoy some form of absolute autonomy from the continental ties with which they have bound themselves. Indeed, when one considers Canada's "de facto" free trade arrangement with the U.S., along with the three-quarters of Canada's import and export trade that is accounted for by the Americans, and the nearly one-half ownership share of our productive instruments that they now enjoy, it is difficult to avoid the conclusion that the Canadian economy now looks less like a distinct national economy and more like a geographically large zone *within* the U.S. economy. To the extent that the logic of the capitalist accumulation process places constraints on political choice, so continental accumulation will limit the autonomy of the Canadian state. This does not imply, however, that the Canadian state has lost either the capacity or the will to manoeuvre within the now larger continental boundaries of its economic life. Since at least the 1850's, the Canadian state could not properly be described as a "client state" no matter how strong or emotional the gravitational pull of allegiance between Canada's political and economic elites and the empire with which they had chosen to associate themselves. Indeed, it would serve no purpose for our economic elites to emasculate Canada's provincial and federal state apparatuses because these can offer them beneficial points of institutional leverage against the elites of other regions within the U.S. economy. The Canadian state will also enjoy considerable autonomy as long as the age-old public fear of being absorbed by our neighbours to the south survives and can be mobilized. While the cry of the 1980's is not likely to be "no truck nor trade with the Yankees," the desire to keep our social and political distance from the Republic shows no sign of abating.

Let us consider in more detail the conditions under which the Canadian state might be prompted in the not too distant future to manifest its relative autonomy in the field of industrial policy. The current free trade initiative is taking place in a highly unstable arena marked by a significant likelihood of political conflict. If our economic elites have convinced themselves that the negotiation of a formal free trade arrangement between Canada and the United States is in the main a *technical* problem related to the political codification and regulation of an already existing continental network of commercial associations, then they are mistaken. Conflict will manifest itself in at least four dimensions: labour and the social distribution of income, the struggle for partisan advantage, federal-provincial relations, and industrial policy. While a discussion of the first three of these dimensions is somewhat outside of the mandate of this chapter, a sketch of the characteristics of the last will suggest some of the elements that might trigger a return to political respectability for the nationalist industrial strategy option.[29]

At an earlier point in this chapter, it was suggested that an underlying factor in the emergence of free trade as a policy initiative was the desire to seize on a simple, practical, and ideologically acceptable formula for "solving" the continuing crisis of Canadian manufacturing after the eclipse of the industrial strategy and megaproject policy options in the early 1980's. Yet, as Chapters 1 and 8 document, our industrial crisis has been building *in spite of* the extensive Canada-U.S. trade liberalization that has already taken place. In its export trade, Canada continues to display an atypical profile for a developed industrial nation, with resource products dwarfing finished manufactures in importance. Accompanied by the fall of our tariff barriers through the 1970's and 1980's, our balance of trade in end manufactures has been hemorrhaging: $87 billion during the 1970's, $60 billion of which were suffered in the last five years of that decade, and $89 billion in the first five and a half years of the 1980's.[30] The figures for the 1980's would be worse if not for the $12 billion surplus posted between 1982 and 1984 in the Auto Pact, a traditional deficit item now enjoying a measure of success due to the lower labour costs in Canada accompanying our devalued dollar. They would also be worse if not for the continuing recession of the early 1980's, which put the brakes on business spending. Since Canada imports more than half the machinery and equipment it needs for production, the investment growth just now beginning to accompany the mid-1980's economic recovery should push us even further into deficit.[31]

To the extent that the free trade negotiations are really about securing and stabilizing a market access already gained, and take place at the level of government to government, they can do very little to address the structural difficulties of Canadian manufacturing. Since the current negotiations, unlike the Auto Pact model, will not result in a three-party agreement between the concerned firms and the two governments, then production, research and development, and export safeguards for Canada cannot be built into them. Because the Conservatives cannot, then, offer guarantees that employment will be protected in any specific manufacturing sector, every plant closure or layoff of significance that in the past might have gone mostly unnoticed is now likely to become a dramatic rallying point for the labour, partisan, and even provincial government opponents of the Mulroney government's trade initiative. In this regard, over time the negotiation process could very well become negatively associated with economic dislocation in the public mind through the pervasive influence of key sectors within the "cultural industries" of broadcasting, publishing, and entertainment who fear that free trade will further erode the already fragile base of the distinct Canadian identity and nationality on which their livelihoods depend.

An attempt by the Mulroney government to protect its flanks through the announcement of generous new government "adjustment" or "transition" assistance programs for "vulnerable" industries is not likely to dispel easily such public concern. Although such programs would certainly provide Tory M.P.'s with a cornucopia of patronage for distribution in their ridings, past Canadian experience recorded in Chapter 8 demonstrates that allocative policies designed to buy or subsidize performance improvements from our manufacturers have been for the most part ineffective. As well, the act of creating adjustment programs could actually serve to heighten public unease about this issue in so far as it represents an implicit admission that there will indeed be industries and regions which will be losers in any Canada-U.S. trade agreement.

While the Tories may be favourably disposed toward free market solutions to Canada's economic problems, we must presume they are also favourably disposed toward winning the next election and so are constrained to maintain a healthy level of industrial production in Canada. If they, or the bureaucrats that advise them, discover that the logic of the current negotiation process can do little to provide them with the leverage they will need to extract a better deal for Canada from the multinationals, or, worse, that a free trade pact will institutionally remove whatever leverage Canadian governments did have in the past to ensure minimum performance standards, we could see our position in the treaty talks evolve into nothing more than a desire for a symbolic statement of free and fair trade principles between the two countries. In the eventuality of a breakdown in the talks, a vacuum would be created in the industrial policy field that would almost certainly lead to a re-examination of aspects of the industrial strategy option. Either way, the Conservatives, or a successor government, might well yet eventually preside over another swing in the nationalist-continentalist pendulum and initiate tentative steps toward some kind of industrial strategy to greet the 1990's.[32]

Notes

Notes to Chapter 1

1. M. Atwood, *Survival* (Toronto: Anansi, 1972), 33.
2. *Globe and Mail,* February 6, 1982, p. B1.
3. J. Britton and J. Gilmour, *The Weakest Link: A Technological Perspective on Canadian Industrial Underdevelopment* (Ottawa: Science Council of Canada, Background Study No. 43, 1978), 26; and *Planning Now for an Information Society: Tomorrow is too Late* (Ottawa: Science Council of Canada, Report No. 33, 1982), 56.
4. W.W. Rostow, *The Stages of Economic Growth* (Cambridge: Cambridge University Press, 1960).
5. K. Levitt, *Silent Surrender* (Toronto: Macmillan, 1970).
6. A.G. Frank, *Capitalism and Underdevelopment in Latin America* (New York: Monthly Review Press, 1969).
7. See I. Lumsden (ed.), *Close the 49th parallel etc.: The Americanization of Canada* (Toronto: University of Toronto Press, 1970); and R. Laxer (ed.), *(Canada) Ltd: The Political Economy of Dependency* (Toronto: McClelland and Stewart, 1973).
8. S. Amin, *Accumulation on a World Scale,* 2 vols. (New York: Monthly Review Press, 1974). The "accumulation process" referred to by Amin, and also used in this text, more commonly goes under the label of "economic growth." As a concept, however, it has the advantage of being a more precise way of capturing what goes on when economic growth occurs. In the capitalist marketplace, firms do not simply become larger and more profitable, thereby adding to aggregate economic activity, or conversely, smaller or bankrupt, thereby subtracting from the aggregate. Rather, when looked at collectively, all this frantic activity tends toward the transformation of the process of production itself. This occurs because the competitive units must "accumulate" in order to survive. That is, they are forced to reinvest a substantial portion of the economic surplus produced by their workers in order to keep up with the new efficiencies and technological breakthroughs being made by other firms in the world economy. Thus, the accumulation process denotes qualitative as well as simply quantitative change.
9. P. Ehrensaft and W. Armstrong, "The formation of dominion capitalism: economic truncation and class structure," in *Inequality: Essays on the political economy of social welfare* (Toronto: University of Toronto Press, 1981), 114-17.
10. G. Williams, "Canada – The Case of the Wealthiest Colony," *This Magazine,* 10, 1 (1976); L. Panitch, "Dependency and Class in Canadian Political Economy," *Studies in Political Economy: A Socialist Review,* 6 (Autumn, 1981).

11. M.J. Brodie and J. Jenson, *Crisis, Challenge and Change: Party and Class in Canada* (Toronto: Methuen, 1980).

12. D.W. Slater has shown that if we use 1913 as an index base year, international trade volume in manufactures rose from 54 in 1896 to 446 in 1965 while trade volume in primary produce rose from 62 to 271 in the corresponding period. It should be noted, however, that it was not until World War II that trade in manufactures began to expand at a more rapid rate than that of primary produce. D.W. Slater, *World Trade and Economic Growth: Trends and Prospects with Applications to Canada* (Toronto: Private Planning Association of Canada, 1968), 8. Slater (p.14) calculates that transport equipment and machinery made up 11.8 per cent of world trade in manufactures in 1899 and 43.2 per cent in 1964. H. Tsyznski's data suggest that motor vehicles, industrial equipment, electrical goods, and agricultural equipment expanded from 8.3 per cent of world trade in manufactured commodities in 1899 to 34.2 per cent in 1950. A.K. Cairncross shows that "engineering products" made up only 13.4 per cent of world manufactured exports in 1899, but 39.5 per cent in 1953. H. Tsyznski, "World Trade in Manufactured Commodities, 1899-1950," *Manchester School of Economic and Social Studies,* 19 (1951), 283. A.K. Cairncross, *Factors in Economic Development* (London: George Allen and Unwin, 1962), 237.

13. For example, the economist Alfred Maizels has argued that "an increasing degree of industrialization of the export structure is . . . to be expected as a consequence of industrial growth." A. Maizels, *Industrial Growth and World Trade* (Cambridge: Cambridge University Press, 1963), 57.

14. *Ibid.,* 17.

15. M. Merhov, *Technological Dependence, Monopoly, and Growth* (Oxford: Pergamon Press, 1969), 167.

16. Cairncross, *Factors in Economic Development,* 237. P. Lamartine Yates estimates that "some dozen countries" provided nine-tenths of the manufactured exports between 1913 and 1953. Slater's data suggest that these ratios remained constant up to the mid-1960's. P. Lamartine Yates, *Forty Years of Foreign Trade* (London: George Allen and Unwin, 1959), 174-5; Slater, *World Trade and Economic Growth,* 30.

17. United Nations Conference on Trade and Development, *Review of Recent Trends and Developments in Trade in Manufactures and Semi-Manufactures* (TD/B/C.2/154), 21 May 1975, p. 6. Only ten of the developing countries account for well over one-half of this total. A.K. Bhattacharya, *Foreign Trade and International Development* (Lexington, Mass: Lexington Books, 1976), 38-9.

18. Maizels, *Industrial Growth and World Trade,* 158, 60-5. Maizels divides manufactured goods into finished manufactures and intermediate products which must undergo further processing. He claims that "a much more accurate picture of the incidence of industrialization can be obtained by excluding these intermediate products from the definition of exports of manufactures." A large proportion of Canada's exports are of intermediate or semi-manufacture (e.g., metals, pulp and paper). For further clarification, see *ibid.,* Appendix D.

19. *Ibid.,* 65-9, 135-7.

20. *Ibid.,* 62.

21. Canada, Statistics Canada, *Statistics Canada Daily,* March 26, 1982, pp. 2-8.

22. Computed from Canada, Statistics Canada, *Summary of External Trade,* various years.

23. OECD, *Labour Force Statistics,* 1963-1974 (Paris, 1976).

Notes to Chapter 2

1. While it would be difficult to isolate the tariff as the only or even the principal

cause of early Canadian industrial growth, it clearly played a central role. During the period following the proclamation of the National Policy tariffs of 1879, many small, inefficient enterprises either disappeared or were merged into more productive units. As a consequence, the total number of industrial establishments engaged in secondary production fell by approximately one-third between 1880 and 1929. Meanwhile, the total capital invested in secondary industry had increased, in relation to constant 1935-39 dollars, by three and a half times between 1890 and 1910 and had doubled again between 1910 and 1929. The decade 1900 to 1910 saw the highest rate of expansion of output in secondary industry before World War II, featuring an average growth rate of 6.2 per cent per year. In summary, by the Great Depression, the basis for Canada's future as a modern industrialized nation had been secured. G.W. Bertram, "Historical Statistics on Growth and Structure of Manufacturing in Canada, 1870-1957," Canadian Political Science Association, Conference on Statistics 1962 and 1963, Tables 1 and 3; and Bertram, "Economic Growth in Canadian Industry, 1870-1915: The Staple Model," in W. Easterbrook and M. Watkins (eds.), *Approaches to Canadian Economic History* (Toronto: McClelland and Stewart, 1967), Table 2. For a celebration of this growth, see D.G. Creighton, *Canada's First Century* (Toronto: Macmillan, 1970). For a critical perspective, see J.H. Dales, "Protection, Immigration and Canadian Nationalism," in P. Russell (ed.), *Nationalism in Canada* (Toronto: McGraw-Hill, 1966).

2. R.T. Naylor, *The History of Canadian Business, 1867-1914* (Toronto: Lorimer, 1975), I, 38. For a critique of some of the more important contemporary approaches see G. Williams, "The National Policy Tariffs: Industrial Underdevelopment Through Import Substitution," *Canadian Journal of Political Science,* XII, 2 (June, 1979), 333-9.

3. A. Gerschenkron, *Economic Backwardness in Historical Perspective* (Cambridge, Mass.: Harvard University Press, 1966), 354.

4. Canada, House of Commons, *Debates,* March 7, 1878, p. 861.

5. *Ibid.,* March 14, 1879, pp. 413-14.

6. S.D. Clark, *Canadian Manufacturers' Association* (Toronto: University of Toronto Press, 1939), 6-7.

7. *Debates,* April 22, 1879, p. 1440.

8. *Ibid.,* p. 1417.

9. *Ibid.,* p. 1442.

10. *Ibid.,* p. 1426.

11. *Ibid.,* May 12, 1887, p. 400.

12. *Journal of Commerce – Finance and Insurance Review,* February 4, 1881, p. 792. Bliss argues that such business publications "were almost certainly faithful representatives of their readers' opinions. They were self-consciously published in the interests of their constituency. Unlike the general press, all their news and editorial columns were designed to appeal to readers in a specific occupation; circulation and advertising depended on the success of that appeal." M. Bliss, *A Living Profit: Studies in the Social History of Canadian Business, 1883-1911* (Toronto: McClelland and Stewart, 1974), 145.

13. H.J. Morgan, *Canadian Men and Women of the Time, 1898* (Toronto: Briggs, 1898), 769, recorded that this journal, originally published by F. Nicholls, president of Canadian General Electric, was "the official organ and spokesman of the manufacturing interests."

14. *Canadian Manufacturer,* August 24, 1883, p. 605.

15. *Ibid.,* pp. 606-7.

16. *Ibid.*, January 2, 1885, p. 866.

17. *Journal of Commerce,* March 11, 1881, p. 111.

18. *Ibid.*, May 25, 1883, p.1305.

19. *Ibid.*, July 26, 1889, pp. 151-2.

20. *Canadian Manufacturer,* August 15, 1890, p. 119.

21. *Ibid.*, June 3, 1892, pp. 324-5.

22. Opposition was by no means universal in this industry. Canada, House of Commons, *Journals,* 1874, Appendix 3, Report of the Select Committee on Manufacturing Interests, pp. 40, 57.

23. *Ibid.*, 1876, Appendix 3, Report of the Select Committee on the Causes of the Present Depression, p. 128.

24. *Ibid.*, p. 127.

25. *Ibid.*, p. 123.

26. *Canadian Manufacturer,* October 5, 1894, pp. 338-9.

27. *Canadian Manufacturer,* July 19, 1895, pp. 55-6.

28. *Ibid.*, July 21, 1893, p. 49.

29. *Ibid.*, November 15, 1901, p. 13.

30. This is based on an estimate of the value of U.S. branch plants in Canada in 1913 of $135 million presented in F.W. Field, *Capital Investments in Canada,* third edition (Toronto: Monetary Times, 1914), 25, and the total value of capital invested in Canadian industries in 1910 of $1,248 million presented in *Census of Canada,* 1911, vol. 3. If other U.S. industrial investments reported by Field of $90 million were included, total ownership share would increase to somewhere between 16 and 18 per cent.

31. E.J. Penrose, *The Economics of the International Patent System* (Baltimore: John Hopkins, 1951), Chapters 1, 3.

32. *Debates,* June 4, 1869, pp. 619-23.

33. Computed from Naylor, *History of Canadian Business,* II, 46, Table X(1).

34. R.T. Naylor exhaustively documents many of the most significant licensing agreements of this period in *History of Canadian Business,* II, Chapter 10.

35. *Canadian Manufacturer,* December 7, 1894, p. 543.

36. *Ibid.*, January 15, 1892, p. 38.

37. M. Wilkins, *The Emergence of Multinational Enterprise: American Business Abroad from the Colonial Era to 1914* (Cambridge, Mass.: Harvard University Press, 1970), 95. Canadian General Electric was organized in 1892 with a majority of shares held by the parent U.S. company. Ownership passed to the Canadian shareholders in 1895 primarily because of a capital shortage in the U.S. firm. However, production in Canada was organized by means of patent and licence agreements with the U.S. firm until 1923, when American General Electric repurchased a majority interest. H. Marshall, F. Southard, and K. Taylor, *Canadian-American Industry: A Study in International Investment* (Toronto: McClelland and Stewart, 1976), 72-3.

38. Computed from K. Buckley, *Capital Formation in Canada, 1896-1930* (Toronto: University of Toronto Press, 1955), 130-1.

39. Computed from Canada, House of Commons, *Sessional Papers,* Trade of Canada, 1886-1915.

40. U.S., 58th Congress, Third Session, *Monthly Consular and Trade Reports*, Document 338, No. 302, November, 1905, pp. 24-5.

41. *Industrial Canada*, March, 1908, p. 619.

42. Naylor, *History of Canadian Business*, II, 59.

43. *Industrial Canada*, June, 1905, pp. 717-18.

44. *Ibid.*

45. *Monetary Times*, November 5, 1926, p. 6.

46. E.J. Hobsbawm, *Industry and Empire* (Harmondsworth: Penguin Books, 1968), 174.

47. All the companies listed as "growth industry" U.S. branch plants may be found in Field, *Capital Investments*, 39-52; and Marshall *et al.*, *Canadian-American Industry*, Chapter 2.

48. Computed from A.K. Cairncross, *Home and Foreign Investment, 1870-1913* (Cambridge: Cambridge University Press, 1953), 185; and *Statesmen's Year Book, 1913* (London: Macmillan, 1913), 107, 123, 242.

49. Computed from Buckley, *Capital Formation in Canada*, 22, 132, 135. Rail investment in the U.S. during this same period was only 7 or 8 per cent of total gross investment and had only been between 16 and 20 per cent during the peak construction era of the 1870's and 1880's. H.G. Vatter, *The Drive to Industrial Maturity, The U.S. Economy, 1860-1914* (Westport: Greenwood Press, 1975), 158-60.

50. India is perhaps the classic case. See P. Baran, *The Political Economy of Growth* (New York: Monthly Review, 1957), 144-50.

51. *Sessional Papers*, 1916, No. 6, pp. 20-1.

52. F.H. Underhill, *The Image of Confederation* (Toronto: Canadian Broadcasting Corporation, 1964), 22.

53. Great Britain, *Parliamentary Debates*, March 20, 1879, p. 1312; *The Times*, March 19, 1879, p. 11.

54. S.B. Ryerson, *Unequal Union* (Toronto: Progress, 1968), 236.

55. Great Britain, House of Commons, *Papers*, "Correspondence Respecting the Canadian Tariff," August, 1887, No. C-5179, p. 4.

56. D. Farr, *The Colonial Office and Canada, 1867-1887* (Toronto: University of Toronto Press, 1955), 193.

57. Great Britain, House of Commons, *Papers*, "Correspondence between the Colonial Office and the Authorities in Canada, on the subject of the Removal or Reduction of the Duties charged on British Goods entering Canada," June 17, 1864, No. 400, p. 12.

58. *Ibid.*

59. *Ibid.*, "Dispatch from the Governor General of Canada respecting the New Customs Tariffs," April, 1879, No. C-2305, p. 19.

60. *Ibid.*, 1887, No. C-5179, pp. 39-40.

61. See C. Berger, *The Sense of Power* (Toronto: University of Toronto Press, 1970); D. Bell and L. Tepperman, *The Roots of Disunity* (Toronto: McClelland and Stewart, 1979), Chapters 2 and 3.

62. Hobsbawm, *Industry and Empire*, 191; S.B. Saul, *Studies in British Overseas Trade, 1870-1914* (Liverpool: Liverpool University Press, 1960), 220.

63. G.A. Montgomery, *The Rise of Modern Industry in Sweden* (London: King and Son, 1939), 104.

64. J. Kuuse, "Foreign Trade and the Breakthrough of the Engineering Industry in Sweden, 1890-1920," *Scandinavian Economic History Review,* XXV, 1 (1977), 1.

65. In Canada, some have alleged that industrialization was inhibited by a form of species hostility toward manufacturers on the part of the merchants and financiers who organized Canadian resource capitalism. The Swedish experience directly contradicts this thesis, at least as it can be found in the work of R.T. Naylor in his "The rise and fall of the third commercial empire of the St. Lawrence," in G. Teeple (ed.), *Capitalism and the National Question in Canada* (Toronto: University of Toronto Press, 1972).

66. L. Jorberg, "Structural Change and Economic Growth in Nineteenth Century Sweden," in S. Koblik (ed.), *Sweden's Development from Poverty to Affluence, 1750-1950* (Minneapolis: University of Minnesota Press, 1975), 110. See also Kuuse, "Breakthrough of the Engineering Industry in Sweden," 7. For the role of merchants and financiers in Japanese industrialization, see J. Hirschmeier, "Shibusawa Eiichi: Industrial Pioneer," and Yasuzo Horie, "Entrepreneurship in Meiji Japan," in W.W. Lockwood (ed.), *The State and Economic Enterprise in Japan* (Princeton: Princeton University Press, 1965).

67. Kuuse, "Breakthrough of the Engineering Industry in Sweden," 5-6.

68. *Industrial Canada,* June, 1905, pp. 717-18.

69. United Nations, UNCTAD Secretariat, *Case Studies in the Transfer of Technology: Policies for transfer and development of technology in pre-War Japan, (1868-1937),* April 25, 1978, p. 16.

70. *Ibid.,* p. 34.

71. *Ibid.,* pp. 4-5.

72. W.W. Lockwood, *The Economic Development of Japan,* second edition (Princeton: Princeton University Press, 1968), 381.

73. *Ibid.,* 539-40.

74. *Ibid.,* 345, 354, 365.

Notes to Chapter 3

1. For more on the institutional development of Trade and Commerce during this and later periods, see O.M. Hill, *Canada's Salesman to the World: The Department of Trade and Commerce, 1892-1939* (Montreal: McGill-Queen's, 1977); G. Williams, "The Political Economy of Canadian Manufactured Exports: The Problem, its Origins, and the Department of Trade and Commerce, 1885-1930," Ph.D. dissertation, York University, 1978, Chapters 3-5.

2. *Canadian Manufacturer,* January 2, 1885, p. 863; February 6, 1885, p. 937.

3. *Industrial Canada,* November, 1901, pp. 131-2. (Report of the Commercial Intelligence Committee to the Annual Convention of the Canadian Manufacturers' Association, November 5-6, 1901.)

4. *Ibid.*

5. Public Archives of Canada (PAC), MG 28, I 230, vol. 36, nos. 154-163, July 16, 1907.

6. *Industrial Canada,* October, 1912, p. 373.

7. *Ibid.,* July, 1909, p. 1179.

8. *Ibid.*

9. *Ibid.,* July, 1903, p. 528.

10. *Ibid.,* July, 1907, p. 924.

11. *Monetary Times,* September 28, 1912, p. 492.

12. *Journal of Commerce,* December 15, 1893, p. 1144.

13. *Industrial Canada,* February, 1902, pp. 219-20.

14. *Ibid.,* November, 1903, pp. 209-11.

15. *Ibid.,* March, 1903, p. 363; April, 1904, p.445; July, 1918, p. 146.

16. Canada, Trade and Commerce, *Weekly Report,* no. 293, September 7, 1909, p. 792.

17. *Ibid.,* no. 416, January 15, 1912, p. 41.

18. *Ibid.,* no. 181, July 15, 1907, pp. 371-2.

19. PAC, RG 20, vol. 1156, no. 5311, June 10, 1897.

20. *Weekly Report,* no. 19, June 6, 1904, pp. 3-4.

21. *Ibid.,* no. 377, April 18, 1911, p. 496.

22. *Ibid.,* no. 353, November 1, 1910.

23. *Ibid.,* no. 381, May 15, 1911.

24. *Ibid.,* no. 331, May 30, 1910, pp. 661-2.

25. *Ibid.,* no. 3, February 15, 1904, p. 12.

26. *Ibid.,* no. 266, March 1, 1909, p. 173.

27. *Ibid.,* no. 338, July 18, 1910, p. 857.

28. *Ibid.,* no. 17, May 23, 1904, p. 4.

29. *Journal of Commerce,* October 25, 1889, p. 718.

30. *Industrial Canada,* July, 1911, p. 1274.

31. *Weekly Report,* no. 252, November 23, 1908, p. 830.

32. *Ibid.,* no. 155, January 14, 1907, p. 31. For additional examples, see no. 122, May 28, 1906, p. 405; no. 128, July 9, 1906, p. 529; no. 541, June 8, 1914, p. 816.

33. *Ibid.,* no. 314, January 31, 1910. p. 136

34. *Ibid.,* no. 432, May 6, 1912, pp. 417-18.

35. *Ibid.,* no. 336, July 4, 1910, p. 308.

36. *Ibid.,* no. 9, March 28, 1904, p. 11.

37. *Industrial Canada,* August, 1906, p. 33.

38. *Weekly Report,* no. 3, February 15, 1904, p. 23.

39. *Ibid.,* no. 139, September 24, 1906, p. 690.

40. *Ibid.,* no. 35, September 26, 1904, p. 13.

41. *Ibid.,* no. 242, September 14, 1908, p. 607.

42. *Ibid.,* no. 316, February 14, 1910, p. 192. See also no. 562, November 2, 1914, p. 1945. On this same subject, the *Monetary Times* pointed out that "the weekly reports of the Department of Trade and Commerce do not appear to receive the serious attention they deserve." (May 1, 1910, p. 1951.)

43. *Weekly Report,* no. 227, June 1, 1908, p. 331.

44. *Industrial Canada,* January, 1911, pp. 630-1.

45. PAC, RG 20, vol. 43, no. 18165, April 11, 1912.

46. *Canadian Manufacturer,* October 19, 1894, pp. 385-6.

47. *Monetary Times,* August 14, 1891, p. 193.

48. *Industrial Canada,* June, 1902, p. 381.

49. *Canadian Manufacturer,* November 2, 1894, p. 440.

50. The *Journal of Commerce* expressed this point elegantly. "Inter-colonial trade or inter-imperial trade should develop equally with imperial sentiment, if it does not there is a screw loose somewhere in the machinery of the British Empire." (January 18, 1901, p. 148.)

51. *Industrial Canada,* September, 1902, p. 71.

52. *Ibid.,* October, 1907, p. 247. See also October, 1905, p. 151.

53. *Ibid.,* October, 1907, p. 283.

54. *Ibid.,* January, 1908, p. 498.

55. *Weekly Report,* no. 198, November 11, 1907, p. 639.

56. *Ibid.,* no. 113, March 26, 1906, p. 232.

57. *Ibid.,* no. 469, January 20, 1913, p. 37.

58. *Ibid.,* no. 542, June 15, 1914, p. 867.

Notes to Chapter 4

1. Williams, "The Political Economy of Canadian Manufactured Exports," Appendix I. Finished manufactures, the reader will recall from our discussion in Chapter 1, are products not normally subject to a further process of manufacture.

2. J.J. Deutsch, "War Finance and the Canadian Economy, 1914-20," *Canadian Journal of Economics and Political Science,* 6, 4 (November, 1940), 535.

3. *Debates,* January 22, 1917, p. 31; Deutsch, "War Finance."

4. Hill, *Canada's Salesman to the World,* 170; J.C. Hopkins, *Canada at War, 1914-1918* (Toronto: Canadian Annual Review, 1919), 66.

5. M. Bliss, in his biography of businessman J.W. Flavelle, chairman of the Imperial Munitions Board, recorded the Board's "impressive" achievement in pushing Canadian manufacturers "into reaching higher standards of precision and efficiency and a far higher volume of production than anyone had thought possible." *A Canadian Millionaire* (Toronto: Macmillan, 1978), 318.

6. R.G. Brown and R. Cook, *Canada 1896-1921: A Nation Transformed* (Toronto: McClelland and Stewart, 1974), 198-200, 239-40.

7. PAC, MG 26 H, vol. 49, no. 22989, May 29, 1915.

8. *Ibid.,* no. 22986, May 27, 1915.

9. *Ibid.,* vol. 50, nos. 23150-23152, June 21, 1915.

10. *Ibid.,* nos. 23060-23062, June 11, 1915.

11. *Ibid.,* nos. 23075-23079, June 12, 1915.

12. *Ibid.,* no. 22998. See also no. 23096.

13. *Ibid.,* vol. 50, nos. 23142-23143, 23150-23152, June 21, 1915.

14. D. Carnegie, *History of the Munitions Supply in Canada* (London: Longmans, Green, 1925), 216. See also *ibid.,* 14, 29, 33, 68, 72, 183, 215, 217; Bliss, *A Canadian Millionaire,* 239.

15. Bliss makes a similar point. "At best . . . Canada's manufacturing contribution to the war was primitive by British and American standards – Canadians made ammunition; others made guns, tanks, and fighting aircraft. The long-term benefits of war industries to Canada in terms of new processes and methods were shared by other industrial countries, resulting in a treadmill situation and no comparative advantage." *A Canadian Millionaire,* 318.

16. Brown and Cook, *Canada 1896-1921*, 236.

17. PAC, MG 26 H, vol. 55, no. 27574, July 22, 1915.

18. *Ibid.,* nos. 27512-27518, June 11, 1915.

19. *Ibid.,* MG 27 II D 7, vol. 18, no. 1871, December 15, 1914.

20. *Ibid.,* MG 26 H, vol. 55, no. 27626, September 4, 1915.

21. J.W. Flavelle, before his appointment as chairman of the Imperial Munitions Board, wrote Borden, "I have frequently reminded my manufacturing friends that the orders which were secured for blankets, knitted goods, saddlery etc. during the early months of the war, originated solely with the Government, and that they, as manufacturers, showed little resource or capacity in finding business for themselves . . . . It occurs to me that where the manufacturing interests have failed, has been in organized effort in harmony with what was being done in Ottawa . . . . " PAC, MG 27 II D 7, vol. 18, no. 1984, June 25, 1915.

22. *Ibid.,* no. 27976, October 15, 1918.

23. *Ibid.,* vol. 19, no. 2550, April 12, 1916.

24. *Weekly Report,* no. 554, September 7, 1914, p. 1460.

25. *Industrial Canada,* July, 1915, pp. 331-2.

26. *Ibid.* For reasons well documented in Hill, *Canada's Salesman to the World* (211-20), this was to prove "an expensive and unproductive venture."

27. Canada, Trade and Commerce, *The German War and its Relation to Canadian Trade,* 1914. A sample of trade commissioner interest in replacing German goods in the Australian market can be found in *Weekly Report,* no. 564, November 16, 1914, p. 2087.

28. *Industrial Canada,* October, 1915, pp. 647-8; *Monetary Times,* February 23, 1917, p. 136; *Weekly Bulletin,* no. 641, May 8, 1916, p. 1020.

29. *Weekly Bulletin,* no. 638, April 17, 1916, p. 853.

30. *Ibid.,* no. 709, August 27, 1917, p. 443.

31. *Ibid.,* no. 669, November 16, 1916, p. 1177.

32. *Ibid.,* no. 832, January 12, 1920, pp. 93, 97.

33. *Ibid.,* no. 672, December 11, 1916.

34. *Ibid.,* no. 732, December 3, 1917, p. 1236.

35. *Industrial Canada,* July, 1918, p. 145.

36. *Weekly Bulletin,* no. 697, June 4, 1917, p. 1308; no. 641, May 8, 1916, pp. 1027-8.

37. *Industrial Canada,* August, 1916, p. 507.

38. *Ibid.*, April, 1918, p. 1754.

39. *Ibid.*, September, 1914, p. 164.

40. *Ibid.*, October, 1914, pp. 267-8.

41. *Ibid.*, March, 1916, p. 1171.

42. *Weekly Bulletin,* no. 633, March 13, 1916; no. 662, October 2, 1916, p. 769.

43. *Industrial Canada,* July, 1916, p. 384.

44. Canada, Senate, *Debates,* July 11, 1917, p. 226.

45. *Ibid.,* June 5, 1917, pp. 94, 97.

46. The Canadian Industrial Reconstruction Association included E.W. Beatty (Canadian Pacific Railway), T. Cantley (Nova Scotia Steel and Coal), H. Cockshutt

(Cockshutt Plow), H.R. Drummond (Canada Sugar), R. Hobson (Steel Company of Canada), W. McMaster (Canadian Explosives), F. Nicholls (Canadian General Electric), and T.A. Russell (Willys Overland and Canada Cycle and Motor). For an examination of its domestic activities, see T. Traves, *The State and Enterprise: Canadian Manufacturers and the Federal Government, 1917-1931* (Toronto: University of Toronto Press, 1979).

47. "A National Policy," An Address delivered by Sir John Willison at Galt, Ontario, July 17, 1918, and published by the Canadian Industrial Reconstruction Association, pp. 6-9.

48. PAC, MG 26 H, vol. 93, nos. 48582-48585, November 7, 1918. Lloyd Harris, chairman of the London Mission, was, among other things: president of Russell Motor Car and of Canada Glue; vice- president of Canada Starch; and a director of the Steel Company of Canada. Sir Charles Gordon, chairman of the Ottawa Commission, was, among other things: president of Dominion Textiles, Penmans, and Dominion Glass; vice-president of the Bank of Montreal and Montreal Cotton; and a director of Royal Trust and Provincial Paper. B.M. Greene (ed.), *Who's Who in Canada and Why* (Toronto: International Press, 1919-20), 454, 351.

49. PAC, MG 26 H, vol. 93, no. 48606, November 15, 1918.

50. *Ibid.*, no. 48610, November 16, 1918.

51. *Ibid.*, RG 20, vol. 85, no. 22038, December 4, 1918.

52. *Ibid.*, MG 26 H, vol. 93, no. 48754, January 28, 1919.

53. *Ibid.*, no. 48622, November 26, 1918.

54. *Ibid.*, nos. 48951-48957, December 6, 1919.

55. *Industrial Canada*, July, 1919, p. 206.

56. PAC, MG 26 H, vol. 93, nos. 48951-48957, December 6, 1919.

57. *Ibid.*, no. 48885, April 14, 1919.

58. *Industrial Canada*, July, 1920, p. 157.

59. *Ibid.*, February, 1921, p. 126.

60. *Weekly Bulletin*, No. 838, February 23, 1920, p. 450.

61. *Ibid.*, no. 842, March 22, 1920, p. 651.

62. *Debates*, March 23, 1920, p. 621.

63. *Debates*, March 29, 1921, p. 1276.

64. *Industrial Canada*, November, 1922, p. 56.

65. Canada, Department of Marine and Fisheries, *Annual Report*, 1922-23, pp. 13-15.

Notes to Chapter 5

1. Examples of the following trade mispractices can be found in the *Commercial Intelligence Journal* of Trade and Commerce: failure to dispatch salesmen to foreign markets, no. 1263, April 14, 1928, p. 567; failure to send catalogues or samples, no. 1054, April 12, 1924, p. 467; refusal to quote foreign delivery prices, no. 997, March 10, 1923, p. 386; unwillingness to advertise, no. 1277, January 21, 1928, pp. 100-1; sloppy packing, no. 1045, February 9, 1924, p. 216. The department's 1924-25 *Annual Report* noted that "the most prolific source of complaint by Trade Commissioners on behalf of foreign business men is inattention by Canadian firms to correspondence." (p. 29) For reasons noted in Chapter 8, critical reports were censored by Trade and Commerce after the 1920's.

2. *Industrial Canada*, July, 1916, p. 384.

3. PAC, MG 26 H, vol. 98, no. 52364, December 12, 1918.

4. *Industrial Canada,* March, 1922, pp. 53-4.

5. *Debates,* October 12, 1932. p. 119. For a descriptive account of the Imperial Conference see Hill, *Canada's Salesman to the World,* Chapter 24.

6. *Monetary Times,* April 2, 1920, p. 15.

7. For example, *Industrial Canada,* July, 1918, p. 238; February, 1919, p. 79; September, 1920, p. 132; March, 1921, pp. 60-3; August, 1922, p. 81; June, 1923, p. 94; October, 1923, p. 78; March, 1927, p. 64.

8. Williams, "The Political Economy of Canadian Manufactured Exports," Appendix I.

9. *Debates,* April 13, 1923, pp. 1828-30. Robbs' trade categories were so loosely defined that they had little meaning. "If we ship wheat that is a raw product. If we ship flour that is a manufactured product. If we ship milk that is a raw product. If we ship butter that is a manufactured product. If we ship pulp-wood it is a raw product. If we ship paper it is a manufactured product. If we ship pulp it is partly manufactured." The issue of classifying exports is taken up again in Chapter 7. For further clarification, see Maizels, *Industrial Growth and World Trade,* Appendix D.

10. *Monetary Times,* April 6, 1928, p. 7.

11. *Debates,* February 11, 1929, p. 34.

12. *Debates,* June 1, 1931, p. 2164.

13. J. Laxer, "Lament for an Industry," *Last Post,* 2, 3 (December-January, 1971-1972), 34.

14. PAC, RG 20, vol. 95, no. 22693 F-1, October 21, 1922.

15. *Commercial Intelligence Journal,* no. 1354, January 11, 1930, p. 60. For automobiles, see no. 1291, October 27, 1928, p. 609.

16. PAC, RG 20, vol. 712, no. 4- U 2-32, February 8, 1947.

17. *Ibid.,* vol. 95, no. 22693 F -1, March 30, 1933.

18. *New York Times,* January 31, 1933.

19. M. Wilkins and F.E. Hill, *American Business Abroad: Ford on Six Continents* (Detroit: Wayne State University Press, 1964), 18, 114-15, 130-1, 159.

20. *Debates,* May 21, 1926, p. 3672; February 21, 1927, p. 507.

21. *Ibid.,* May 21, 1926, p. 3644.

22. *Ibid.,* April 27, 1926, p. 2847.

23. *Ibid.,* May 21, 1926, p. 3655. G.H. Boivin, Minister of Customs, also stressed this point, pp. 3668-9.

24. C.H. Aikman, *National Problems of Canada: The Automobile Industry of Canada,* McGill University Economic Studies, No. 8. (Toronto: Macmillan, 1926), 31, 40-1.

25. PAC, RG 20, vol. 124, no. 25007: C (1), March 26, 1934.

26. *Ibid.,* RG 2, 1, vol. 1778, no. 109, January 22, 1927; vol. 1818, T. 127996 B, April 19, 1929.

27. Canada, Advisory Board on Tariff and Taxation, Record of Public Sittings, Iron and Steel, vol. 3, Automobiles and their Parts, December 12, 1929; January 22, 23, 1930, p. 99.

28. Australia, House of Representatives, *Debates,* October 2, 1924, p. 5084.

29. Canadian automakers were disappointed that the content quotas were so high and

that only certain parts had been included in the treaty, but they hoped for a future moderation in the regulations that would allow them preferential entry into the Australian market. T.A. Russell, president of Willys-Overland, wrote King: "I do not know that the Treaty at the present moment can be taken advantage of by any Canadian motor firm except the Ford Company, but we have all felt that it more or less prepared the way for the maintenance of preference within the Empire and were glad indeed to see a start made with Australia. Perhaps at some later date it may be possible to secure some further advantage, which would benefit the motor industry more directly." PAC, MG 26 J 1, vol. 123, no. 104625, July 17, 1925.

30. New Zealand, House of Representatives, *Debates*, September 30, 1924, p. 15.

31. PAC, MG 26 J 1, vol. 80, no. 67893, December 6, 1922.

32. *Ibid.*, no. 67895.

33. Australia, House of Representatives, *Debates*, October 2, 1924, p. 5073.

34. *Industrial Canada*, January, 1929, p. 222.

35. PAC, RG 20, vol. 162, no. 26725(3), July 23, 1932.

36. *Ibid.*, vol. 712, no. 4- U 2-40 A, January 27, 1950.

37. *Weekly Bulletin*, no. 858, July 12, 1920, pp. 70-1; no. 869, September 27, 1920, p. 890.

38. I.M. Drummond, *Imperial Economic Policy, 1917-1939* (London: George Allen and Unwin, 1974), 33-6

39. PAC, RG 20, vol. 162, no. 26725 (2) (3).

40. *Ibid.*, MG 26 J 1, vol. 104, no. 87927, January 15, 1924.

41. *Ibid.*, MG 26 E 1 (a), vol. 96, no. 7, February 1, 1894

42. Australia, House of Representatives, *Debates*, August 27, 1925.

43. Union of South Africa, House of Assembly, *Debates*, July 1, 1925, pp. 5286-7.

44. Wilkins and Hill, *American Business Abroad*, 242. The trade commissioners recorded this decline. *Commercial Intelligence Journal*, no. 1152, February 17, 1926, p. 283 (South Africa); no. 1195, December 25, 1926, pp.748-9 (New Zealand); no. 1225, July 23, 1927, p. 101 (Australia).

45. Sun Life Assurance Company of Canada, *The Canadian Automotive Industry*, prepared for the Royal Commission on Canada's Economic Prospects, September, 1956, p. 7.

46. J.V.T. Baker, *The New Zealand People at War: War Economy* (Christchurch: Whitcombe and Tombs, 1965), 19-20; D.H. Houghton, *The South African Economy*, fourth edition (Cape Town: Oxford University Press, 1976), 122-6; A.E. Safarian, *The Canadian Economy in the Great Depression* (Toronto: McClelland and Stewart, 1970), Table 50; A.G.L. Shaw, *The Economic Development of Australia*, seventh edition (Melbourne: Longman Cheshire, 1980), 155-6.

47. *Debates*, February 21, 1927, p. 507

48. PAC, RG 20, vol. 94, no. 22693: E, December 27, 1924, and January 5, 1925.

49. *Ibid.*, vol. 162, no. 26725 (2), October 13, 1930, October 21, 1930, and May 4, 1931.

50. *Debates*, March 13, 1928, p. 1262

51. See Traves, *State and Enterprise*, Chapter 6. He observes, "the auto tariff revisions greatly appealed to King's imagination; at one stroke he increased jobs and reduced prices for the working man, he strengthened the Liberals' popular political base, and he furthered the Liberal-Progressive party alliance." (p. 108)

52. Advisory Board on Tariff and Taxation, Automobiles, pp. 68-9, 146.

53. *Debates,* April 26, 1932, pp. 2378-9.

54. *Monetary Times,* October 24, 1919, p. 11.

55. For example, *Weekly Bulletin,* no. 898, April 18, 1921, p. 627; no. 919, September 12, 1921, p. 433; *Commercial Intelligence Journal,* no. 968, August 19, 1922, p. 319; no. 1362, March 8, 1930, p. 368.

56. PAC, RG 20, vol. 178, no. 27725 (1), April 13, 1939, and November 7, 1947.

57. *Ibid.*, no. 27491, February 25, 1926.

58. *Ibid.,* March 30, 1926.

Notes to Chapter 6

1. Dominion Bureau of Statistics, *Indexes of Real Domestic Product by Industry* (1961 Base), July, 1968; Statistics Canada, *Fixed Capital Flows and Stocks,* 1926-1978, October, 1978; *National Income and Expenditure Accounts,* vol. 1, Annual Estimates, 1926-1974, March, 1976.

2. Ontario, *Debates,* June 13, 1968, p. 4427. For a thorough and insightful discussion of foreign investment after World War II, see D. Wolfe, "Economic Growth and Foreign Investment: A Perspective on Canadian Economic Policy, 1945-1957," *Journal of Canadian Studies,* 13, 1 (Spring, 1978). For a defence of foreign investment during this era, see R. Bothwell, I. Drummond, and J. English, *Canada since 1945: Power, Politics and Provincialism* (Toronto: University of Toronto Press, 1981), Chapters 5 and 28.

3. Canada, Information Canada, *Foreign Direct Investment in Canada,* 1972, Tables 9 and 10, p. 25.

4. C.P. Kindleberger, *Foreign Trade and the National Economy* (New Haven: Yale University Press, 1962), 87.

5. *Industrial Canada,* July, 1939, pp. 100-2. The trade commissioners also remarked on the changing character of market demand as ISI became established in the countries where they were posted. For example, one wrote Ottawa that "in view of the apparent desire of both Chile and Bolivia to develop their own national industries of a secondary nature, we would be well advised, I believe, to centre our efforts toward the supply of those materials which entered into these said secondary industries, for I do not think that the tariff would permit much in the way of market development in the sale of finished consumers' goods." PAC, RG 20, vol. 270, no. 35226, May 27, 1943. See also *ibid.,* July 8, 1943.

6. *Industrial Canada,* May, 1939, pp. 39, 49.

7. Canada, Department of Reconstruction and Supply, *Canada's Industrial War Effort,* 1939-1945, 1947. See Chapter 4 for a review of Canadian technological dependence in World War I. Not only on the terrain of technology was the export performance of Canadian manufacturers during World War II to be closely patterned on their Great War experience. Here again, their trade was export in destination only. The state, under the auspices of the Hyde Park arrangements, collected foreign orders and organized domestic production. Indeed, at the end of hostilities, C.D. Howe, Minister of Munitions and Supply, had to lecture manufacturers grown prosperous on guaranteed markets in the virtues of private enterprise. See R. Bothwell and W. Kilbourn, *C.D. Howe* (Toronto: McClelland and Stewart, 1979), Chapters 10-12; C.P. Stacey, *Arms, Men and Governments: The War Policies of Canada, 1939-1945* (Ottawa: Queen's Printer, 1970), Part VIII.

8. Stacey, *Arms, Men and Governments,* 489. He also reports that "largely because so many Canadian firms were subsidiaries of American or British corporations, comparatively little industrial research or development was then conducted in Canada,

and of what was done a quite negligible amount had any military significance." (p. 507)

9. *Industrial Canada,* November, 1942, pp. 93-5.

10. Trade and Commerce, Economics Branch, *Canadian Machinery and Equipment Market,* September 1, 1949.

11. PAC, MG 27 III B 20, vol. 87, no. S. 48-10, August 15, 1947. For an informative discussion of Howe's role in economic policy formulation, see Bothwell and Kilbourn, *C.D. Howe.*

12. PAC, *ibid.,* September 2, 1947. W.A. Mackintosh, another important economic adviser to Howe and a figure more fully discussed in Chapter 7, was to write about the process of getting economic theories through to his boss that "Howe agrees but he does not know what he is agreeing with." Quoted in J.L. Granatstein, *The Ottawa Men: The Civil Service Mandarins, 1935-1957* (Toronto: Oxford University Press, 1982), 166.

13. For a more complete discussion of this legislation, see H.C. Eastman, "Recent Canadian Economic Policy: Some Alternatives," *Canadian Journal of Economics and Political Science,* XVIII, 2 (May, 1952); Wolfe, "Economic Growth and Foreign Investment."

14. *Debates,* March 1, 1949, p. 1002; *Industrial Canada,* February, 1948, pp. 49-52; PAC, MG 27 III B 20, vol. 86, no. S 48, January 15, 1948.

15. *Industrial Canada,* February, 1948, pp. 49-52.

16. PAC, MG 27 III B 20, vol. 87, no. S. 48-10, October 23, 1947.

17. *Montreal Star,* June 27, 1979, p. D2.

18. C. Vaitsos, "Patents Revisited: Their Function in Developing Countries," in C. Cooper (ed.), *Science, Technology and Development* (London: Frank Cass, 1973).

19. *Foreign Direct Investment in Canada,* p. 118. For general reviews of Canadian technological dependence, see Canada, Science Council of Canada, Background Studies no. 23, P.L. Bourgault, *Innovation and the Structure of Canadian Industry,* October, 1972; and no. 43, J. Britton and J. Gilmour, *The Weakest Link: A Technological Perspective on Canadian Industrial Underdevelopment,* 1978.

20. Canada, Science Council of Canada, Background Study no. 35, A.J. Cordell and J. Gilmour, *The Role and Function of Government Laboratories and the Transfer of Technology to the Manufacturing Sector,* April, 1975, pp. 45-6.

21. Canada, Science Council of Canada, Background Study no. 22, A.J. Cordell, *The Multinational Firm, Foreign Direct Investment and Canadian Science Policy,* December, 1971, p. 56.

22. Industry, Trade and Commerce, Technological Innovation Studies Program, Research Report, D.A. Ondrack, *Foreign Ownership and Technological Innovations in Canada: A Study of the Industrial Machinery Sector of Industry,* October, 1975, pp. 29-30.

23. Canada, Department of Justice, Combines Investigation Commission, Report of the Commissioner, *Canada and International Cartels,* October 10, 1945, p. 49. It is unfortunate indeed that all the data collected by the Commission in preparing this report is missing and has either been destroyed or lost. Although the author was given permission to examine these documents, he was informed by an official of the Department of Consumer and Corporate Affairs that two extensive searches had produced no satisfactory results.

24. *Ibid.,* p. 43

25. *Ibid.,* pp. 20-1.

26. PAC, RG 20, vol. 718, no. 7-983, June 5, 1945.

27. *Ibid.*, vol. 716, no. 7-C 1-1, March 2, 1949. For other examples see vol. 650, no. 7-1586-F, October 24, 1961; vol. 722, no. 11872, September 15, 1947; vol. 723, no. 7-389, May 23, 1947; vol. 724, no. 19838, January 11, 19, 1950.

28. *Ibid.*, vol. 718, no. 7-983, June 3, 1946, Garner to McLeod.

29. *Ibid.*, vol. 665, no. 18-590-1 D (1), February 8, 1963; "Special Study on Export by Canadian Subsidiaries," pp. 11, 13.

30. *Ibid.*, vol. 650, no. 7-1586-E-1, May 2, 1961. Industry, Trade and Commerce kindly opened certain of their records from 1952 to the mid-1960's held by the Public Archives for the examination of the author. This exception to the thirty-year secrecy rule was granted on condition that the identities of individuals and corporations not be disclosed.

31. *Ibid.*, vol. 665, no. 18-590-1 D (1), March 15, 1963: "Special Study on Export by Canadian Subsidiaries," p. 2.

32. *Ibid.;* also "Main Report Special Study on Export by Canadian Subsidiaries," Trade Commissioners' Conference, Ottawa, April 4-11, 1963, p. 2.

33. *Ibid.*, vol. 694, no. 18-171-3, April 15, 1958: "Universal Export Rights for U.S. Subsidiaries," Item 3.

34. *Ibid.*, vol. 650, no. 7-1586-E-1, May 11, 1961: "Summary of Discussions United States Group, 1960 Export Trade Promotion Conference."

35. "Special Study on Export by Canadian Subsidiaries," February 8, 1963, p. 4.

36. *Ibid.*, p. 3.

37. "Main Report Special Study on Export by Canadian Subsidiaries."

38. PAC, RG 20, vol. 921, no. T-7-1582, December 22, 1964.

39. *Financial Post,* November 29, 1947, p. 1.

40. Bothwell and Kilbourn, *C.D. Howe,* 219-20.

41. *Debates,* December 16, 1947, pp. 354-5, 398-9.

42. *Ibid.*, pp. 345-6.

43. *Ibid.*, June 10, 1954, p. 5768.

44. *Financial Post,* October 20, 1956, pp. 28-9; *Globe and Mail,* October 16, 1956, p. 22.

45. *Debates,* July 9, 1956, p. 5777; February 11, 1957, p. 1157.

46. *Ibid.*, July 15, 1959, p. 6096.

47. *Ibid.*, December 11, 1962, p. 2527.

48. *Ibid.*, June 13, 1963, p. 1001.

49. W. Gordon, *Walter L. Gordon: A Political Memoir* (Toronto: McClelland and Stewart, 1977), 256.

50. *Debates,* June 17, 1963, p. 1246; *Globe and Mail,* June 15, 1963, p. 4.

51. *Debates,* March 24, 1964, pp. 1398-9.

52. *Ibid.*, March 31, 1966, pp. 3713-14; November 18, 1966, p. 10052.

53. *Industrial Canada,* July, 1947, p. 121.

54. *Industrial Canada,* July, 1938, p. 107; July, 1939, pp. 104-5.

55. PAC, RG 20, vol. 718, no. 7-983, March 5, 1946.

56. *Industrial Canada,* January, 1939, p. 53.

57. *Ibid.*, July, 1944, p. 238.

58. *Ibid.*, January, 1948, p. 112.

59. *Ibid.*, July, 1958, pp. 44-50.

60. *Ibid.*, June, 1958, pp. 50, 54.

61. *Ibid.*, p. 61; September, 1958, p. 62.

62. *Globe and Mail*, September 21, 1963, p. 3; *Financial Post*, January 19, 1963.

Notes to Chapter 7

1. R. Whitaker, "Images of the state in Canada," in L. Panitch (ed.), *The Canadian State: Political Economy and Political Power* (Toronto: University of Toronto Press, 1977), 28-9.

2. See D. Drache, "Rediscovering Canadian Political Economy," *Journal of Canadian Studies*, XI, 3 (August, 1976).

3. W.A. Mackintosh, "Economic Factors in Canadian History," in W.T Easterbrook and M.H. Watkins (eds.), *Approaches to Canadian Economic History* (Toronto: McClelland and Stewart, 1967), 4. Although Mackintosh made no such formal division into stages, they are easily deduced from a careful reading of his work. The similarities are striking between Mackintosh's theory and the later economic "take-off" theory of U.S. economist W.W. Rostow in his *Stages of Economic Growth.*

4. W.A. Mackintosh, "Some Aspects of a Pioneer Economy," *Canadian Journal of Economics and Political Science* (November, 1936), 460.

5. W.A. Mackintosh, "Canadian Tariff Policy," *Canadian Papers, 1933* (Toronto: Canadian Institute of International Affairs, 1933), 17.

6. W.A. Mackintosh, *Agricultural Co-operation in Western Canada* (Toronto: Ryerson, 1924), 3.

7. Mackintosh, "Economic Factors in Canadian History," 14. Again, the parallel to Rostow is obvious. He argues that this same period produced "take-off" in the Canadian economy. *(Stages of Economic Growth,* 8-9.)

8. Canada, Royal Commission on Dominion-Provincial Relations, Appendix III, W.A. Mackintosh, *The Economic Background of Dominion-Provincial Relations,* 1939, Chapter 8.

9. Mackintosh, "Canadian Tariff Policy," 16-17.

10. H.A. Innis, *The Fur Trade in Canada* (New Haven: Yale University Press, 1930), 388.

11. H.A. Innis, *Essays in Canadian Economic History* (Toronto: University of Toronto Press, 1956), 20.

12. *Ibid.,* 127, 174, 405.

13. H. Laureys, *The Foreign Trade of Canada* (Toronto: Macmillan, 1929), 75, 78. It is instructive to contrast Laureys' pessimism here to the optimistic comments of Canada's political leaders in his era on the international performance of our manufacturers. Prime Minister King, it will be remembered from Chapter 5, was not alone in remarking that "we are getting away from the stage of a country which is simply selling its raw materials to the stage where as a country we are developing a large manufacturing industry as well . . . we have reached a higher stage in our manufacturing development in Canada, having regard to the age of the country and its population, than has, I believe, any other country in the history of the world." *(Debates,* February 11, 1929, p. 34.)

14. Laureys, *The Foreign Trade of Canada,* 80-3.

15. *Ibid.*, xiv.

16. Innis believed that "institutions," including the state, "act as channels through which civilization bears with persistent corroding effects on the position of the social scientist." "The Role of Intelligence: Some Further Notes," *Canadian Journal of Economics and Political Science*, 1, 2 (May, 1935), 282. See also B. Ferguson and D. Owram, "Social Scientists and Public Policy from the 1920s through World War II," *Journal of Canadian Studies*, 15, 4 (Winter, 1980-81); C. Berger, *The Writing of Canadian History* (Toronto: Oxford University Press, 1976), 106-7, 110.

17. W.A. Mackintosh, "Canadian Trade Policy," *Queen's Quarterly*, 41 (Spring, 1934), 86-7.

18. Mackintosh, "Canadian Tariff Policy," 17.

19. *Industrial Canada*, July, 1939, pp. 99-100.

20. W.A. Mackintosh, "An Economist Looks at Economics," *Canadian Journal of Economics and Political Science*, 3, 3 (August, 1937), 316.

21. Granatstein, *The Ottawa Men*, 153-68.

22. T. Cole, *The Canadian Bureaucracy: A Study of Canadian Civil Servants and other Public Employees, 1939-1947* (Durham: Duke University Press, 1949), 269-70.

23. Innis, *Essays in Canadian Economic History*, 307.

24. D.H. Fullerton, "Survey of Canadian Foreign Trade," *Annals of the American Academy of Political and Social Science* (September, 1947).

25. D.H. Fullerton and H.A. Hampson, *Canadian Secondary Manufacturing Industry*, Study prepared for the Royal Commission on Canada's Economic Prospects, May, 1957, pp. 37-8, 181.

26. H.G.H. Aitken, "The Changing Structure of the Canadian Economy with Particular Reference to the Influence of the United States," in H.G.H. Aitken *et al.*, *The American Economic Impact on Canada* (Durham: Duke University Press, 1959), 9, 11.

27. R. Dehem, "The Economics of Stunted Growth," *Canadian Journal of Economics and Political Science*, 28, 4 (November, 1962), 509.

28. I. Brecher and S.S. Reisman, *Canada-United States Economic Relations*, Study prepared for the Royal Commission on Canada's Economic Prospects, July, 1957, pp. 143-5.

29. G. Huson, "Foreign Control of Canadian Business (Part II)," *Business Quarterly*, 22, 3 (Fall, 1957), 356. See also E. Curwain, "Trade – Round the World and Round the Clock," *ibid.*, 20, 3 (Fall, 1955).

30. M.G. Clark, *Canada and World Trade* (Ottawa: Economic Council of Canada, Staff Study no. 7, 1965), 3. Clark (pp. 35-6) was also alive to the problem of branch plant administered markets.

31. B.W. Wilkinson, *Canada's International Trade: An Analysis of Recent Trends and Patterns* (Montreal: Canadian Trade Committee, Private Planning Association of Canada, 1968), 17-18, 43.

32. Levitt, *Silent Surrender*, 127-8.

33. For an outline of the Waffle positions on these questions, see Laxer (ed.), *(Canada) Ltd.*

34. *Foreign Direct Investment in Canada*, 154, 179. Export blocking as a result of licensing technology was also documented in the Gray Report. In a sample of 208 such arrangements entered into by Canadian manufacturers between 1965 and 1969, only 5 per cent granted unrestricted export rights and 58 per cent were confined to the Canadian market (p. 168). For a similar finding, see Industry, Trade and

Commerce, Technological Innovation Studies Program, Research Report, J.P. Killing, *Manufacturing under License in Canada,* February, 1975, pp. 113, 128. Herb Gray, the cabinet sponsor of these opinions, became a human barometer of the changing political climate on foreign investment. He suffered political isolation after this report was published but was rehabilitated as the nation's first ITC Minister of the 1980's only to subsequently suffer yet other demotions. For further discussion of Gray, see Chapter 8.

35. *Foreign Direct Investment in Canada,* 163-4.

36. Bourgault, *Innovation and the Structure of Canadian Industry,* 40-2.

37. *Ibid.,* 42-52, 95.

38. *Ibid.,* 96. For a more recent discussion of inadequacies in the small domestic market argument, see B.W. Wilkinson, *Canada in the Changing World Economy* (Montreal: C.D. Howe Research Institute, 1980), 159-61.

39. *Ibid.,* 74.

40. Britton and Gilmour, *The Weakest Link,* 26, 42-9.

41. *Ibid.,* 92, 110, 126.

42. *Ibid.,* Chapter 7.

43. *Ibid.,* 162-4.

44. A.W. Currie, *Canadian Economic Development,* fourth edition (Toronto: Nelson and Sons, 1963), 303-4.

45. J.D. Gibson, "Some Problems of Canadian Trading Policy," in R.M. Clark (ed.), *Canadian Issues: Essays in Honour of Henry F. Angus* (Toronto: University of Toronto Press, 1961), 121.

46. W.A. Mackintosh, "Canadian Economic Policy from 1945 to 1957," in *American Economic Impact on Canada,* 62, 68. See also his "The Canadian Economy and Its Competitors," *Foreign Affairs,* 34, 1 (October, 1955).

47. H.G. Johnson, *The Canadian Quandry* (Toronto: McGraw-Hill, 1963), 31, 108, 126-8.

48. H.E. English, *Industrial Structure in Canada's International Competitive Position* (Montreal: Canadian Trade Committee, Private Planning Association of Canada, 1964), 40.

49. R.J. and P. Wonnacott, *Free Trade Between the United States and Canada* (Cambridge: Harvard University Press, 1967), 177-9.

50. H.C. Eastman and S. Stykolt, *The Tariff and Competition in Canada* (New York: St. Martin's Press, 1967), Chapter 5.

51. Mackintosh, "Canadian Economic Policy from 1945 to 1957," 67.

52. A.E. Safarian, *Foreign Ownership of Canadian Industry* (Toronto: McGraw-Hill, 1966), 137.

53. W.A. Dimma, "The Canada Development Corporation: Diffident Experiment on a Large Scale," D.B.A. thesis, Harvard University, 1973, p. 113.

54. Canada, Privy Council Office, Report of the Task Force on the Structure of Canadian Industry, *Foreign Ownership and the Structure of Canadian Industry,* January, 1968, pp. 197-207.

55. D.G. McFetridge and L.J. Weatherley, *Notes on the Economics of Large Firm Size,* Study no. 20 for the Royal Commission on Corporate Concentration, March, 1977, pp. 81, 90.

56. R.J. Wonnacott, *Canada's Trade Options* (Ottawa: Economic Council of Canada, 1975), 182.

57. Economic Council of Canada, *Looking Outward: A New Trade Strategy for Canada* (Ottawa: Information Canada, 1975), 34-7, 55. Interestingly, a more recent (1978) Economic Council study by R. Dauphin, *The Impact of Free Trade in Canada*, concluded that "such an arrangement would render Canada subject to exploitation by the U.S. manufacturers . . . the so-called reorganization effect and the often mentioned gain to Canada from the formation of a free trade area with the United States were, in fact, myths. On the contrary, the de facto partial free trade area now existing between Canada and the United States already involves a net cost to Canada." (p. 116)

58. Canada, Senate, Standing Committee on Foreign Affairs, *Canada-United States Relations, Volume II, Canada's Trade Relations with the United States*, June, 1978, pp. 45-6, 116.

59. R.J. Wonnacott, "Industrial strategy: a Canadian substitute for trade liberalization?" *Canadian Journal of Economics*, 8, 4 (November, 1975), 546.

60. M.J. Gordon, "A World Scale National Corporation Industrial Strategy," *Canadian Public Policy*, 4, 1 (Winter, 1978), 47. Britton and Gilmour also predict a "devastating scenario" including "unemployment and massive industrial dislocation" would follow a Canada-U.S. free trade agreement. *The Weakest Link*, 61, 153-4.

61. *Ibid.*, 105.

62. A.E. Safarian, "Foreign Ownership and Industrial Behaviour: A Comment on The Weakest Link," *Canadian Public Policy*, 5, 3 (Summer, 1979).

63. K.S Palda, *The Science Council's Weakest Link: A Critique of the Science Council's Technocratic Industrial Strategy for Canada* (Vancouver: The Fraser Institute, 1979), 7-9; S. Globerman, "Canadian Science Policy and Technological Sovereignty," *Canadian Public Policy*, 4, 1 (Winter, 1978), 43-4.

Notes to Chapter 8

1. For a descriptive survey of these new trends in the world economy, see OECD, *The Impact of the Newly Industrializing Countries on Production and Trade in Manufactures* (Paris, 1979); OECD, *International Investment and Multinational Enterprises: Recent International Direct Investment Trends* (Paris, 1981).

2. Britton and Gilmour, *The Weakest Link*, 51.

3. Canada, Senate, Standing Committee on Foreign Affairs, *Canada-United States Relations, Volume III, Canada's Trade Relations with the United States*, March, 1982, p. 33.

4. See, for example, Science Council of Canada, Committee on Industrial Policies, *Uncertain Prospects: Canadian Manufacturing Industry, 1971-1977*, October, 1977; Britton and Gilmour, *The Weakest Link;* J. Laxer, "Canadian Manufacturing and U.S. Trade Policy," in *(Canada) Ltd.*

5. *Globe and Mail*, April 2, 1980, p. B4.

6. PAC, RG 20, vol. 718, no. 7-983, February 18, 1949.

7. The potential advantages to Canada of this production regime are becoming widely known. To illustrate, on the occasion of the announcement of the terms of the Tokyo GATT, the *Financial Post* was moved to editorialize that "world product mandating is what we need to push hard for now . . . . So there's more research and development done in Canada. So that production can be rationalized. Given this environment, many Canadian subsidiaries can export more." (July 21, 1979, p. 6.)

8. Canada, Science Council of Canada, Working Group on Industrial Policies, Multinationals and Industrial Strategy, *The Role of World Product Mandates,* p. 11.

9. The case of the small appliance plant of Canadian General Electric in Barrie, Ontario, illustrates this point. Under severe attack from Japanese and other Asian producers of these products, both this branch plant and its U.S. parent have suffered dramatic reverses in the last decade. In order to weather the storm, this multinational rationalized its continental production to increase efficiency and lower costs. For the Canadian plant, this meant a reduction in product lines from twenty-five to ten and decreased employment. Presumably, the fifteen abandoned lines will henceforth be imported from the U.S. In order to keep the Barrie factory alive, it was ceded, "in exchange," a mandate for the production of two relatively unimportant lines which are more popular in Canada than the U.S. – electric frying pans and electric kettles. See *Globe and Mail,* June 16, 1980, pp. B1, B7.

10. Canada, Statistics Canada, *Statistics Canada Daily,* March 26, 1982, pp. 2-8.

11. For a comparative summary of some of these policies, see Canada, International Development Research Centre, Science and Technology for Development, STPI Module 6, *Policy Instruments for the Regulation of Technology Imports,* and STPI Module 7, *Policy Instruments to Define the Pattern of Demand for Technology* (S. Barrio). Two excellent case studies of the difficulties in administering multinational compliance to these initiatives can be found in D. Bennett and K.E. Sharpe, "Transnational Corporations and the political economy of export promotion: the case of the Mexican automobile industry," *International Organization,* 33, 2 (Spring, 1979); and L.K. Mytelka, *Regional Development in a Global Economy: The Multinational Corporation, Technology, and Andean Integration* (New Haven: Yale University Press, 1979).

12. E.J. Dosman, *The National Interest: The Politics of Northern Development, 1968-75* (Toronto: McClelland and Stewart, 1975), 213.

13. See G. Toner and F. Bregha, "The Political Economy of Energy," in M. Whittington and G. Williams (eds.), *Canadian Politics in the 1980s* (Toronto: Methuen, 1981); and G.B. Doern, "Energy, Mines and Resources, the Energy Ministry and the National Energy Program," in Doern (ed.), *How Ottawa Spends Your Tax Dollars: Federal Priorities 1981* (Toronto: Lorimer, 1981).

14. *Industrial Canada,* November, 1901, pp. 131-2.

15. *Debates,* June 5, 1929, p. 948.

16. PAC, RG 20, vol. 81, no. 21879(2), April 9, May 28, 1926.

17. A thorough discussion of these trends may be found in Melissa Clark, "The Canadian State and Staples: An Ear to Washington," Ph.D. dissertation, McMaster University, 1979.

18. *Ibid.*

19. Department of Trade and Commerce, *Annual Report,* 1947-1960.

20. Department of Trade and Commerce, Information Division, *Expand with Canada,* 1951, p. 1.

21. PAC, RG 20, vol. 694, no. 18-187-1: Conference of Heads of Posts from Canadian Government Trade Commissioner Offices in the United States at the Seigneury Club, Montebello, P.Q., 19-22 February 1962, Background Paper no. 6A, Licensing Arrangements (Industrial Promotion Branch), p. 1.

22. *Debates,* June 7, 1963, pp. 802-3.

23. *Ibid.,* March 11, 1969, p. 6493.

24. *Financial Post,* January 30, 1982, p. 9.

25. Department of Industry, Trade and Commerce, *Annual Report,* 1979-80.

26. *Globe and Mail,* March 4, 1980, p. B3.

27. PAC, RG 20, vol. 665, no. 18-590-1 D (1): "Main Report Special Study on Exports by Canadian Subsidiaries," p. 3.

28. *Ibid.:* "Summary Report on the Special Study on Exports by Canadian Subsidiaries," pp. 2, 4.

29. *Ibid.,* vol. 718, no. 7-983, June 3, 1946, Garner to McLeod.

30. See Chapter 6, note 38.

31. Department of Trade and Commerce, Press Release, Excerpts from an Address by the Hon. Robert H. Winters, Minister of Trade and Commerce, on Foreign Ownership and the Multinational Corporation Delivered at the 42nd Canadian Purchasing Conference, Montreal, P.Q., July 10, 1967, p. 10.

32. R. French, *How Ottawa Decides: Planning and Industrial Policy-Making, 1968-1980* (Toronto: Lorimer, 1980), 103-18.

33. Department of Industry, Trade and Commerce, Export Promotion Review Committee, Final Report, *Strengthening Canada Abroad,* November 30, 1979, pp. 12, 17.

34. F.J. Fletcher and R.J. Drummond, "Canadian Attitude Trends, 1960-1978," Institute for Research on Public Policy, Montreal, Working Paper no. 4, August, 1979, pp. 38-9. The current offensive by business, provincial and Conservative Party politicians, and the media on the Foreign Investment Review Act seems designed to reverse this trend in public opinion. The mainly ineffectual FIRA is being blamed for almost all of Canada's ills in this campaign. For example, the *Globe and Mail* recently editorialized that "one reason why Canada has consistently turned in a poorer [unemployment] performance than the United States – our inflation and interest rates are also much higher – is that the Canadian government persists in discouraging foreign capital. The Foreign Investment Review Agency has been busy since 1974 preventing foreign capital from creating Canadian jobs." (August 9, 1982, p. 6.) It remains to be seen whether public attitudes will change as a result of this assault.

35. *Ottawa Citizen,* June 21, 1980, p. 14.

36. Department of Industry, Trade and Commerce, *Framework for Implementing the Government's New Industry Development Policy During the Next Four Years and Proposals for Immediate Action,* July 3, 1980, pp. 7, 12, 13, 47.

37. *Globe and Mail,* September 17, 1980, p. 10. For an interesting insight into how the position of the continentalist faction within the cabinet was strengthened during this period by U.S. government and business pressure on Ottawa to "shelve" these attempts to reform branch plant performance through industrial strategy, see S. Clarkson, *Canada and the Reagan Challenge* (Toronto: Lorimer, 1982), Chapter 4.

38. Government of Canada, *Economic Development for Canada in the 1980s,* November, 1981.

39. *Globe and Mail,* February 13, 1982, p. 1.

40. *Economic Development for Canada,* 3, 8. The hand of the industrial strategy faction of cabinet in writing these phrases and fighting to see them included seems obvious. For his part, Gray argued, as he read the statement, that the door was still open for government to monitor subsidiary performance with a view to improving the export problem. (*Financial Post,* December 19, 1981, pp. 1, 2.)

41. G. Williams, "Trade Promotion and Canada's Industrial Dilemma: The Demise of the Department of Industry, Trade and Commerce," in G.B. Doern (ed.), *How Ottawa Spends Your Tax Dollars, 1982* (Toronto: Lorimer, 1982).

42. *Strengthening Canada Abroad.*

43. French, *How Ottawa Decides*, 131.

44. C. Offe, "Theory of the Capitalist State in the Problem of Policy Formation," in L.N. Lindberg *et al.* (eds.), *Stress and Contradiction in Modern Capitalism* (Lexington: Lexington Books, 1975).

45. *Globe and Mail*, November 15 and 16, 1982, p. B1. Some are already warning, however, that these moves may be too late. A recent study of Canada's prospects in the glamour industry of the 1980's, computers, concluded that "American domination of the [Canadian] market and the steady flow of imports has led to a significant trade imbalance, which many observers consider will reach $5 billion by 1985." The research manager of one Toronto firm that tracks the computer hardware industry asserted that in this key sector "Canada never even got off the starting line and the window has closed in many areas." *Globe and Mail*, January 8, 1983, p. B2.

Notes to Chapter 9

1. The argument developed in this chapter relies heavily on material previously published in my "Still Not for Export," *Canadian Forum* (October, 1983), and "Symbols, Economic Logic and Political Conflict in the Canada-U.S.A. Free Trade Negotiations," *Queen's Quarterly* (Winter, 1985).

2. Department of Industry, Trade and Commerce, Memorandum from an Assistant Deputy Minister to the Deputy Minister, *Export Performance of Canada-based Foreign Subsidiaries* with Annex 1, "Examples of Export Market Limitations of Canadian Based Subsidiaries in Capital Equipment Manufacturing," April 13, 1977. Access to this document was granted to the author by an unofficial source on the condition that the identities of individuals and corporations not be disclosed. Ian Waddell, a New Democratic MP, had his request to view this memorandum denied by James Kelleher, Minister of State for International Trade, in a letter dated January 28, 1985, "because of the commercial confidentiality of the information on which the report was based."

3. R. Mahon, from the vantage point of the vulnerable and somewhat marginalized textile industry, approaches the question of tariff liberalization differently, emphasizing that it has been an arena of intra-class conflict in the sense that it "began to undermine the old basis for the accord between the staples faction and capital based in manufacturing, raising the prospect of trade-induced deindustrialization." See her *Politics of Industrial Restructuring: Canadian Textiles* (Toronto: University of Toronto Press, 1984), p. 17.

4. For examples of both of these strategies, see L. Muszynski, *The Deindustrialization of Metropolitan Toronto: A Study of Plant Closures, Layoffs and Unemployment* (Toronto: Social Planning Council of Metropolitan Toronto, 1985), Chapter 3. For an informative critique of Auto Pact production, see Clarkson, *Canada and the Reagan Challenge*, pp. 126-133.

5. *Globe and Mail*, January 30, 1984, p. B12.

6. K.C. Dhawan and L. Kryzanowski, *High Technology Plant Location Decisions: U.S.-Based Multinationals in the Canadian Computer Industry* (Montreal: Concordia University, Faculty of Commerce and Administration, November, 1983), pp. 144-45.

7. M. Atkinson, "If You Can't Beat Them: World Product Mandating and Canadian Industrial Policy," in D. Cameron and F. Houle (eds.), *Canada and the New International Division of Labour* (Ottawa: University of Ottawa Press, 1985), p. 144.

8. Speech of H.W. Joly, President, Canadian Manufacturers' Association, to the 1967 Annual Meeting, *Industrial Canada*, July, 1967, p. 12.

9. *Industrial Canada*, March, 1972, pp. 8, 9, 28.

10. Canada, Senate, Standing Committee on Foreign Affairs, *Proceedings*, December 9, 1980, p. 14:50.

11. Canada, *Report of the Royal Commission on the Economic Union and Development Prospects*

for Canada, Volume 1 (Ottawa: Supply and Services, 1985), p. 336.

12. Special Joint Committee of the Senate and of the House of Commons on Canada's International Relations, *Minutes of Proceedings and Evidence*, August 1, 1985, p. 15:33.

13. *Ibid.*, July 15, 1985, pp. 2:62-63.

14. For an insightful discussion of the factions represented within the modern Conservative Party, see M.J. Brodie and J. Jenson, "The Party System," in M. Whittington and G. Williams (eds.), *Canadian Politics in the 1980s*, Second Edition (Toronto: Methuen, 1984).

15. Prime Minister's Office, "Canada-U.S. New Bilateral Trade Initiative Communications Strategy," 1985. (Draft document, excerpted in the *Toronto Star*, September 20, 1985, pp. A1, A21.)

16. Special Joint Committee of the Senate and of the House of Commons on Canada's International Relations, *Minutes of Proceedings and Evidence*, July 26, 1985, p. 11:6.

17. *Ibid.*, July 17, 1985, p. 4:10.

18. *Ibid.*, p. 4:36.

19. *Ibid.*, p. 4:46.

20. *Ibid.*, August 8, 1985, pp. 17:43-44.

21. *Ibid.*, July 26, 1985, p. 11:6.

22. *Ibid.*, July 15, 1985, p. 2:73.

23. *Ibid.*, August 8, 1985, p. 17:62.

24. *Ibid.*, July 17, 1985, p. 4:10.

25. *Ibid.*, July 18, 1985, p. 5:24.

26. *Ibid.*, July 17, 1985, p. 4:34.

27. See the Canadian Institute of Public Opinion, *The Gallup Report*, September 9, 1985. This change in public attitudes followed a concerted campaign at the beginning of the present decade by business leaders in conjunction with provincial and Conservative Party politicians to link the severe economic recession of that period to the aborted Liberal Party challenge to foreign investment in the form of the NEP and a strengthened FIRA.

28. No judgement is being offered here as to either the scope or effectiveness of policies related to the industrial strategy option that might emerge from the political process. The argument merely holds out the possibility that our state elites could be driven in their direction.

29. These dimensions are more fully outlined in my "Symbols, Economic Logic and Political Conflict in the Canada-U.S.A. Free Trade Negotiations," *Queen's Quarterly* (Winter, 1985). It should be noted that any political conflict and instability manifested in these three dimensions is likely to contribute additional pressure for a reformed industrial policy.

30. Computed from: Canada, *Summary of External Trade*, various years.

31. *Globe and Mail*, October 12, 1985, p. B1.

32. Curiously, one can find support for this position from even the unabashedly continentalist 1985 Macdonald Royal Commission. After deprecating claims as lacking "authoritative evidence" that Canadian industrialization has been arrested by the export and research and development deficiencies of branch plant production, the commission nonetheless noted that "in the light of potential conflicts of interest" over Canadian sourcing and WPMS "some form of government regulation would seem reasonable." *Report of the Royal Commission on the Economic Union and Development Prospects for Canada*, Volume II, p. 236.

Index